Praise for *How I Built*

'If only this book would have come out [...] business would have been so much simpler [...]'

Simon Sinek, author of *Start With Why*

'Guy Raz has an extraordinary talent for not only unearthing the most powerful ideas in any story, but also translating those ideas into wisdom accessible for everyone'

Chris Anderson, head of TED

'Now, more than ever, we need dreamers and builders – this book is full of them and their stories of inspiration'

Alexis Ohanian, co-founder of Reddit

'This book is all about inspiration – told with blood, sweat and tears. You'll come away refreshed. And ready to hit the ground running'

Mark Cuban, entrepreneur

'Truly remarkable stories . . . about truly remarkable people. Guy Raz captures their stories on the page to incredible effect'

Jennifer Hyman, CEO of Rent the Runway

'If you're determined to reach for your dream, read this book'

Barbara Corcoran, founder of The Corcoran Group

'Through stories of passion, audacity and courage, Guy weaves together a shared business-building experience that's both inspiring and real'

Lara Merriken, founder of LÄRABAR

'What's so remarkable about Guy's book is not so much that all these individuals saw their dreams come true, but that as their stories of overcoming frustrations and hurdles unfold, you end up cheering for them to succeed'

Tony Hsieh, author of *Delivering Happiness*

HOW I BUILT THIS

The Unexpected Paths to Success from
the World's Most Inspiring Entrepreneurs

GUY RAZ

with Nils Parker

MACMILLAN

First published 2020 by Houghton Mifflin Harcourt

First published in the UK 2020 by Macmillan
an imprint of Pan Macmillan
The Smithson, 6 Briset Street, London EC1M 5NR
Associated companies throughout the world
www.panmacmillan.com

ISBN 978-1-5290-2630-6

This book presents the ideas of its author and his interviewees.
It is not intended to be a substitute for financial, legal, or other professional
advice. The publisher and the author disclaim liability for any adverse effects
resulting directly or indirectly from information contained in this book.

3 5 7 9 8 6 4 2

A CIP catalogue record for this book is available from the British Library.

Book design by Chrissy Kurpeski

Printed and bound in India by Replika Press Pvt. Ltd.

Visit **www.panmacmillan.com** to read more about all our books
and to buy them. You will also find features, author interviews and
news of any author events, and you can sign up for e-newsletters
so that you're always first to hear about our new releases.

FOR SALE IN THE INDIAN SUBCONTINENT ONLY

For builders and those dreaming of building.

CONTENTS

PART III THE DESTINATION

INTRODUCTION

On an otherwise normal summer Monday in 2018, my wife, Hannah, returned home from her daily run with tears streaming down her cheeks. As she came into the kitchen of our Berkeley, California, home where I was making breakfast for our boys, she pulled the earbuds from her ears and said through deep breaths, "Why didn't . . . you prepare me . . . for this episode?"

That morning, the team at *How I Built This* — the business podcast I created and have hosted since September 2016 — released our most recent episode, about Stacy Brown and her company, Chicken Salad Chick. I had forgotten this was the episode airing that day because the lag time between an interview and its release is usually many months. What I had *not* forgotten was how much of an emotional roller coaster my interview with Stacy Brown was. And it was clear from Hannah's reaction that it had resulted in a very powerful episode. Here's the basic outline of the story.

Stacy starts making chicken salad out of her home in Auburn, Alabama, as a way to make ends meet after her husband walked out on her and their three children, all under the age of six. Her goal is to earn $500 a month to pay the bills.

She finds small-time success right away selling her chicken salad door-to-door for several months, until someone calls the health department on her. (Apparently making food out of an unlicensed kitchen and selling it in off-the-shelf storage containers, basically out of the back of your car, is, technically speaking, not legal.) In response, the health department shuts her down.

As this is happening, she enlists the help of a business-savvy family friend named Kevin Brown, who convinces her not to give up, but to double down and open a restaurant instead, in an 800-square-foot shack. The rent is $800 a month. So with his help, she does just that, and it's successful, too. On their first day in business, they sell out of their chicken salad by 2 p.m.

The intensity of the business and their partnership brings Stacy and Kevin closer together. Eventually, they fall in love and get married. Now as partners in life *and* in business, they steadily grow Chicken Salad Chick and use the cash flow to open two additional locations in Auburn, since no bank will even give them the time of day, let alone a small-business loan.

After four or five years of bootstrapping their way to sustainability, they realize it's time to find someone who can help them pivot to a franchise model where they'll have a shot at turning a real profit and taking some cash out of the business.

Unfortunately, they end up partnering with a less-than-honorable couple to whom they foolishly, in retrospect, sell 51 percent of the company, and who threaten to fire Stacy and Kevin from their own business just a few months later when the two couples' visions for the future of Chicken Salad Chick diverge.

Unwilling to let go of all they've built, Stacy and Kevin negotiate a buyout — except the partners want a 3× return on their initial investment, which amounts to $1.3 million(!), and they want it in thirty days(!!), or they are going to take over the company, and Stacy and Kevin will get nothing(!!!).

Needless to say, Stacy and Kevin don't have $1.3 million, so they travel all over Alabama pitching to anyone who will listen to them, trying desperately to raise the money. They get nowhere until the very last day — day 30 of thirty — when a man named Earlon Mc-Whorter, who made his money building Lowe's Home Improvement stores, calls them up after attending their pitch meeting at the Auburn Chamber of Commerce and tells them that he believes in them, that he loves their chicken salad, and that he will write them a check for every penny they need.

Earlon's investment doesn't just give Stacy and Kevin their company back; it propels them into a franchising model that catches fire immediately. They start opening stores all over the South. Everything is going amazingly well. And then, in the middle of their expansion, Kevin is diagnosed with stage 4 colon cancer that has metastasized to his liver. He immediately begins an aggressive chemotherapy treatment regimen and, astoundingly, never misses a single day of work.

It's the beginning of another fight. This one, tragically, they will not win. But that does not stop them. Not only do they continue growing Chicken Salad Chick, but they also start the Chicken Salad Chick Foundation to support colon cancer research. As part of their fundraising efforts, Kevin has the idea to put on a huge benefit concert at Auburn University's Jordan-Hare Stadium and to have Kenny Chesney (the biggest star in country music at the time) headline it. It's a crazy idea, but then so was a restaurant dedicated exclusively to chicken salad. He helped make that happen, so why not this?

Why not, indeed. They get Kenny Chesney. They sell 50,000 tickets. And on that night in April, they fill Jordan-Hare Stadium. Except Kevin will not be among the crowd, not in his physical form, at least. He passes away six months before, on November 21, 2015, surrounded by family.

For Stacy, it's an unfathomably painful loss. One that comes after nearly a full decade of very high highs and incredibly low lows, in both her personal life and her professional life. And yet, Stacy, like her husband, continues fighting. She perseveres. Not just for herself and her children, but for the memory of what Kevin meant to her and to their business. Later that year, all of their effort is rewarded: Chicken Salad Chick is listed in the Inc. 5000 as one of the fastest-growing restaurant brands in America.* Today, it is a $100 million business.

---

* It was number 37 among *all* privately held companies.

This tumultuous, inspiring story is, in many ways, a quintessential entrepreneurial story. It's also a classic hero's journey. If you've ever read any Greek mythology or the Bible or watched *Star Wars,* you have experience with the "hero's journey," the concept — identified by the author and philosopher Joseph Campbell — that most great epic stories follow a similar narrative arc: a hero has a crazy idea; people doubt her; she leaves the village to pursue her vision, faces untold obstacles, falls into an abyss, barely escapes death, but manages to come out the other side with whatever she was looking for and continues on her journey to an eventual triumphant return.

This is obviously a gross oversimplification of the structure of the hero's journey, but those are the basic ingredients of a great classic story. They're also the key elements of many great business stories — Stacy Brown's included. It was a discovery I made entirely by accident while taking a business school class during the year I spent at Harvard as a Nieman journalism fellow in 2008. It was in that class that I was first exposed to the case study method and to the idea that you could learn about business through stories. Time and again I found classic heroic journeys embedded in these case studies. There were calls to adventure, trials and errors, all-is-lost moments, the ultimate boon — all told through the prism of business.

What was even more surprising, to me at least, was that I was at all interested. In high school and college, I used to think that "business" was a dirty word. To me, it was the realm of hucksters and pitchmen selling cheap consumer products on late-night infomercials. Even though my generation produced people like Elon Musk and Larry Page, most of my cohort subscribed to an anticorporate, anticommercial ethos, perhaps best illustrated in a famous 1992 cover of *Rolling Stone* featuring Kurt Cobain wearing a shirt that read CORPORATE MAGAZINES STILL SUCK.

Why would I care about the story of some business? It's not like business was ever going to be my thing. Especially because I watched the ups and downs of my parents' pearl-importing business and how much time and energy it sucked out of them. I have vivid memories of my parents grinding away at the kitchen table late into the evening, combing through customer lists, making cold calls that more often than not ended with the proverbial door being slammed in their faces — all in the service of providing a stable life for me, my younger brother, and my two older sisters.

I didn't want that life for myself. Watching my parents endure what entrepreneurship demanded of them, I could not think of any career less suited to my temperament and my interests than talking about businesses all day, let alone starting one. That's why I went into journalism, then into radio, and eventually into hosting at NPR. And yet, here I am. I have somehow managed to create or co-create five podcasts that, together, generate millions of dollars in revenue and are heard by 19 million people a month. It's a lot of work, more than I ever imagined, and to make sure it all gets done, I started a production company. An *actual* company! Who would have guessed it? In truth, I'm still not sure how it all came (or stays) together, but we're a small, nimble, tight-knit outfit, and I freely admit that I love it.

What I love most is the journey of coming up with a big idea and turning it into something tangible — though it would take me until my late thirties to start to feel even a tinge of confidence about some of my ideas or my ability to execute them. For most of my career before then, I struggled with the kinds of worries I thought charismatic entrepreneurs never confronted: anxiety, fear, imposter syndrome, even depression.

But over the course of my time doing deep-dive interviews with hundreds of business founders and CEOs for my shows, I've come to understand that, for the most part, they are just like you and me. Which is to say, they're human. They all have sleepless nights and midnight terrors. Most of them, at some point, feel like imposters. They are not natural superheroes; they are all Clark Kents. The only difference between them and you, at this moment, is that when opportunity presented itself, they went into the phone booth and put on the cape. They took the leap. That's basically it.

How I Built This was not my first leap, but it was my biggest, and the one that took the longest to make. It was a slow burn that began with the epiphany inside that Harvard Business School classroom. As a former war reporter, I knew that the most compelling human stories are journeys, and I had a hunch, now that I could see the hero's journey inside most business stories, that there was a tribe out there that would relate to these journeys in a business context.

That was how the idea for *How I Built This* evolved. And like the birth of the show, most of the ideas you will read about in this book didn't begin with a big explosion either ... but rather with a little spark. A spark that got nurtured, sometimes very slowly, until one day the person who would eventually bring that idea to life woke up to realize the thing that used to get them out of bed in the morning was no longer the thing that fired them up. It was something else now.

An idea, as it was for Lara Merriken, Gary Erickson, and Peter Rahal, who all wanted to make a better energy bar.

A desire to strike out on their own to see if they could do it, as it was for Angie and Dan Bastian when they moved back to Minnesota from Florida and decided to buy a $10,000 kettle corn starter kit that would eventually become Angie's BOOMCHICKAPOP.

An opportunity that leverages one's skill set and experience, as it was for Randy Hetrick of TRX, when the homemade workout system he'd cobbled together to stay in shape while deployed overseas as a Navy SEAL captured the attention of his fellow SEALs, and then his friends, and then other fitness fanatics, including one very famous Super Bowl–winning quarterback.

Or sometimes, *a lucky (and perfectly timed) pivot,* as it was for Stewart Butterfield when the internal messaging system his team developed to help build a massively multiplayer online game (MMOG) actually turned out to be more promising than the game itself. The game was scrapped. The messaging system became Slack.

In short, this book is for people who aren't natural-born entrepreneurs or even entrepreneurs at all, but instead are dreamers whose lack of experience is inversely proportional to the force of their ambition and the momentum of their desire to bring something new into the world and to make the world a better place. People who are idealistic but may not have found an idea worth going out on a limb for just yet. People who appreciate success if it comes, and who can find ways to learn from failure when it happens (oh, yes, failure will happen). People who learn the hard way — through experience — though the wisdom in those lessons may not always be immediately self-evident to them. People who still have no idea how they ended up where they are, with a product or a service, with employees and customers, but who want to make a real go of it, because they don't want to let anyone down, least of all themselves.

This book is organized to help those people — people like you and me, like Stacy Brown — succeed. It is the product of in-depth interviews with hundreds of the most successful and inspiring entrepreneurs from across the business landscape — from the food industry to consumer packaged goods to the tech world, and more. It is a synthesis of the lessons I have learned from those founders, and it is structured to follow the path we took as we traced their entrepreneurial hero's journeys from the call to found their businesses (part I), through the tests and trials of their growth phases (part II), and finally to their destination as the mature, global brands we know today (part III). My goal is to pull back the curtain on entrepreneurship, to shed light on the black box of entrepreneurial success, and to provide an architecture for how to think creatively about building something, whether that's an idea, a movement, or, of course, a business.

Each chapter explores a discrete moment that nearly every founder faces in the life of their business — from coming up with an idea to getting their story straight; from finding funding to finding a co-founder; from pivoting their product to building their culture; from surviving catastrophe to figuring out how to grow and scale a business that lasts and leaves them feeling good about who they are and what they have done for the world.

That said, not everything in this book will apply to your specific situation. Maybe you are trying to build something small. Maybe you don't want to scale. Maybe you're an employee trying to build something *inside* your company. And that's totally fine! This book is not an all-or-nothing proposition. I just hope you're able to find something in these pages that leaves you with a sense of both possibility and relief, since almost every story in the book describes a real problem that needed to be solved and an entrepreneur who found a way to solve it.

My hope in structuring the book in this way is to show anyone who has the courage to pursue an idea but is struggling with the fear of failure that every mistake that could be made in business has been made, that solutions to your problems have already been found — many of them by the founders you will meet in the pages to come — and that to learn from other people's mistakes instead of going through them yourself is, perhaps, the only shortcut that exists in all of entrepreneurship.

Now that you know how I built this book, let's dive into how these brilliant innovators, entrepreneurs, and idealists built some of the world's greatest businesses, so that one day soon, you can build your own.

Let's start writing *your* hero's journey.

Guy Raz
Spring 2020

PART I

THE CALL

ENTREPRENEURSHIP ISN'T VERY NATURAL. It defies many of our most human instincts. Our desire for security. Our fear of crazy risks. Our tendency to go with the flow and not make too many waves. As much as we think of ourselves as unique individuals, we also like to fit in and to be chosen — by those who fit in and were chosen before us.

And yet, there is always that one person we know who goes the other way. Who embraces a different set of instincts. The kind that have driven humans for millennia to leave home, to push boundaries, and to build. For most of history we have called that kind of person an explorer. But in the twenty-first century, with the frontiers that are still open for exploration no longer physical, but technological, social, intellectual, and economic, we have given that person a new name: *entrepreneur*.

The entrepreneur is a person who strikes out on their own to reach these frontiers of progress, aware of both the risks and the rewards of going it alone. They are driven to discover what might be found out there. They feel the call to make something out of what they find — something new, better, faster, more efficient — and to make it accessible to the rest of us in a way that we can use. It could be a product or a service or an idea that spurs its own kind of exploration, starting the cycle anew.

It doesn't matter. What matters is that anyone can be an entrepreneur. Entrepreneurs aren't chosen, they are made. *Self*-made. You could be an entrepreneur. Maybe you already are. Maybe you have already heard the call: Of an idea that gets you excited. Of a problem that needs a solution. Of a friend who needs help that you are uniquely suited to provide. Either way, what follows is a critical set of things to think about as you prepare to cross the Rubicon of entrepreneurship into truly uncharted territory.

1

Be Open to Ideas

People start businesses for all kinds of reasons. They do it to satisfy a dream or to solve a problem or to fill a void in the market. Some people want to improve on something that seems obsolete, and others want to reinvent an entire industry. There are literally dozens of on-ramps to the entrepreneurial journey. But no matter which one you take, at some point you are going to need an idea. Something specific. Something concrete and unique and new. An idea that makes life better or more interesting and delivers on the reason you wanted to start a business in the first place.

Sounds simple enough, right? After all, ideas are a dime a dozen. Or at least that's what many of us are led to believe: That ideas are easy and abundant. That what matters is *execution*. And all of that is true to some extent. It's just not the whole truth, because coming up with a *good* idea is hard. Good ideas are hard to find and hard to get right. But once you find one, they are also very hard to turn away from. That's what makes good ideas so intimidating. Not that you won't ever find one, but that one day you will, and when you do, it's very possible that your life will never be the same again.

So where do you find one of these good ideas? Where do you look? *Can you look?* Or do you have to wait for the angels to sing in your ear and the light bulb to go on over your head? Some people are lucky, and this epiphany happens for them early. An idea hits them out of the blue and sends them on their way. For most of us, though, it isn't so simple. We have to look for a good idea, or at least be open to receiving it.

It's one of the eternal entrepreneurial questions: Can you actually find a good idea, or does it have to find you? The answer is the same for both options: yes.

Chef and restaurateur José Andrés told me that ideas happen "when you are actively moving and searching." When I asked him how he came up with his first restaurant concept in the early 1990s — a small-plates restaurant called Jaleo that revolutionized Washington, DC, dining, and then launched a thousand competitors nationwide — his answer was simple: "I was looking."

Lisa Price, on the other hand, wasn't actually looking for the idea that would become Carol's Daughter, her beauty brand, which the makeup and personal care giant L'Oréal would eventually snap up for north of mid–eight figures in 2014.

"I thought that I had found the career that I was going to do for the rest of my life," Lisa told me. A graduate of the High School of Music & Art in New York City, she was in her late twenties and had just come through a decade-long gauntlet of unrewarding clerical jobs — first at American Express, then at the United Nations, then in health care — along with a brief and emotionally devastating attempt at a singing career in between. She was living with her soon-to-be husband in a one-bedroom apartment in Brooklyn when, in the late 1980s, through a friend, she found herself in what she thought was her dream job: writer's assistant on *The Cosby Show*.

This was, of course, long before the tragic drama surrounding the show's eponymous star that has changed how we think about everything Bill Cosby created. *The Cosby Show* was then the most popular sitcom on television, and for African Americans arguably one of the most important television shows ever made.

"It was particularly incredible being an African American woman and what that show meant to me and my family," Lisa told me. "To see African Americans depicted in such a positive light, and for me to be standing in the Huxtable kitchen the morning of my first table read, as I'm listening to the cast read the script, I could have just floated off at that point."

In the years that followed, she could have floated off to any number of television production jobs: script supervisor, production coordinator, producer. "And that is what I thought I was going to do," she recalled.

Then one day Lisa read an article about one of the greatest — and apparently best-smelling — musicians of all time. "I'm a huge Prince fan," Lisa said. "And this article talked about how he always smelled very good. And the reason for it was he kept an assortment of fragrances on his bureau. He put Chanel No. 5 in his boots."

Lisa happens to love fragrance. She always has. But her fascination had never gone much beyond the appreciation of a consumer. Prince made her realize that fragrance was so much more than an accessory. It was a form of creative expression. *An art.*

"I just loved the idea of this blending of fragrances and creating these unique scents," she said, reflecting not just on an interest that she shared with Prince (which was obviously totally cool) but also on the moment that really got the ball rolling for her.

Over the next few years, Lisa started to read and research the different kinds of scent notes in perfumes — top notes, heart notes, base notes — and how to combine them. She learned the art of application. "The way that your fragrance lasts on your body is you layer it," she explained to me casually during our conversation, as I'm sure she'd done for thousands of people before me. "You wash with it, you moisturize with it, then you spritz it on." Early on she tried blending drugstore lotions with various fragrances from her collection to make her own scented moisturizer, but she only ended up making a mess. "They weren't balanced from a chemistry perspective, so things would just separate," she said. Eventually, browsing the shelves of a new age bookstore with her husband one Sunday afternoon in Brooklyn's Park Slope neighborhood, she came across a book on essential oils that also included recipes for things like massage oil, hair oil, creams, balms, and butters. Everything she liked.

"I thought, 'This is great, I can make my own lotions,'" Lisa recalled. "The recipes were very bare-bones, and they used things like paraffin and lanolin, which I wasn't too crazy about using. I wanted to use beeswax, and I wanted to find cocoa butter. So I used the skeleton of the recipes within the book, and then I just started adding my own combinations. I could go back and tweak it if something came out runny or too thick or too oily or too stiff, and adjust the recipe accordingly."

By the early 1990s, Lisa had her formulas down: Lotions and body butters that held together just the way she wanted. Lotions she could actually use. Now, if you are anything like me when Lisa first told me this story, you would assume that these first lotions were the beginning of the Carol's Daughter empire as we know it. Not quite. In those first few years, none of Lisa's creations were for public consumption. They weren't for sale. They were only for *her*. They were made with fragrances *she* liked, with ingredients like aloe vera and cocoa butter that *she* preferred, that addressed the moisturizing needs of *her* skin. This was her hobby, after all. *It was for fun.* She wasn't trying to please anyone else. She was, well, scratching her own itch. Why *wouldn't* her creations match her preferences? Plus, it wasn't like she was making this stuff as a diversion from, or a fast track to, a different life. She was very happy with her career.

"I was ecstatic. It was wonderful," Lisa said. "And I think because I was very happy at what I was doing with work, when I had my downtime I didn't have that desperate feeling that you feel when you're like, 'Oh, God, I'm finally not at work, and I just want to relax and veg out.' So I became creative when I was at home."

The sheer joy of tinkering and stretching her creative limits sustained Lisa all the way through the end of *The Cosby Show,* which went off the air in 1992. She spent the next year as a freelance production assistant, bouncing from show to show until the summer, when the television business in New York traditionally gets very slow and work dries up. That's when her mother, Carol, suggested Lisa try to sell her lotions and creams at their church's upcoming flea market.

It was May 1993, and Lisa thought it would be nice to make some money and contribute more toward household expenses during the summer lull. But still she was skeptical: "I said, 'Really, Mommy? Do you think people would pay for this?'" We know the answer to that question now, and with hindsight it seems self-evident. But in the moment, Lisa's apprehension would have been a totally reasonable reaction for someone who, for the first time, was being asked to think about her personal creation as a product marketed to other people. *As a business idea.*

In this way, at least as entrepreneurial stories go, Lisa Price is the most like the rest of us. She was so passionate about what she did, it was so intrinsically rewarding just as an activity, that it didn't even occur to her to take the next step with her idea — to sell it, or to turn it into a business. It was almost weird for her, as her response to her mother clearly illustrates, to even think other people would be interested.

I've heard numerous variations of this story from a number of entrepreneurs. I even lived it myself when, in a nod to the growing popularity of the podcast, we decided to take the show on the road and do live interviews in big theaters. I mean, for the majority of my career, I have come to audiences as a disembodied voice through their car radio speakers or their earbuds. No one wanted to *see* me, I thought. For weeks, often months, before each of these initial live events, I worried whether enough of our fans would be interested in watching two people talk onstage. I wondered aloud to anyone who would listen, much as Lisa Price did to her mother, whether people would actually pay for this. And not just the $50 for a ticket, but also the cost of childcare and parking and all the other things that go along with a night at the theater.

As luck would have it, we sold out nearly every one of those early live shows, and each time it happened, it was a genuine shock to me. Because when you're not looking for a good business idea, it just doesn't seem real when one finds *you,* even when the proof is staring you in the face. This is especially true, I learned in talking with Lisa, when the idea involves a consumer product. Products are things on shelves in stores, with labels and bar codes on them, and prices that end in ".99." In 1993, Lisa was making these lotions in her kitchen and storing them in Tupperware containers she had in the cupboard. She didn't have *names* for them — they were just whatever they were. And let's say she took her mom up on this crazy idea to set up a table at the flea market, what was she going to sell them in?

Of course, none of that was really important. Those issues would be easy enough to address with a little bit of time and ingenuity (for example, she used old baby food jars as packaging in the early days). What *was* important was something Carol understood that Lisa had never really considered: *her stuff really worked.* And Carol would know. Lisa produced a number of lotions specifically for her mother and for her younger siblings, and they worked brilliantly. Carol's skin had never looked better, and her kids' dry, irritated skin had never felt better. These lotions may have started as a personal passion project that gave Lisa a creative outlet, but soon enough they served a greater purpose. They solved real problems: hers, her mom's, and her siblings'. Her customers, if they were out there as Carol believed, would benefit from her products in much the same ways.

And that is the key to finding an idea, whether you are actively on the hunt for one or simply open to the possibility. No matter what kind of business you are thinking of starting — whether it's a product or a service, whether it's your side hustle or your main thing, whether it's for men or women, kids or adults — the intersection of personal passion and problem solving is where good ideas are born and lasting businesses are built.

Trusting her mother's instincts, Lisa invested $100 in materials, table rental, and flowers for decoration, and then put her items up for sale for the first time. And guess what? She sold out. But just like the creative process up to that point, this, too, was all about fun. It still wasn't a business.

Then, in August of that year, something revelatory — possibly fated — appeared on Lisa's TV screen. I'll let her describe it, because it's too good not to share in its entirety.

"I was watching an episode of *The Oprah Winfrey Show,* and she was talking to people who had started businesses with little or no money and one person said, 'Well, you have to know that you're passionate about what you do. If you're not passionate about it, you will quit before you make any money.' And I remember thinking, 'I'm really passionate about this stuff. I like doing this.' And then somebody else said she would define passion as, if someone woke you up out of your bed in the middle of the night, would you go and do this thing? And I honestly could answer yes to that question. And I remember sitting on the edge of my bed and saying, 'Wait a minute. Maybe this could be a business.' And that day was the day that I realized this just doesn't have to be a hobby. This can be more."

Actually, a lot more.

As the summer drew to a close, and buoyed by her success at the church flea market, Lisa expanded her marketing that fall to street fairs, arts and crafts festivals, and other flea markets throughout the city's five boroughs. But it wasn't raw entrepreneurial ambition that spurred her expansion. It was the two greatest forms of organic growth: repeat customers and word of mouth. Or to put it another way, it was Lisa's passion reflected back to her in the form of consumer demand.

"People would call and say, 'Hey, I bought a jar of cream from you at such and such street fair, and I'm running out. How can I get some more?' And I would look at my schedule, and if I knew I was going to be home on a Saturday, I said, 'Well, I'm working the rest of the week, but if you want, come by my apartment on Saturday. What time would you like to come by?'"

And when those people came to her apartment, they almost never came alone.

"My husband called it the 'sister-girl network.' Somebody always brought a friend with them. And if you brought a friend, you'd get a free gift, or I'd give them [a discount]," Lisa said, recounting the early growth of Carol's Daughter. "It was all that grassroots kind of stuff."

This is where so many aspiring entrepreneurs get tripped up when thinking about startup ideas. They forget about igniting this kind of passion in their customers and instead use only their own passion as the North Star for their search. Passion is important — you will never hear me say otherwise — but the trouble with passion by itself is that it can lead you down rabbit holes that only you care about, or to problems that only you have.

Watching a few episodes of the immensely popular business television competition show *Shark Tank* is all you need to do to see this phenomenon play out in real time. There was the funeral concierge service called Good Grief Celebrations; the custom bobblehead company called The Bobble Place; a better tanning and massage pillow called the Podillow; an energy drink for women called Cougar Limited; a ticketless coat-checking system called CoatChex; and, perhaps the idea most diametrically opposed to Lisa Price's scented skin care products, the No Fly Cone, a flytrap that used dog poop as bait to catch annoying flies in an effective, nontoxic way.

One of the judges, Daymond John (whom we will meet later, in chapter 3), immediately identified the central challenge of that particular idea. "So the dog has to defecate outside, and you put the trap over this, and that attracts the flies. But if you clean up the dog's mess and put it away . . . you're kind of creating the problem by leaving the poop outside, aren't you?"

The product's inventor, a Colorado-based horse trainer named Bruce Gaither, who was tired of dealing with horseflies all day, gave an impassioned answer to the question, but the explanation wasn't convincing enough for any of the Sharks. Passion for the idea may have gotten Bruce out of bed every morning, and it surely helped him persevere whenever he felt like he might quit, but it was never going to sell his product, nor would it make the Sharks any money, because customers don't pay for passion. *They pay for things they can use.*

The same month the episode of *Shark Tank* with Bruce Gaither aired, Paul Graham, co-founder of the startup accelerator Y Combinator and a kind of entrepreneurial Confucius, wrote a long essay titled "How to Get Startup Ideas" for his blog. It opens with a discussion of problems and reads like Graham had just watched Bruce on *Shark Tank* and was talking directly to him.

"The way to get startup ideas is not to try to think of startup ideas," Graham wrote. "It's to look for problems, preferably problems you have yourself . . . It sounds obvious to say you should only work on problems that exist. And yet by far the most common mistake startups make is to solve problems no one has."

The reason this mistake happens so often, as far as I can tell, is that looking for problems — *looking for ideas* — tends to take time, sometimes a fair amount of luck, and always hard work. If you aren't searching smartly, or at least open to the possibilities and perspectives around you, it becomes that much harder to find something that works.

Bruce Gaither found a problem to solve — he got that part right — it just wasn't a problem enough people had. It was, in many ways, a solution in search of a problem, or as Daymond John might have put it, a solution that required Bruce to create the problem he was trying to solve.

Lisa Price, on the other hand, was open to her mother's perspective, she heeded the advice in that *Oprah* episode, and she managed in the process to solve problems that not only she had, but that millions of African American women and other people of color also had, though that was not her original intent.

"I was not deliberately saying this is for African American women. I was deliberately saying this is for dry skin, and subsequently, when you have more melanin in your skin, that dry skin will show. You look dull. You look a little bit gray. You look, as people say, ashy. And you cannot get away from that. And that's how I probably at that time ended up with that audience of people who were more brown, because they found something that took away that ash."

There is a name for a person who creates something purely out of passion: *hobbyist*. There is a name for a person who creates something out of passion that solves a problem only they have: *tinkerer*. There is a name for a person who creates something out of passion that also solves a problem they share with lots of other people: *entrepreneur*.

At one point or another, Lisa Price was all three of these people. Prince turned her into a passionate hobbyist. Experimenting with ingredients to solve her dry skin problem made her an inveterate tinkerer. Once she combined her passion as a hobbyist with her problem-solving skills as a tinkerer, and then applied that to the needs of the women of Brooklyn and beyond, what she ended up with was a great idea. What she built was an amazing business. What she became was . . . an entrepreneur.

But there was an additional layer of genius to Lisa's lotions as well. They didn't just solve the problem of dry skin for women of color; they created a brand-new market that Lisa could dominate. "This was not something that you could walk into a drugstore and say, 'Oh, look at that. This is fantastic,'" she remembered. "It wasn't there. There was definitely a community that was not being served."

And now it would be. A community that continued to grow in size and purchasing power and would ultimately demand more and better options in other areas as well; including skin care brands like Bevel, designed for *men* of color by Walker & Company,* which was founded in 2013, just a year before L'Oréal's acquisition of Carol's Daughter. That's twenty years of steady growth in a segment of the market that had been systematically ignored for generations.

The French novelist Victor Hugo famously wrote in 1862, "One withstands the invasion of armies; one does not withstand the invasion of ideas." Lisa Price, open to inspiration from all quarters, identified this surging idea whose time had come before anyone else. Then she embraced it and made the decision to harness its power and lead the charge into a new market, all from the front.

---

* We'll meet Tristan Walker, the founder of Walker & Company, in chapter 15.

2

Is It Dangerous or Just Scary?

W hy is it that so many of us are so bad at differentiating between things that terrify us and things that present a real hazard? We're scared of flying, but we have no problem zipping down the highway in our cars at eighty-five miles per hour, even though you're *eighty-six* times more likely to die in a car accident than a plane crash; the odds of which are nearly 1 in 10,000, which itself is three times less likely than choking on food. We're afraid of letting our children go in the ocean on summer beach days because of sharks, but we demand they take baths on a regular basis, even though bathtubs claim one American life every day and sharks claim only one per year on average.

"Bathtubs should be 365 times as frightening as sharks, but it's the reverse. We don't have 'Bathtub Week' on the Discovery Channel," the brilliant writer-scholar James Fallows wrote in a 2014 article for *The Atlantic* on this very subject of the difference between danger and fear. The reason for this is fairly simple: we're more relaxed around things we're more acquainted with.

How many car rides have you taken this year? How many flights? How many showers or baths have you taken in your life? How many sharks have you come across in open water? The number of shark encounters is so minuscule in comparison that their rarity turns them into mysteries, which then turn into uncertainty within our-selves. And most of us do not do well with uncertainty. We worry. We fill the gap in our knowledge with our worst-case-scenario thinking. We get scared. And then we refuse to step even one foot in the water.

This is a position that many first-time entrepreneurs find them-selves in as they contemplate leaving the relative safety of stable everyday employment to start a new business. They are forced to reckon with the gap in familiarity between a regular paycheck and a boss who tells them what to do on the one side, and being their own boss with no guarantees on the other. For some, that gap can look like a canyon — or, worse, an abyss. And crossing it seems like the scariest, most foolish thing anyone could consider.

In 1984, the creator of Sam Adams beer, Jim Koch, was staring long and hard across the chasm. It was spring. It was the beginning of the baseball season in Boston, and it was about to be "morning in America." Ronald Reagan was preparing for what would be a land-slide reelection to the presidency, the economy had finally turned around after years in recession, the US Olympic team was about to run away from the competition at the Summer Games in Los Angeles, and Jim was in the middle of his sixth year as a management consul-tant for Boston Consulting Group (BCG), already earning $250,000 per year (that's more than $600K in 2020 dollars) before his thirty-fifth birthday.

By all accounts, Jim Koch had it made. His feet were planted se-curely on the terra firma of the business consulting world. "We flew first-class. You consulted with CEOs. Everyone treated you really well," Jim recalled. These were interesting, heady times at BCG. The company had just become fully employee owned, complete with an employee stock ownership plan (ESOP) that forged a real path to truly significant wealth for consultants like Jim. At the same time, he had already worked alongside a quartet of future luminaries: a young Mitt Romney; a thirtysomething Benjamin Netanyahu; the soon-to-be-legendary business school professor and author Clayton Chris-tensen, whose seminal work, *The Innovator's Dilemma,* helped shape twenty-first-century entrepreneurship; and future hedge fund billionaire John Paulson, who would make his fortune virtually overnight betting against the subprime lending market with credit default swaps some twenty-five years later. Jim Koch was no slouch either. He's triple Harvard (BA, JD, MBA), and to anyone who was paying attention — which included BCG's founder, its current CEO, and the man who would be next in line — the sky was the limit for this kid from the east side of Cincinnati.

"It was a great job for a while," Jim said with trademark understatement.

For a while? At Jim's salary, with the stock options still ahead of him, he was closing in on "pay off your parents' mortgage and start a foundation" territory. What more could one person possibly want from a job? Well, for Jim Koch, it wasn't about more; it was about different. In the beginning at BCG, Jim was being paid to learn about business strategy, product categories, organizational issues, and business problems. But once he entered management, his job became ... well ... boring. He was selling BCG's services rather than diving into problems and finding solutions. "The learning stopped," he said. "And then I had this epiphany. I asked myself, 'Do I want to do this the rest of my life?' And the answer came back: 'No.' And the corollary to that was, 'Well, if I don't want to do it for the rest of my life, I probably don't want to do it tomorrow.'"

It was a pretty abrupt turn for someone who had three degrees from Harvard and every reason in the world to wrap himself in the security and the creature comforts of his job. Yet something had to change. "I knew I did not want to work in the corporate world anymore," he said. So he started to think about quitting. Then, not unlike what happened with Lisa Price, a fortuitously timed article, this one in *Inc.* magazine, about a small but successful craft brewery in San Francisco called Anchor Brewery, triggered something in Jim, and it developed into an idea: a new craft beer.

Like any good consultant, Jim did his research into the current state of the beer industry, and once he settled on that as the very thing he wanted to pursue, he went home to visit his father to tell him of his plan to start a brewery. His father's response was unequivocal: "He looked at me and he said, 'Jim, you have done some really stupid things in your life. This is the stupidest.'" And Jim's father would know, because beer was the Koch family business.

Jim Koch's father was a fifth-generation brewmaster. Five generations of eldest Koch sons had been brewers. Jim would be the sixth — if his father wasn't able to talk him out of it. And there would be ample reason for him to do that. When Jim's dad got out of brewmaster school in 1948, there were a thousand breweries all over the United States. By 1984, that number had dwindled to *fifty*. In the intervening years, his father had to move the family from town to town as breweries closed, before finally leaving the brewing industry entirely.

"My dad told me that it was a miserable way to make a living," Jim said. "The last thing that he wanted for me to do was to go back into brewing." Jim was married with two small children. He was making a good living. That much was undeniable. To leave now, with everything looking up? It was too risky. Too scary.

Or was it?

Now, here's the thing about Jim Koch when it comes to fear and risk: this was not the first time he had taken a significant jump away from the safe, familiar path. In his midtwenties, while pursuing a joint JD and MBA, he dropped out of Harvard to become an Outward Bound instructor. "I just didn't want to make decisions that would bind me for the rest of my life [while still] having more to do," he explained. "And I also realized that there are things you can do in your twenties that if you don't do them then, you will never be able to do them."

For the next three and a half years, Jim spent his life outdoors, rock climbing, kayaking, backpacking, doing adventurous things that probably scared his parents half to death. But in doing them he learned that "you don't need that much to live on if you're really enjoying what you're doing." He also learned that nothing is permanent and that you can always go back once a different path has run its course. It was an experience that changed Jim's life. It shaped his entire perspective on the decision, some ten years later, to ignore his father's advice, to leave his job at Boston Consulting Group, and to create Sam Adams and the brewery that would become Boston Beer Company.

For anyone who possesses even a modicum of risk aversion, myself included, this seems from the outside like it must have been a terrifying decision. Think of the old proverb "A bird in the hand is worth two in the bush." Well, the bird in Jim's hand wasn't just any bird. It was a golden goose. It provided money and power and influence. He was going to let all that fly away? To brew beer? To have the same job that his father and grandfather had had? When precisely what they had always wanted for him was a better life? To Jim's mind, though, that golden goose looked more like golden handcuffs. It wasn't leaving BCG that carried all the risk; it was staying.

"It is the difference in life between things that are scary and things that are dangerous. There are plenty of things that are scary but aren't dangerous. And there are things that are dangerous but not scary. And those are the things that get you," Jim said by way of explanation. I understood in theory what he was saying, but he offered a climbing analogy from his Outward Bound days to really drive it home.

"One of the things we taught people to do was rappel off a cliff. It is a very scary thing to do, but you are also held by a belay rope, and that rope would hold a car. So walking off the cliff backwards is scary, but it's not dangerous. Walking across a thirty-five-degree-angle snowfield on a beautiful late May afternoon with bright blue sky, on the other hand, is not scary at all, but it is very dangerous, because the snow is melting, eventually it is going to find a layer of ice, the water will lubricate that ice, and then you have an avalanche. That is dangerous but not scary."

Jim was describing to me the exact same kind of comparative scenario that James Fallows had for his readers a few years earlier. We've all gone on walks when the weather is beautiful. Of course it's safe! But how many of us have rappelled off a cliff? And how many more than once? The whole thing just *sounds* dangerous. Like swimming in the ocean where, similar to rappelling, you can't really see the bottom. Except Jim Koch didn't need to see the bottom to know what was there — or, more likely, *not* there — and he wasn't at all concerned about hitting it.

"In my situation," he said, it was "staying at BCG that was dangerous but not scary. The danger was continuing to do something that didn't make me happy and getting to sixty-five years old and looking back and going, 'Oh my God, I wasted my life.'"

Failing is scary. Wasting your life is dangerous.

The great irony, of course, is that the history of modern entrepreneurship is littered with the stories of founders whose success we roundly celebrate today but whose loved ones worried in the beginning about the same thing that Jim did — that they'd waste their lives — but only if they *did* take that leap in pursuit of their ideas.

When Steve Jobs and Bill Gates dropped out of college in 1972 and 1975, respectively, to go on to found Apple and Microsoft, you can be sure their parents weren't high-fiving and sleeping soundly those first years, just as Mark Zuckerberg's parents weren't a generation later when he left school to start Facebook. Or Evan Williams's parents, when he left the University of Nebraska after a year and a half to work in the nascent tech startup sector before eventually founding Blogger and Twitter and then Medium.

Leaving a stable, well-paying career or dropping out of a prestigious university has simply never been something you did if you wanted to be successful in life, even if you did have a world-altering idea. Despite many success stories to the contrary and a laundry list of self-made billionaires who never donned a cap and gown, this conceit is as true today as it was in 1984. And not just for Jim Koch, but also for an eighteen-year-old freshman at the University of Texas named Michael Dell, who had just endured from his parents a harsher version of the talking-to that Jim was about to receive from his father later that spring.

Just as Jim came from a long line of brewers, Michael came from a long line of physicians. "I was a premed major," Michael told me, "and some of this was [a result of] the programming from my parents, because my father was a doctor, my older brother was a doctor, a lot of my cousins were doctors, and I always thought I'd be a doctor."

Except Michael had discovered computers several years earlier as a junior high school student, and they had quickly become his passion. He bought his first computer, an Apple II, when he was fifteen years old, and he took the whole thing apart to see how it worked. He was one of *those* kids. Then, as a premed freshman, he started upgrading off-the-shelf computers out of his dorm room. "It was just sort of a fun thing to do, a way to make some money," he said. "I was buying new computers and souping them up and then reselling them. I would upgrade them with more memory, and that actually became the main business — putting hard drives in those machines."

Today, we take memory and computing power for granted. Companies give away two-gigabyte thumb drives as swag at conferences like they are breath mints. But in late 1983 and early 1984, when Michael Dell was a freshman, machines like the original IBM microcomputers didn't even have hard disk drives.

"So what I would do is, I would make a hard disk drive system that you could put inside an IBM computer, and then instead of two 160K or 320K floppy disk drives, it would have a 10-megabyte hard drive, which at that time was something amazing."

It was so amazing that Michael quickly found customers at area universities and in lawyers' and doctors' offices, architecture firms, and other high-dollar, tech-savvy professions. ("Students weren't really buying computers at the time, and most of the students that I knew weren't really interested," Michael said.) He was even bidding on state contracts, which is just fantastically precocious. Before too long he was doing $50,000 to $80,000 per month in sales. That's nearly a million-dollar business. From a dorm room. *In 1983.*

Sounds like a pretty great business, right? Well, there were two people who would have disagreed: their names were Mom and Dad. And Michael knew it, which is why he never told them what he was doing or how much money he was making. They only found out when he had to explain why his grades that first semester were so poor.

"They became very upset with me and said, 'You have to stop this and focus on your studies.' They said, 'You've gotta get your priorities straight. What are you doing with your life?' All that stuff," Michael recounted. To Michael's credit, he gave it a shot. He tried to do what his parents asked of him.

It lasted about ten days.

"I actually realized that this was more than a hobby or a nice way to make some extra cash on the side while I was going to school," Michael said. "It was actually something I was very passionate about. So during those ten days, I sort of mapped out the beginnings of how I was going to finish up my freshman year but then launch this as a real, official business. And I eventually made a deal with my parents that I would do that, and if it worked out I would continue, and if it didn't I'd go back to school."

In January 1984, he registered his little dorm room Skunk Works as "PC's Limited." In May, just a month after Jim Koch decided to quit his job at BCG to start Sam Adams, Michael Dell finished his freshman year, officially incorporated as Dell Computer Corporation, moved his operation into office space in North Austin, and left school forever.

The disconnect between Michael Dell and his parents, and the key issue that I suspect has thwarted many young, aspiring entrepreneurs, is misapprehending the difference between something being dangerous and something being scary. It is mistaking fear for folly, risk for recklessness. It is the presumption that if something has never been done before, that is because it can't or it shouldn't be done. If you have a good idea that excites you, that compels you to take a detour from the comfort of a normal existence along the beaten path, you will first need to navigate this minefield of misunderstanding, whether it lives within you or sits between you and those whose opinions you value and respect. Because while you can never fully know what you're getting yourself into when it comes to building a business, you should at least know whether you can get yourself out of it if everything goes south. That is the difference between dangerous and scary.

For Michael's parents — coming from a family of well-educated people at a time when personal computing was mostly a curiosity that was often dismissed as a fad — leaving school to tinker with computers and resell them must have felt like their son was in danger of throwing his life away. What is more dangerous to a parent than a child taking their first steps out onto the high-wire act of adulthood and doing so without a net?

But for Michael, there was nothing at all dangerous about this idea. He loved working on computers. He knew them well enough as a teenager that professional adults with even more to lose than he did trusted his insight and his work. *He was solving their problems.* Moreover, having found early success and having seen what was on the other side of this big leap, it was impossible to go back and see the world in the same way again, to *ever again* see it as his parents had. He knew the rules of this new world, and because of that, any last vestiges of danger melted away. And, hey, if it didn't work out for whatever reason, he could always just go back to school and slot right back into the premed program. He was nineteen years old; he had his entire life ahead of him.

The reality was, the scariest part of starting Dell Computer Corporation was the same thing that is scary about starting any business: it's the unknown. What did a teenage Michael Dell know about running a business? About hiring? About leading people? About finding and leasing office space? About corporate taxes? What do any of us know about that stuff before we confront it? Nothing. That is truly terrifying to any first-time entrepreneur. But it is also eminently knowable — if you choose to learn it.

The danger for Michael was in relenting to his parents' demands that he become a doctor, in hating every waking second of it while he watched the personal computing revolution unfold in front of him, and then in resenting his family for the rest of his life because they pushed him down a path that he knew in his heart was wrong for him.

If there is one thing I am certain of from my time interviewing entrepreneurs, it is that anyone who found their success after leaving the relative security of higher education or their previous profession would be utterly unsurprised by the choices that Jim and Michael made in 1984. When entrepreneurs of that type think back to the moment they took the leap — when, swinging on the monkey bars of life, they finally took one hand off the bar behind them and swung forward to reach for the next bar in front of them — they all talk about that initial uncertainty and the scariness of the unknown. But then those concerns melt away as they reflect on the even greater dangers of regret and squandered opportunity, and, as Jim put it, waking up at sixty-five years old only to realize that they'd wasted their lives.

Even though it comes from an old French word, "entrepreneur-ship" is a fairly new term in the vocabulary of business. Founders to-day self-identify as entrepreneurs in a way that the generations who came before them struggle to understand, mostly because they didn't have the language back then to describe what they were doing as they built their businesses. Fundamentally, though, they were doing the same thing. They were taking the detour, taking the leap — away from the type of professional life they didn't want, and toward something new and exciting and their own.

As a group, they have made entrepreneurship both less scary *and* less dangerous. By developing a lexicon for the process of starting a business, by giving it a name, many of the modern founders whom you will meet in this book have helped to demystify the prospect of taking the leap. By breaking new ground, the older generation of founders — of which Jim and Mike are a part — have made taking the leap seem almost normal.

They are why you can trust the rope threaded through your har-ness by experts and counterweighted by mentors, and have faith that the anchors hammered into the cliff face by those who came before you will hold, as you take that first big step backward off the cliff and into the unknown. Because they know what it means to take your fate into your own hands and to feel that you've got a real grip on this idea that has its own grip on your soul.

3

Leave Your Safety Zone . . .
but Do It Safely

PayPal alumnus and LinkedIn founder Reid Hoffman captured the romance of entrepreneurial daring perhaps better than anyone when he said, "Starting a company is like throwing yourself off the cliff and assembling an airplane on the way down."

There is something romantic about the struggle to do something new, isn't there? About taking the leap. At one point or another, all of us who are enamored of the pursuit of big ideas have found ourselves enthralled by the origin story of a successful enterprise: the marathon coding sessions; the all-nighters that stretch across an entire week; the four friends stacked on top of one another inside a one-bedroom apartment, meeting every evening at the kitchen table in the "boardroom." In commencement addresses and keynote speeches, famous founders talk wistfully about these memorable and crucial moments. Being down to their last dollar; maxing out their credit cards; eating nothing but ramen noodles and drinking nothing but Mountain Dew for months on end.

Those were the good old days.

There are some people who find those stories exhilarating; others, terrifying. For the longest time, I would have counted myself as one of the latter. And to an extent, I still do. I mean, what kind of maniac would just throw caution to the wind as Reid described? Who in their right mind would ever take such a huge risk? If building a company or creating something big and new is like jumping off a cliff and *hoping* to put enough pieces together before it, and you, die a horrible death, the question I always want to ask founders and creators is, *Why do it? What are you thinking? Why would you ever jump?*

Okay, maybe I have more than one question.

The reassuring thing I've discovered, though, is that for every blind leaper, there is another type of entrepreneur. One who doesn't walk backward off the cliff like it was a gangplank. One who doesn't just close their eyes, hold their nose, and hand their fate over to gravity. This entrepreneur's eyes are wide open. They have already measured the jump. Like a trained gymnast, they've already picked a landing spot. More important, they know that if they aren't able to stick the landing, if they can't build the entire plane in time and the business goes up in flames, their whole life won't get wiped out with it. They're taking the leap of faith knowing they have carefully packed, checked, and triple-checked their parachute.

At the risk of torturing this metaphor beyond recognition, what I'm saying is that most of the successful entrepreneurs I've met left the comfort of their previous lives as safely and smartly as possible. And they did this in one of two ways: either they stayed in their "real jobs" until their startups demanded more time than they could spare, or they went for it with a fallback plan in their hip pocket, which made the risks inherent in entrepreneurship manageable enough for them to be able to sleep at night.

Daymond John did both.

In 1989, long before he was one of the most savvy sharks on *Shark Tank,* Daymond John was one of the most ambitious waiters at Red Lobster. Twenty years old, living with his mother in Hollis, Queens, Daymond spent his evenings serving Cheddar Bay Biscuits to the seafood lover in you, and his days working on an idea for a new hip-hop clothing brand. He called it FUBU — from "for us, by us" — in response to certain high-end clothing companies that didn't like "rappers, inner-city kids, African Americans" wearing their clothes. "I started to get fed up hearing about all these types of brands," Daymond told me. "I wanted to create a brand that loved and respected the people who love and respected hip-hop."

His first product was more or less an accident. It was a particular kind of tie-top wool ski cap ("not with the ball on top, but with a little tie like a shoestring") that was relatively inexpensive and was becoming popular with a lot of rappers, but that was still impossible to find anywhere in the city where everyday people shopped for clothes. "I went all over uptown Manhattan," Daymond remembered. "When I finally found one, if you added the gas and tolls, I paid $30 for this thing. I showed my mother, and she said, 'You can't afford to just pay that kind of money for something you can make for $2.'"

The light bulb went on. There was opportunity here. Daymond's mother sent him to a fabric store to buy $40 worth of fabric and then taught him how to sew the caps himself. Within three hours, he had eighty caps. Forget $2; he'd made a bunch of caps for 50 cents apiece. Now he just had to sell them.

The next day was Good Friday. Everyone from the neighborhood would be headed over to the Jamaica Colosseum Mall to shop for Easter, so that's where Daymond went. "I caught people when they walked in and out of that mall, standing on the corner," he said. "I sold the hats for $20, but if you didn't have $20, it would be $17. If you didn't have $17, it would be $15. And if you didn't have $15, they were $10. My last two hats, they were $3." By the time the day was done, Daymond was holding $800 in cash, $760 of it pure profit. A 20× return on investment. Within a couple months, he'd used the money from some of these early sales to refine the quality of his hats and his FUBU logo, and then move into shirts.

Daymond was onto something. He started by purchasing simple Champion T-shirts and sweatshirts from local clothing stores, then stitching his own FUBU label *over* the Champion insignia. When he sold enough of those, he took the proceeds and sourced high-quality blank jerseys and sweatshirts from around the country. He hired embroidery shops and silk-screen printers to elevate the quality of the craftsmanship.

"My plan at the time involved the big black guys in the neighborhood," Daymond explained. "They had little options to be very stylish, so they had to go to Rochester Big and Tall and get a big white shirt or a black shirt, or they had to pay a lot of money to get their stuff custom-made. So we found a place that made 4X-, 5X-, 6X-sized shirts, and we made twenty of them." Just imagine: that's sixty massively large shirts with FUBU's logo emblazoned across the front in an equally massive font. It would be hard to miss, right? That's what Daymond thought, too. "We knew that if we gave them [for free] to these guys, who were bodyguards and bouncers standing out in front of the clubs, they would not just wear it once. We knew these guys would wear it forever. So for the first six months, that's what we did. And before you know it, these guys were walking billboards."

But these were not your run-of-the-mill bouncers or bodyguards. They were not just ID checkers or crowd control managers. These guys were glued to the hips of rap artists who were redefining American pop culture. They were the gatekeepers of what were becoming the hottest clubs in New York — the Studio 54s of their generation. Which meant, when outfitted in gear provided directly from Daymond, each one was the living, breathing equivalent of a Times Square billboard for FUBU. One that managed to get the attention of Ralph McDaniels, the influential co-founder of the iconic New York public access TV show *Video Music Box,* which had been responsible for breaking nearly every single hip-hop artist on the East Coast as far back as 1983. Ralph put Daymond and his partners on the show in 1993 and told everyone who was watching that FUBU was the next big thing.

"He really put us out there, and after that all the rappers — all of them — were ready to wear our stuff because Ralph gave us the thumbs-up," Daymond said.

This was not an exaggeration, and it was a very big deal. You have to remember, in 1992–1993 rap and hip-hop were exploding into the mainstream. These were the years when the world was introduced to the first albums from iconic hip-hop artists like Dr. Dre, Arrested Development, Common, House of Pain, UGK, Snoop Dogg, E-40, Bone Thugs-n-Harmony, and the Roots. Not to mention follow-up albums from seminal artists like the Beastie Boys, Eric B. & Rakim, Public Enemy, Too Short, and Ice Cube. I don't mean for this to turn into a VH1 *Behind the Music* episode about the history of rap, but it's important to understand that FUBU began its ascendancy as the defining brand in hip-hop fashion during the same years that many of the artists who defined the golden age of hip-hop rose to prominence wearing the company's clothes.

Daymond was four-plus years into his FUBU journey at this point. He had strung together a number of wins for his fledgling business, some of them big enough that, if they were to happen in the modern entrepreneurial environment, they very well might inspire their beneficiaries to drop out of college or quit their jobs, move to Silicon Valley, and try to raise a bunch of money. Basically, to take that running jump off the cliff that Reid Hoffman talked about.

But that was never on the spectrum of possibilities for Daymond. Even the rush of attention and sales that came from his appearance on *Video Music Box* couldn't get him to quit his "real job" — only to reduce his hours. He eased himself into the entrepreneurial life. "It was forty hours at Red Lobster and six hours at FUBU. Then it was thirty hours at Red Lobster and twenty hours at FUBU, because money started to come in," he told an audience of entrepreneurs at one of CNBC's iConic conferences in 2017.

A number of great business minds who found themselves in comparable positions early in their careers took similar approaches to balancing their old jobs with their new entrepreneurial ventures. When Phil Knight started Blue Ribbon Sports, the company that would become Nike, he spent five years as a certified public accountant, "putting in six days a week at Price Waterhouse" and all of his free time at Blue Ribbon. "Most days I didn't mind," he recounted in his memoir, *Shoe Dog,* because "I invested a healthy portion of my paycheck into Blue Ribbon's account at the bank, padding my precious equity, boosting the company's cash balance."

The shoe business is hard, but where money is concerned, there are few industries riskier than the airline business. As Virgin Atlantic's founder Richard Branson famously quipped, "If you want to be a millionaire, start with a billion dollars and launch a new airline." The graveyard of defunct airlines is a testament to the essential truth at the core of Branson's joke.

That makes the late Herb Kelleher's achievement all the more impressive as co-founder of Southwest Airlines. For much of Southwest's early existence, Herb, a practicing attorney, kept his private law practice open. For the first four and a half years, as he helped get the airline off the ground with funding and FAA approvals and aircraft leases, he also defended the company against a litany of lawsuits.

In 1969, in fact, it got so bad that the company ran out of money, and the Southwest board of directors talked seriously about shutting down the airline. It was Herb's willingness to "litigate for nothing and to pay all the court costs out of [his] own pocket" that kept the lights on. In keeping his day job for as long as he did, he gave Southwest the runway it needed to take flight as the newest (and only, at the time) no-frills, low-cost airline. Today, it carries more passengers than all but two airlines in the entire world.

Herb didn't give up his law practice until 1981, fourteen years after the founding of Southwest Airlines, and he only did it at the request of the board of directors. Daymond John didn't hang on for quite so long. He quit Red Lobster completely in 1995, six years into the life of FUBU. But even then it was only after he'd secured a multimillion-dollar round of financing from the head of the textiles division inside the South Korean tech giant Samsung, as part of a deal Daymond and his partners were seeking in order to fulfill $300,000 in orders he'd booked a few months earlier at the MAGIC fashion trade show in Las Vegas.

And it's here that we get to the heart of Daymond's decision to stay at Red Lobster for as long as he did, and why he concluded his talk at the iConic conference by exhorting the crowd *not* to quit their day jobs. Despite its early successes, despite all the attention from media and tastemakers, despite the rising profile of the brand in the hip-hop community, FUBU was never too far from insolvency. It was always in need of cash.

"Through 1989 and 1992, I closed the business three times because, with all the development costs, I ran out of money," Daymond told me. "Like many businesses, my partners and I leveraged our credit cards above $50,000 with a very high interest rate, which is not the smartest thing to do." That trade show in Vegas? Daymond and his partners snuck in every day wearing half the FUBU gear they were trying to sell to retailers, because they couldn't afford floor passes, let alone the fee for an exhibitor's booth. Oh, and that deal they struck with Samsung? It was the product of a classified ad that Daymond's mother took out in the *New York Times:* "Million dollars in orders. Need financing." The ad cost $2,000. Daymond worked for a month at Red Lobster to pay for it.

Daymond will tell you that his job at Red Lobster did for FUBU what Herb Kelleher's legal practice did for Southwest: it gave his business the runway to take off, and once it did, he poured himself into it completely. But in the same breath, Daymond will also say that the Red Lobster job was the rip cord he could have pulled any time he felt like FUBU was going down. One could argue he should have pulled it more times than he did; he certainly would have been better off in the short run. "If [FUBU] would have failed [early on]," he told the iConic audience, "I wouldn't have been owing everybody; I wouldn't have had this huge deficit; my credit wouldn't have been ruined for seven years." He also would have had a job that kept him housed, fed, and clothed. A job he was good at, that he actually liked. "I was having a great time as a waiter," he said of those early years.

Knowing that he could always go back to something he was good at, where he had a lot of experience, didn't make the leap into FUBU any less scary, but it did remove a lot of the danger. It gave him a cushion, a fallback plan. The same was true for Jim Koch. The knowledge that he could go back to Boston Consulting Group or some other management consulting firm whenever he wanted, made the insane decision (at the time) to start a craft brewery seem less crazy. For Sara Blakely, the billionaire founder of Spanx, selling fax machines was her fallback. For Mark Cuban, internet entrepreneur and Daymond John's fellow shark, it was bartending. The founder of JetBlue

Airways, David Neeleman, knew that if his idea for a low-cost airline that flew out of big markets didn't take off, he could always go back to being a travel agent.

These fallback plans offered varying degrees of psychological security to the brilliant founders who had them, but how much money they could make was far less important than the fact that they could at least be assured of making enough money to live. This was the idea that Jane Wurwand, the creator of Dermalogica, learned from her mother growing up in the United Kingdom. "The five words that changed my life were my mom saying to my sisters and myself, 'Learn how to do something!'" Jane said. "She was absolutely adamant that each of us had to get a skill so that no matter what happened, if we were somewhere, anywhere, in the world, we would have a skill set in our hands that we could go to work [with] immediately and earn money and keep food on the table."

Jane's skill was skin care. She began her career in that field by teaching skin care treatments to licensed aestheticians in Marina del Rey, California, at a little place called the International Dermal Institute, that she founded with her husband. Three years later, she recognized an opportunity to create a whole skin care line — twenty-seven products in all — that she could sell to her students and that they in turn could use on their clients at salons around the country. It was a good idea. But in 1986 there was no guarantee that a skin care line wouldn't completely flop. Fortunately for Jane, if that happened, she still knew how to teach skin care, and with the International Dermal Institute still up and running, she would always have a place to teach it. She would always have money coming in.

That is the buoying effect of not quitting your job right away and having a fallback plan for when you do. It's not so that you'll have another way to do something *new* and possibly get rich. Rather, it's a way to have another shot at doing something you've already done *before* so that you don't go broke while you gather yourself to try again. By doing things smartly and safely like this, you'll give yourself more time and more room to operate, while simultaneously reducing the chances that failure can ruin your life.

Having a fallback plan does not mean you are building an escape hatch from your dream. It's not an excuse not to try hard, nor is it a ready-made reason to quit. It just means you've given yourself a cushion at the bottom of your entrepreneurial leap of faith so that if you do crash, you can bounce back to fight another day.

4

Do Your Research

I really love talking to creators and digging into the granular details of how they built their products. Every time I learn something new or unexpected from them, which is usually something totally impressive, it makes me sit back in my chair and simply say, "Wow!" I live for those "wow" moments. I love to be blown away by people who were already so inspiring before they walked into my studio or onto whatever stage we were set to share in conversation.

Each founder I've met has been uniquely impressive, but if there is a characteristic they share that continually grabs me, it's that all of them have done their homework — about their product, their business, their customers, their industry as a whole — and it has imbued them with a deep confidence in the viability of their ideas. I've asked these innovators and idealists thousands of questions over the years, and I can probably count on one hand the number of times they doubted the things they'd built. They knew their ideas would work, because *they knew their stuff.* I suppose I shouldn't be surprised by this. If most successful founders looked before they leapt off Reid Hoffman's entrepreneurial cliff, it only makes sense that they also figured out what kind of plane they were going to build in the process of falling.

To do that — to know what you're going to do before you've done it — is to do your research. Lots and lots of research. Every founder does it. They *have* to. But there is one kind of founder in particular whose story, I think, speaks most strongly to the impact of research. It's a story that offers the greatest motivation to apprehensive creators and aspiring entrepreneurs, because it involves those who found themselves starting a business within an industry they had absolutely no experience in.

Sometimes it's a product of passion, as it was for Lisa Price and her skin care line, Carol's Daughter.

Sometimes it's the result of a lack of options, as it was for the founders of Ben & Jerry's, middle school friends Ben Cohen and Jerry Greenfield. Ben, an underemployed cabdriver in New York City and a serial college dropout. Jerry, a multiple medical school rejectee working as a lab technician in North Carolina. Both of them willing, in the late 1970s, to "put our fortunes together" for a few years, as Jerry wryly described it, "to open up a little shop."

But just as often, it is a consequence of curiosity and coincidence. Someone goes looking for something that they are sure already exists — a product, a service, a TV show, even a video game, it doesn't really matter — only to discover that it is nowhere to be found. So they start talking about it in casual conversation to whoever will listen — friends, family, Uber drivers, baristas, professional acquaintances — and they learn that they are not the only one who has been looking for this thing and has come up empty-handed. Then, in realizing that they are not alone, something else happens: the absence of this thing evolves from a minor inconvenience in their life to a real-world problem that, in their estimation, *needs* to be solved. And they have an idea for how to solve it.

It is the stories that follow this particular arc that I am consistently enthralled by. They almost sound like parables — like Icarus crossed with *The Little Engine That Could*. And what I find to be most thrilling of all — most startling, really — about the heroes of these stories is that their lack of subject matter expertise or institutional knowledge or industry experience was never a deterrent to them. It was actually a blessing. It was *freedom*. Because without the traditional constraints of standard operating procedures or the expectations created by prior generations of similar offerings, these curious individuals were free to ignore all the basic assumptions about the business they were preparing to enter and to figure out how to create the best possible version of the thing they were looking for, in whatever ways made the most sense to them.

This is what Jen Rubio did when she created the luggage company Away with her friend Steph Korey.

In early 2015, Jen Rubio was in her midtwenties and, by any measure, a total rock star. She was also unemployed. A few months earlier, she'd quit her job as the global head of innovation for the British fashion retailer AllSaints—a position for which she had moved to London from New York in the summer of 2013 after leaving the online eyewear retailer Warby Parker, where she was head of social media. Jen was in between jobs and in between cities. She was also about as far away from the center of the luggage business as you can get for someone with hundreds of thousands of frequent-flier miles under her belt.

Then she went skiing in the Swiss Alps with her friends for a week. "I was completely just on a tear around the world, splitting my time between interviewing for jobs that I probably had no business applying for and going on vacation," Jen said. That's when, on the way back home, luggage became her life.

"I'm in Zurich airport, and my bag breaks," she recalled. "I'm leaving a trail of my underwear behind me as I'm running through the airport. It was so embarrassing. When I get home, I decide I'm just going to buy a really nice bag that I love and this won't happen again for a long time. So I go on Facebook and ask my friends what they recommend. Every single person is like, 'I don't know,' or 'I have this, but don't get it, it's awful.'"

Not a single person in her large and diverse network of taste-making, style-setting friends had a good answer for her. It was either buy a Tumi bag that costs more than most plane tickets; spend $100 on an American Tourister from a big-box store that looks like everybody else's luggage; or spend nothing at all for a poorly made piece and hope it makes it down the baggage carousel before totally falling apart. Those were the options, and none of her friends had any opinion on them, one way or the other, besides *don't.*

"It was so crazy to me that all of these people, including myself, who love to travel really had no connection to this thing that they brought with them on every single trip," Jen said. So she set out in search of the perfect bag. "I was on a mission. I was like, 'There has to be an amazing luggage brand that exists.' And I couldn't find one."

Immediately, she began digging into the luggage industry, asking big, open-ended questions both to herself and to everyone she met:

"Why doesn't this luggage brand exist?"

"How come buying luggage is so awful?"

"How come you have to go into the basement of a department store or, like in New York, all these crazy luggage stores in Midtown that are massive, and there's a $500 bag next to a $50 bag and they look exactly the same and the luggage salesman is whispering in your ear, 'I can give you 30 percent off if you buy it right now.'"

"Why is this so horrible?"

That is when she called her friend Steph Korey, whom she worked with at Warby Parker in the company's early days. Steph was now in New York, in business school at Columbia University. Simultaneously, she was consulting with the mattress startup Casper in her capacity as a supply chain specialist. It was just going to be one of those friendly check-in calls to see how Steph was doing and maybe take her temperature on an idea. Jen and Steph were supposed to talk for ten minutes. They talked for three hours.

"I basically called her with my little baby idea to start a luggage brand," Jen said, "and she was like, '*This is it*. What we did at Warby Parker, we can do with luggage.'"

To be clear, neither woman was really seriously considering starting a new business. Jen was in the final stages of interviewing for (and ultimately getting) a position as vice president of marketing for a big fashion company. Steph was courting offers to become vice president of supply chain for a couple different startups. All Jen really wanted, or so she thought, was a suitcase that she truly loved. From her end, Steph was mostly interested in finding another industry to disrupt in much the same way Warby Parker had disrupted eyeglasses.

And yet, without telling each other, when they got off the phone after this marathon conversation, each of them started intensely researching the luggage idea on their own — Jen from the marketing and brand side, Steph from the supply chain and product development side. They couldn't help themselves. With the dearth of luggage options out there, the more questions these two women with unique skill sets and experience building out trendy yet accessible brands asked, the greater the opportunity they saw.

A few weeks later, Jen was in New York to interview for yet *another* job (she'd turned down the previous one, but she still wasn't sure if Steph was really into this venture), and so she decided to go hang out at Steph's apartment once her interview was over. Then she decided to spend the night. They ended up talking about this luggage idea deep into the morning. When Jen woke up the next day, she didn't leave — *for another three weeks.* During that time, sitting right there on Steph Korey's living room sofa, they essentially founded the company that would become Away.

"The first few weeks were just like our intense version of market research," Jen recalled, "which basically meant we went shopping every single day. We went to every department store. We went to every luggage store. We made these Google maps of different luggage stores around New York and compared all the experiences and all the prices. We kept very meticulous notes on what was out there."

At the same time, they researched and visited factories to figure out what it would take "to cut out the department stores and the bargain basement luggage stores and all of the weird wholesale and retail and licensing markups," which, according to Jen, is more or less how Warby Parker is able to "make something really high quality at a much more affordable price." They cut out the middlemen. This was more or less the same business model Steph was helping Casper implement in their attempt to disrupt the mattress market.

At this juncture, Jen and Steph still had to figure out the look and feel and function of their bag. "Neither of us had experience making luggage," Jen said. "Our only experience with luggage was that we owned it." So they created a survey asking what consumers wanted. It included a list of "every feature imaginable based on what we knew from our research, and we sent the survey out to, like, 100 friends," Jen told me.

Smart, right?

"It was the stupidest idea ever," she said. Wow, okay. "If you have a survey that says 'What would you like to see in your luggage?' everything gets checked. It's not at all indicative of what people actually want or what they would pay for."

Their research had revealed every possible combination of features that could ever exist in a piece of luggage, but the usefulness of that information was inherently limited if they didn't know how consumers felt about each feature individually and in relation to all the others. It's like pineapple and pizza: Yes, pineapple is delicious. And, sure, technically you *can* put it on pizza. But should you, really? Jen and Steph quickly figured out that they had to narrow the universe of potential features from what *could* go into their luggage to what *should* go into it. To do that, they had to figure out how people actually used their luggage — on business trips, on vacation, on family holidays, on travel of any and every kind. So over the next few months, they talked to nearly 800 people and asked them just that:

How do you pack?
What do you do right when you get to the hotel?
What do you do with your luggage?
What do you put in it?
What are your biggest pain points when you're traveling?

"We would talk to them about travel and ask them all these open-ended questions," Jen said. The same kinds of questions Jen asked of the industry as a whole when she first tried to understand it. "With some people who we knew, we would actually go over to their house and watch them pack. And that's how we figured out all of the things we needed to make . . . our one perfect suitcase."

Of course, the suitcase wasn't actually perfect. Jen and Steph would go on to iterate and improve on the luggage several more times after the first version, like any smart creator does. That doesn't mean the research they did was faulty or that it was less valuable than it could have been. In fact, it was *in*valuable. It was the first concrete step they took in a multipart process that helped them refine their design, home in on what really mattered, and leave out all the stuff that wasn't going to move the needle. It eventually put them in a position to take the next step and pull the trigger on their idea as a full-fledged business.

That is exactly what research is supposed to accomplish. It is not meant to be leaned on like a crutch, or deferred to unequivocally, as though it is more relevant than experience or instinct or talent. When a creator goes down that pathway, as I have learned by talking to creators from across industries and disciplines, they risk falling into the trap of crowdsourcing the creative process. And while there is often wisdom in the crowd in certain instances, creativity is not one of them. With look and feel and function, which can involve intensely personal preferences, the crowd can become a shapeless mob with a gravity that even the most experienced entrepreneur can't predict. Just imagine what could have come from that original list of features Jen and Steph used to survey their 100 friends: zippers and pockets and ports everywhere, infinite color options inside and out, rows of wheels, telescoping handles with shoulder straps and carabiners. It would have looked like a *frankencase!*

There is a famous line from Steve Jobs about this pitfall: "Some people say, 'Give the customers what they want.' But that's not my approach . . . People don't know what they want until you show it to them." What a lot of people don't know is that there is an important insight at the end of that quote that, inexplicably, always gets cut off, and that statement from Jobs is particularly relevant here: "That's why I never rely on market research."

All the market research Jen and Steph accumulated — all the comparison shopping they did on price, design, and purchase experience — it wasn't so they could just collate it and regurgitate it back out into the marketplace to give people what they *said* they wanted. Rather, it was to build a foundation of knowledge on which they could leverage their creative instincts and their professional judgment, in order to truly innovate and deliver what dissatisfied luggage customers like them really *needed*.

Talking to Jen Rubio about the role that research plays for creators and entrepreneurs reminded me of how athletes talk about practice, or how actors approach rehearsal. It's deep work and repetition that sear the fundamentals into your muscle memory. They help you understand how to do things and why you should do them in a certain way, so when the lights come on and it's time to do something for real, you can put all that prep work away and just act or play or build. You can create freely, without reservation or hesitation.

When Jen and Steph introduced their first bag—what would become "The Carry-On" in the language of their simply named product lines—it had a USB charger, a removable laundry bag, an indestructible outer shell, and 360-degree wheels. Each of these features, along with the $225 price tag and direct-to-consumer delivery, was deliberately selected as part of a product marketing strategy that was developed from all their research but not defined or decided by it. Jen and Steph didn't blindly follow the whims of the first 100 friends they polled or the 800 people they interviewed afterward. Instead, they banked all that knowledge and then applied their own judgment, instincts, aesthetics, skills, and experience to it.

The results were undeniable. They officially formed Away as a real business in early 2015. By February of the following year, they had seed funding, a big feature piece in *Vogue* magazine, and 2,000 suitcases in hand from a manufacturer in China—each piece of luggage spoken for by customers who'd never touched or even seen one of the suitcases up close. That first full year in operation, they sold 55,000 suitcases. Not long after, they added "The Bigger Carry-On," "The Medium," and "The Large," to create a full line of suitcases. Within three years, they sold *a million* pieces.

Wow.

In many ways, this is a model for creativity, whether you are inside a company as an employee or you're an industry outsider with a good idea and an itch for entrepreneurship. It is a playbook for innovation, no matter who you are or what you want to build. This is not a playbook Jen and Steph wrote themselves, to be sure. It's not as if they were trying to reach new heights in data-driven product development with their research. But the nature of their research is not what makes their story so inspiring and relevant; it's the relatability.

When Daymond John enlisted the help of local silk-screen printers and embroidery shops in the early days of FUBU, he didn't know where to go or what to do. He was a waiter from Queens. So he pulled out the yellow pages (remember those?) and cold-called every listing he could find. He researched them. Then he got up every morning at 6 a.m. and took the train to New Jersey — which was the self-proclaimed "embroidery capital of the world" at the time — checking out all the shops until he found the right one for his budget and his needs.

Little more than a decade earlier, when Ben Cohen and Jerry Greenfield decided to open their "little shop," they "sent away for thirty SBA [Small Business Administration] pamphlets on all the different aspects of running a business," Ben recalled. When they decided their shop would serve ice cream (because bagel-making equipment — their other idea — was too expensive), they spent most of their time "doing a lot of research on a business plan for an ice cream shop ... and taking this correspondence course in how to make ice cream." Like Daymond, they "spent a lot of time with the yellow pages."

Twenty years after Daymond's march through the "E" and "S" sections of the phone book, a professional soccer player from New Zealand named Tim Brown did something very similar in his quest to make a simple, clean, comfortable lace-up sneaker. "A creative problem that feels like it needs to be solved," as Tim put it, sent him in search of a footwear factory that would let him visit so he could learn the ins and outs of how shoes are made. "It was like the university application process: I was spraying and praying." Eventually, a factory in Indonesia opened its doors to Tim, and he "walked into this world that was intriguing and surprisingly complicated and incredibly old-fashioned in the way that it worked. And I realized my innovation alarm was going off, because I'd ask these really, really simple questions, and no one could give me a clear answer." Like

Jen and Steph, Tim decided he was going to be the one to solve this creative problem and answer the questions the shoe manufacturers couldn't. Five years later, he launched the idea on Kickstarter. Two years after that, barely a month after Away delivered its first 2,000 suitcases, Tim, now with a partner named Joey Zwillinger, turned that idea into a company called Allbirds. And two years after that, it was worth $1.4 billion.

Apparel. Ice cream. Footwear. Luggage. They're all different, but they're all the same. There is nothing special about any of these industries that makes them uniquely suited for new entrants or for disruption. Similarly, there isn't anything innate in Jen and Steph, or Daymond or Tim, or Ben and Jerry, that made them uniquely suited as creators to be the new kids on their respective blocks. But they are fantastic examples of founders who did their homework to fill in the gaps in their understanding, so that the things they set out to build did not topple for lack of a sturdy foundation.

They relied on research to teach them how to build a plane — which gave them the confidence to lean on their instincts and trust their creative visions when it came time to decide exactly what kind of plane they wanted to build and fly. This has been a winning combination countless times in the history of new ideas. It's one any of us can commit to when we set out to create something new — when we decide to take our own leap off the cliff of entrepreneurship.

5

Find Your Co-founder

When we think about the founding of our most famous modern companies, it's amazing how often only a handful of names come to mind: Zuckerberg. Jobs. Bezos. Musk. Gates. Ellison.

The truth is, we love origin stories almost as much as we love heroes and the idea of singular exceptionalism. So we tend to exalt many of our modern founders. We regard them as mythical figures of unique ability. We even call their companies *unicorns* when they become super successful. And yet, time and again, when I meet the founder of an amazing company that has done wonderful things, I find myself listening not so much to the story of a great idea born of singular brilliance, but to the triumph of a good idea in the hands of a perfect partnership. In my experience, it seems that partnerships have been the rule, not the exception; and as Paul Graham wrote in his famous 2006 essay about the mistakes that kill startups ("single founder" being number one), "It seems unlikely this is a coincidence."

It makes sense when you consider that we are not solitary creatures. Human beings are social animals. We live in groups. We work in teams. We mate in pairs. We thrive when we are together. It is as true in life as it is in business. "Even companies you think of as having one founder, like Oracle, usually turn out to have more," Graham wrote. Indeed, the truth is that virtually no company is the creation of a single individual, but rather the product of a partnership, or even a group of co-founders. Just look at the entrepreneurs we've met so far.

Jen Rubio probably didn't *need* Steph Korey to design the first Away bag. After all, Jen was the one with the marketing and design sensibility. It's possible Jen didn't even need Steph to get the bag made. But to get it manufactured at scale? At the right price point? And distributed seamlessly directly to consumers? Well, that was all Steph. Heck, Steph probably didn't need Jen either. Jen once joked to me that if Billy McFarland had recruited Steph in 2015 instead of Jen recruiting her, Steph probably would have saved the infamous Fyre Festival with her logistics acumen. Regardless, without Jen there would be no bag. And without Steph there would be no distribution model. And without *both of them* there would be no Away, period.

Lisa Price made fantastic lotions and butters, but she didn't even think about selling them as *products* until her mother pushed her to set up a table at their church flea market. And the fledgling business probably never would have gotten the traction it needed within the "sister-girl network" without Lisa's husband, Gordon, who not only helped Lisa identify them as her first, core market, but also worked hard in scribbling down orders off their answering machine so she could fulfill them.

Jim Koch had five generations of brewers' wisdom to lean on as well as an old family recipe to tinker with as he created Samuel Adams Boston Lager, but the secret ingredient in Sam Adams as a startup business came in the form of Rhonda Kallman, his twenty-three-year-old assistant at Boston Consulting Group. At first glance, a management consultant and an assistant quitting their jobs to start a company together sounds like something yanked straight out of the logline of a Hollywood romantic comedy. It has a very *Jerry Maguire* vibe to it. In reality, of all the people Jim knew, there was no one better suited than Rhonda to join him on this entrepreneurial journey.

"I looked around BCG, full of the best and the brightest from the top business schools," Jim recalled, "and I realized there was this person here who was energetic, talented, resourceful, a great people person — she had all of the skills I don't really have. She was my secretary. We were the perfect complement." Jim was the brewmaster; Rhonda was the practical one. Together they founded Boston Beer Company, which was profitable from its very first month.

Whether he knew it at the time or not, Jim had arrived at the most powerful reason every entrepreneur should look for a cofounder when they have an idea and are thinking about starting a business: You need a partner whose skill set complements yours. Someone who not only shares your vision but elevates it and holds you accountable to it; who does what you cannot; who thinks and sees things in a way you don't; whose strengths compensate for your weaknesses, and vice versa.

This kind of yin-yang approach happens all the time. For example, you could not find two more different yet complementary people than Adam Lowry and Eric Ryan. They're the co-founders of the household cleaning product manufacturer Method, which is famous for its teardrop-shaped soap bottle that's pretty enough to keep out on the counter instead of hidden away under the sink with all the other industrial-strength cleansers.

Childhood friends from Grosse Pointe, Michigan, Adam and Eric went to college on opposite sides of the country for very different purposes — Adam to Stanford for chemical engineering, Eric to Rhode Island for business — before reuniting in San Francisco in the late 1990s, entirely by chance. "It was Thanksgiving one year, maybe 1997 or 1998. I walk onto the plane, and I see Eric," Adam told me of their encounter on the way home for the holiday. "He'd only moved to San Francisco a couple weeks prior. There was an open seat. I ended up sitting next to him on the plane, and for five hours we got all caught up. It turned out we were living on the exact same block."

Within a year, they were roommates, Eric joining Adam and three other guys in a house that Adam described as "exactly as clean as you would expect it to be." Still, despite the convergence of their lives, their career paths continued in different directions. Adam was at the

Carnegie Institution for Science working on environmental issues. Eric was at an advertising agency called Hal Riney & Partners working on product campaigns. Their perspectives on entrepreneurship were equally dissimilar.

"I knew since the third grade I wanted to be an entrepreneur," Eric said. "I was the annoying neighborhood kid who was constantly selling buttons or anything else I could. So I always knew I wanted to start a company." Which was a big part of the reason he gravitated toward advertising and branding after college.

Adam's path, however, was "less predestined," as he put it. Not only was he a "big believer in that you don't need to figure out what you need to do with your life," but he was also "motivated by creating some sort of good change in the world." Today, that is practically the entrance exam for entrepreneurship, but back in the 1990s, not so much.

Then over Christmas in 1999, their professional journeys began to converge, this time on a ski trip. Months earlier, Eric had been working on a big project for Colgate Palmolive, spending a lot of his time in grocery stores, specifically in the cleaning aisle. "It was such a big category but a sea of sameness," Eric said. "Everything looked and smelled the same. The brands were pretty dated. And so that was kind of a clue to dig there."

Which he did, much the way Jen Rubio and Steph Korey did ... except more quietly.

Eric bought a variety of items from different cleaning product categories and took them home to do his own version of a competitor analysis — which he then hid under his bed because he didn't feel like he had anyone to talk to who would understand what he was thinking. "It's pretty dorky," he said about his idea. "I didn't want anybody to know I was even thinking about this category." Not even his mom, who said to him at one point early on, "I've never even seen you make a bed. Are you sure you're the right person to start a cleaning products business?"

By himself? Maybe not. But with a partner, who knows?

The famous American writer and polymath Oliver Wendell Holmes Sr. wrote in 1872, "Many ideas grow better when trans-

planted into another mind than in the one where they sprang up."*
On their drive to their ski vacation, Eric planted the seed in Adam's
mind.

"I felt like Adam was somebody I could share an idea with, so I
mentioned that, hey, there may be an opportunity in this space,"
Eric said. "And I remember Adam looked over at me as he's driving
and goes, 'You know, I have a degree in chemical engineering . . .'"
It hadn't even occurred to Eric that Adam's degree would be useful.
But, of course, it was not only useful, it was essential.

Adam then made another point. "I said, 'Well, you know, not only
are these products really ugly, but did you know they're super toxic
as well?'"

"That was the thing that Adam brought up that really opened my
eyes," Eric said. "You mean, you actually pollute when you clean, and
you use poison to make your home healthier?"

By the time they'd finished their first couple runs on the mountain that morning, the idea that Eric had planted in Adam had already sprouted and begun to grow. This wasn't just about better-
looking, better-smelling cleaning products anymore; it was about
making them better for you and for the environment.

When they got back to San Francisco a few days later, Adam
moved a desk into Eric's room, where he spent his days researching
the different cleaning product categories from the chemistry side,†
while Eric finished up work on the Colgate project at his agency
job, getting more brand experience in that world and learning even
more about consumers. Together, both at night and on weekends,
they worked on their business plan. Things moved quickly after that.
By mid-2000, Eric was busy searching for the ideal bottle type and
shape, along with someone to design, tool, and produce it. At the
same time, Adam was working to perfect his cleaning formulas, mixing in five-gallon buckets a host of different substances that he had

---

* If that name rings a bell, it should: he was the father of the famous Supreme
Court justice of the same name.
† Adam had quit his job at the Carnegie Institution several months earlier in an
attempt to qualify for the 2000 Olympics with the US sailing team.

stored in individual sixteen-ounce jars, all of this in the kitchen of the home they still shared with three other guys.

"I came home one day, and Adam was mixing things in beer pitchers, and I was like, 'We're going to kill one of our roommates here,'" Eric recalled. "Luckily, the stuff was nontoxic," he said, laughing at the craziness of the scene. That "stuff" eventually became a four-product line of surface cleaners that combined beautiful design and nontoxic ingredients. In 2001, it, and they, officially became Method.

Method was the perfect marriage of Adam's and Eric's differing skill sets and sensibilities. "Our joke was 'style and substance': Adam working on basically everything in the bottle, and me doing everything around the bottle," Eric said. "A lot of it just came down to our own dumb luck of Adam's passion for sustainability and mine for design."

You can never discount the importance of luck — even dumb luck — in the success of any new idea. But luck certainly doesn't fully explain how Method cleaning products landed on Target shelves within a year, or how the business became profitable within five years, or how it reached $100 million in sales within the decade. For that, I believe, you have to look at this perfect partnership between Eric Ryan and Adam Lowry. Two men, one an extrovert, the other an introvert; one who runs at a problem, the other who "needs a little bit more space to think it through"; one an aesthetically driven businessman, the other a socially conscious, purpose-driven engineer. Both of them equally committed to a vision for a beautiful, environmentally friendly line of cleaning products — "eco-chic," as the category came to be called — and to doing everything it took to execute that two-pronged mission. "Traditionally, green products didn't look beautiful, and beautiful products weren't necessarily green," Eric explained. "That's the paradigm we really broke."

In the end, my favorite part of Eric and Adam's story is all the serendipity and the bits of interesting timing that are baked into it. Growing up together. Moving away in different directions. Bumping into each other on a plane, only to find out they now lived on the same block. Coming up with an idea for, of all things, *soap* — or as Eric put it, "an idea that was hot 120 years ago" — at a time and in a place where investors were throwing suitcases full of money at tech startups. But at the same time, consumers were also "starting to think more about their homes as reflections of themselves," especially with the recent introduction of IKEA to America and HGTV (Home & Garden Television) to national cable packages. It all just seems so unlikely!

Adam Lowry may have felt like his path to entrepreneurship was less than predestined, but to me stories like his and Eric's, stories like Method's, always feel as though they have a bit of that fatefulness to them: the right idea in the right place, at the right time, with the right people. And it is the people part of that equation that is most interesting to me about Method, at least as it relates to bringing new ideas into the world. Because just as Away is a prime example of how doing your research opens any industry to the inexperienced and uninitiated if they have a good idea, Method shows that finding the right partner can unlock *any* good idea, no matter how arcane or esoteric or beyond its sell-by date it may seem.

This is not some revolutionary insight on my part. Many of the same founders I talked about at the beginning of this chapter, whom we have now elevated to godlike status in our culture, have talked openly about the importance of the partners they had in their early fight to bring their ideas to fruition, many of them while the fight was still happening.

"My best business decisions really have to do with picking people," Bill Gates said in a 1998 conversation with Warren Buffett on the campus of the University of Washington. "Deciding to go into partnership with Paul Allen is probably at the top of the list ... Having somebody who you totally trust, who's totally committed, who shares your vision and yet has a little bit different set of skills, and also acts as a check on you — and just the benefit of sparking off of somebody who's got that kind of brilliance — it's not only made it fun, but it's really led to a lot of success."

In a 1985 *Playboy* interview, Apple co-founder Steve Jobs talked about the importance of both his partner Steve Wozniak's differing interests and their shared *lack* of a vision. "Neither of us had any idea that this would go anywhere," Jobs said. "Woz was motivated by fig-

uring things out. He concentrated more on the engineering and proceeded to do one of his most brilliant pieces of work, which was the
disk drive that made the Apple II a possibility. I was trying to build
the company ... I don't think it would have happened without Woz
and I don't think it would have happened without me."

The power of partnership is not just a modern tech phenomenon.
Partnerships are a hallmark in the history of innovation, regardless of the industry. Many of them are cultural icons we know by the
name on the door: Ben and Jerry. Hewlett and Packard. Harley and
Davidson. Wells and Fargo. Procter and Gamble (with whom Adam
and Eric were in direct competition, incidentally). As for Warren
Buffett and his part in that conversation with Bill Gates in 1998, he
was in complete agreement about the importance of picking people:
"I've had a partner like that, Charlie Munger, for a lot of years, and it
does for me exactly what Bill is talking about."

As unlikely as many of these successful partnerships seem, to
me at least, they do not appear to be entirely the product of chance.
Adam and Eric were childhood friends. Gates and Allen went to
high school together. Steve Wozniak lived across the street from
Steve Jobs's only friend at the Cupertino, California, high school
Jobs attended. Jen Rubio and Steph Korey worked together. Charlie Munger worked in Warren Buffett's grandfather's store. There
are also countless marriages at the center of the founding of great
brands: Kate Spade, Dermalogica, Stacy's Pita Chips, Drybar, Lonely
Planet, Melissa & Doug, to name just a few. I suppose you could say
there is a faithfulness behind the fatefulness of their success. A commitment to a preexisting relationship that was proof, by virtue of its
very existence, that each partner could trust the other to have their
best interests at heart. Knowing that they always had a port in the
storm. A port much closer to home than you might expect for something like an entrepreneurial venture.

This is the other reason to find a co-founder. A reason whose impact you cannot really divine from the market research and whose
value you cannot track on a P&L statement. It's the real reason Jim
Koch was looking for a partner when he found Rhonda Kallman right
under his nose. His father, with no shortage of his own experience

trying to get small breweries off the ground in the 1950s and 1960s, had advised him to find someone to partner with because starting a business is lonely, "full of ups and downs" that are hard to stomach when you're on the entrepreneurial roller coaster by yourself.

It was a piece of advice echoed unequivocally by Paul Graham more than twenty years later, when he wrote, "Starting a startup is too hard for one person. Even if you could do all the work yourself, you need colleagues to brainstorm with, to talk you out of stupid decisions, and to cheer you up when things go wrong . . . The low points in a startup are so low that few could bear them alone."

Partners don't just help your idea survive the fickleness of consumers, the ruthlessness of competitors, the scrutiny of investors, or the uncertainty of world events. They help *you* survive as well. And if your idea is ever to become a real business, it needs you alive and kicking. Which means it needs your partner — your co-founder — too.

6

Fund the Business, Part 1: Bootstrapping

Adam Lowry and Eric Ryan found their first retailer for Method in February 2001, with a chain of family-owned grocery stores along the San Francisco peninsula called Mollie Stone's Markets. The first location was in Burlingame, just off El Camino Real, which runs like an artery down the peninsula, through two of the richest counties in California and into Silicon Valley, crossing Sand Hill Road along the way. That road's famous concentration of venture capital firms had all basically snubbed Adam and Eric when they first went out looking for investors.

This was a time, just as the dot-com bubble was preparing to burst, when if you had ".com" in the name of your business, there was a line out the door to give you money. But if you were doing something more analog, like trying to disrupt a stagnant consumer goods category dominated by two multibillion-dollar conglomerates — in this case, Procter & Gamble and Unilever — that door wasn't just closed, it was locked and dead-bolted, and the lights were turned off inside.*

---

* Between the time Adam and Eric reconnected on their flight home in 1998 and they got their first product on store shelves in 2001, Pets.com would be born, raise eight figures in venture capital, be acquired by Amazon, IPO, crater, and then be shuttered.

Adam and Eric didn't worry too much about the initial rejections they received from the Sand Hill Road guys (and make no mistake, it was almost all guys on Sand Hill back then), because they knew they wouldn't actually need that much money to get their business off the ground. These were not dangerous industrial solvents they were trying to make, after all. They were creating natural, nontoxic cleaners with water, vinegar, baking soda, plant extracts, and essential oils — "very common, everyday, mild chemicals . . . that don't require a professional lab in order to mix," as Adam described it. So they began by each putting in $45,000 of their life savings — Eric's bequeathed by his grandfather, who had recently passed away — and used that to start experimenting.

Those first couple years, they did most everything themselves: perfecting their formula, guiding the design and manufacture of the bottles, printing Eric's personal cell phone number on the bottle as the customer service number,* doing in-store demos to get customers (Eric even wore a lab coat), pitching investors like the Sand Hill Road firms, calling on retail accounts like Mollie Stone's Markets. They even handled inventory management. Every day, as they expanded into more Mollie Stone's and then into additional boutique groceries, Adam and Eric would take turns driving around to each store to check inventory levels and restock the shelves as necessary. They called it their paper route.

And the subsequent costs attendant to all these tasks, if money from friends and family wouldn't cover it, Adam and Eric would just put on their credit cards. They leaned so heavily on personal credit, in fact, that when they finally landed their first professional money ($1 million from a single investor), they couldn't afford to pay the restaurant bill at the traditional closing dinner because they'd already maxed out all of their cards.

If you've never started a business, this sounds like the height of irresponsible money management. But there is a name for what Adam

---

* A surprising number of founders I interviewed used their own mobile phone numbers as the customer service line and printed them on the packaging of their products. Even more surprising is how long they did it for!

and Eric did. It's called *bootstrapping*. Bootstrapping is what you do if you don't have a Rolodex of billionaires to flip through and ask for money; if it's your first company and you're going it alone, just you and your partner(s). More specifically, bootstrapping is using what you have at your disposal to get yourself where you want to be.

Typically, when we talk about bootstrapping, it's a financial conversation, and to an extent that will always be true. Without other people's money to stand up your business — whether it's from friends and family, venture capital, or something like an SBA loan — you have to find other ways to pay for things: credit cards, personal savings, cycling profits back into the business. But having spoken to hundreds of brilliant entrepreneurs, I know that bootstrapping is more than simply using alternative sources of personal financing as a last resort. It's also about keeping control of your business as long as you can. It's about using other nonmonetary assets to solve problems that you would otherwise hire someone else to solve or throw money at — assets like your time, your effort, your network, and your own talent and ingenuity.

Joe Gebbia, Brian Chesky, and Nathan Blecharczyk leveraged every one of those resources in 2007 and 2008 to bootstrap their way into the peer-to-peer online hospitality platform that we know today as Airbnb.

Airbnb began as a website called Airbedandbreakfast.com that was designed to offer a place to stay for attendees of large conferences once all the hotel rooms in the host city were sold-out. The idea came to Joe one day in September 2007 as he sat at home surfing the internet, wondering how he was going to make rent and not lose a friend. See, Joe's landlord had just raised his rent by 25 percent mere weeks after Joe had convinced his new roommate, Brian Chesky, to quit his job down in Los Angeles and move up to San Francisco to start a company together. What company? Well, that part they hadn't figured out yet.

As luck would have it, there was an industrial design conference coming to San Francisco a couple weeks later that they were thinking about attending — he and Brian were both graduates of the Rhode Island School of Design (RISD) — and when Joe navigated to the conference website to check if passes were still available, he saw right there on the front page, in big red letters, the words HOTELS SOLD OUT.

The idea became clear to Joe right away: "I'm thinking, 'What a bummer. Designers are going to come last minute, and they're not going to have a place to stay.' In that instant, I'm looking around the living room, and I go, 'Wait, we have so much extra space here, and I have air beds in the closet.' And so the idea of hosting people on air beds gradually became natural to me."

He brought the idea to Brian, his roommate. Brian had $1,000 to his name when he moved up to San Francisco that month. His portion of the rent was $1,050 per month. Even I can do that math. As odd an idea as this may have seemed in the moment, it was a no-brainer to someone who had no money.

"It'll be more than just a place to sleep," Joe thought at the time. "We can cook breakfast in the morning, we'll pick them up from the airport and give them a neighborhood guide and maps of San Francisco."

This is how he pitched it to Brian, in an email made famous when it was presented on the TED stage in 2016.

> Brian
> i thought of a way to make a few bucks — turning our place into designers bed and breakfast — offering young designers who come into a town a place to crash during the 4 day event, complete with wireless internet, a small desk space, a sleeping mat, and breakfast each morning. Ha!
>
> joe

Brian was in. Together, they used their design chops to quickly build a simple website. It described who they were, what the idea was — sleep on our living room floor on an air mattress for $80 per night, basically — and all the other stuff they would provide as part of the deal.

And when Joe said "they," he meant *they:* Joe and Brian. Which is exactly how it all worked out for the three guests they had space for. "They stayed with us, and we got to show them San Francisco. They got to feel like they belonged there in the sense that they didn't feel like outsiders," Joe said.

Everything their guests did outside of the conference was arranged for or guided by Joe and Brian. If this had been a cruise, they were the shipbuilders, the captains, the social directors, the navigators and engineers, the cooks, and the housekeeping staff, all rolled into two guys. "I'll never forget saying goodbye," Joe recalled, "and watching the door click closed and thinking, 'What if we made it possible for other people to also share their experience and to host guests in their home and show off their city?'"

To do that, they would need a much more robust website that required a level of technical expertise that neither Joe nor Brian possessed. With no money to hire programmers, they would need to leverage their network to find one. Fortunately, Joe knew a guy. An engineer with a computer science degree from Harvard named Nate Blecharczyk, who just happened to be the roommate that Brian replaced when he moved in with Joe.

After the holidays, Joe gave Nate a call and they met for a drink. "So here we are in January 2008, with an idea and no engineer," Joe said, "and I tell him about this weekend experiment with these three guests, and he loved the idea."

Eventually, the three of them decided that the perfect time to relaunch Airbedandbreakfast.com would be at the next big tech conference, which happened to be South by Southwest (SXSW) in Austin, Texas, in March. By the time they came to this strategic decision, the conference was less than a month away. The turnaround would be tight, but the opportunity was ideal.

"It's the place where some of the tech greats had launched before us. Twitter had launched there, Foursquare, and others. We were just going to follow the rocket ship that all of them did," Joe explained. Plus, "every year the same thing happens. The hotels sell out months in advance, [and] people scramble for housing."

What better scenario for an online hospitality platform born from a total lack of hotel room capacity? For the next three weeks, they worked out of Joe and Brian's apartment, day in and day out, rebuilding the website — Joe doing the design, Nate doing the coding, and Brian doing everything else required to turn an idea into a business. With no money. On "half a shoestring," as Joe said.

They launched the site with six listings, just in time for the conference. Unfortunately, only two people booked. And one of them was Brian.

"It was completely demoralizing," Joe said. "Here was this idea that we were so excited about, and nobody took us up on the idea." But they realized a couple key things in the process. One was that exchanging money in person, especially in a home, is really weird, so they should probably have the financial transaction piece online. The second was that there may be people who like to travel for reasons other than conferences, who are also interested in the idea of staying in someone's home — with or without the air mattress, ostensibly — so maybe this idea shouldn't just be tied to conference sites.

"We said, 'Well, let's add payments, and let's make this a travel site," Joe said. "And that's when we had an idea, which was to relaunch this new version of our service at the crest of a tidal wave of press."

In 2008, there was a tsunami of attention spreading across the country. It was following the historically seismic candidacy of Barack Obama for the presidency of the United States, and that summer it was set to crash into Denver, Colorado, at the Democratic National Convention, where Obama was going to speak and accept the Democratic nomination for president. This presented a unique opportunity.

"A hundred thousand people were anticipated to see Obama speak, and there were less than 30,000 hotel rooms, most of which were picked up by delegates," Joe remembered. It was a legitimate housing crisis. At one point, Denver's mayor even considered opening the city's parks to campers. Suddenly, there was a real need for the service that Joe, Brian, and Nate were trying to bring into being. They just had to get the word out.

"We thought what if we timed the relaunch of our service during the DNC? We can ride the coattails of all the Obama press to bring a lot of awareness to this marketplace," Joe said.

So that's exactly what they did. While Nate worked on shifting the website from its conference orientation to a travel focus and then adding an online payment function, Joe and Brian flew to Denver. They talked to anyone who would give them ten minutes until they finally started to get some traction.

"We got local press, which turned into the regional press, which turned into national press," Joe said. Joe and Brian even did a live interview with CNN from their living room. Within a matter of four weeks after the convention, they managed to add 800 homes to their website and process 100 bookings.

"I thought that this was it," Joe said. "This was our rocket ship to the moon." And they'd bootstrapped the entire thing. More than that, they'd shown proof of concept; they'd evinced their own worthiness as smart, agile entrepreneurs; and best of all, they controlled 100 percent of the business.

What better time to pursue investment (like the Method guys did) than when it feels like your new venture is headed into the stratosphere and you're in control at the helm? Through their connections in San Francisco, Joe and Brian were introduced to twenty different investors from Sand Hill Road. They emailed each one of them their pitch deck.

But it didn't go great. "Ten of them reply to our email. Five of them meet us for coffee. Zero invested in us." Joe rattled off the decreasing cascade of increasingly horrible numbers like they'd been stitched into his entrepreneurial DNA. "I didn't have anything else going on in my life except this. And to put it in front of very credible investors — the guys who have picked the Googles and PayPals and YouTubes of the world — and have them look you square in the eye and go, 'Well, this is weird,'" Joe said, his voice trailing off, "Two thousand eight was the worst year of my life."

In theory, this should have been the end of Airbedandbreakfast .com. And in a way, it was. Or at least it was the beginning of the end. That's because within eight months, the name would be shortened to Airbnb; the trio of co-founders would be accepted to, and then graduate from, the Y Combinator startup incubator; and their fledgling website would have 10,000 users and 2,500 listings. This all happened, ironically, all because of two boxes of cereal and a binder full of credit cards.

"You know those binders where you keep baseball cards?" Joe asked me when I was curious how they managed to keep going after striking out with investors. "I had one of those, except there weren't baseball cards in it. There were credit cards. We would go through Visa after Visa to Mastercard and finally to Amex, just maxing out the credit cards. And that's how we funded ourselves."

They called it "the Visa round." It kept the lights on and the servers running, but that was about it. "There's no worse feeling than getting a credit card statement that's only going up, with no hope of ever paying it down," Joe said. Then late one night, during the lead-up to the 2008 presidential election, Joe and Brian were sitting in their kitchen, spitballing ways to add value to their service. They'd handled the "bed" part of Airbedandbreakfast.com, they figured, but what about the "breakfast" part? What had they really done on that end?

"Maybe we give our hosts some breakfast cereal to give to their guests," Joe said, recapitulating his conversation with Brian. "Wouldn't it be funny if it was politically themed? We could call it 'Obama O's: The Breakfast of Change.' Or maybe 'Captain McCain's: A Maverick in Every Bite.'"

If you think that sounds more like the product of a 2 a.m. pity party than a focused brainstorming session, you're right. "We were just trying to keep each other's spirits up at this point," Joe said. Except for one small detail: they actually went forth and made the breakfast cereal!

They didn't just make the cereal either. They merchandised and promoted it. Brian went out and bought 500 bags of generic cereal. Joe art-directed and hired an illustrator, again from their network — a RISD alum who would work on commission as a favor. Realizing that they had a limited edition series on their hands now, they built a website for each brand of cereal; sent 100 boxes to every media outlet they had contact information for, including the ones they'd gotten press coverage from during the Democratic National Convention a month earlier; numbered the boxes 1 to 500; and then sold them online for $40 apiece.

The idea worked. They got a ton of press *and* they sold all the cereal.

I was absolutely blown away by this part of the Airbnb story. But it triggered a question: What was the point? How was this really going to help Airbedandbreakfast.com? Joe's answer was that it wasn't. Or, more precisely, that it didn't really matter. "At $40 a box times 500 boxes, we made $20,000 in breakfast cereal," Joe explained, "which was just enough to pay off our credit cards."

Obama O's and Cap'n McCain's didn't fuel the Airbnb rocket ship, but it kept them going long enough for them to get accepted into Y Combinator's winter class that year. In fact, it was the ingenuity they displayed in making the cereal, not actually their Airbnb idea, that convinced Y Combinator co-founder Paul Graham to find a place for them in the program. "Through the breakfast cereal, we had proven to him that we had hustle, we had grit," Joe said. "If we could figure out how to sell breakfast cereal for $40 a box, we could figure out how to make our website work."

With Graham's guidance, they got even grittier, even scrappier. He gave them permission to do things that didn't scale in order to solve the immediate problems that were standing in the way of their growth. They began by digging into the website's search results, looking for positive trends they could exploit and negative trends they could nip in the bud. The first pattern they recognized was that the listings that did the poorest tended to have the worst photos.

"People were using their camera phones. They were taking pictures of their homes at night. They were not merchandising their home in a way that made people want to stay there, so no one was booking them," Joe said. Most of the picture issues were occurring with listings in New York City, which, at the time, was their biggest market. This presented them with a unique opportunity to cut off a negative trend while building on a positive one. Joe had taken some photography classes while he was enrolled at RISD. He was "willing to bet that if we just flew out there for a weekend, we could probably take some nicer photos. We wouldn't charge them for it. We'd do it for free."

So Brian and Joe got on a plane to New York, rented a really nice camera, emailed all thirty of their New York City–based hosts with their offer, and then went door-to-door across the city's five boroughs: Brian and Joe as Airbnb co-founders. Joe also as their professional in-house photographer. And the photos he ended up taking were very good. "I'm getting the lighting right, the composition," he explained. "I'm kind of staging the place a little bit, and I show the photos on the back of the camera, and these hosts are like, 'Oh my God, my apartment looks amazing, I can't believe it! Do you want to stay for some tea or coffee?'"

Of course they'd say yes, and end up spending, in some cases, hours in the homes of their earliest adopters, talking to them about their lives and their experiences with the website. It pushed Brian and Joe right into what Joe called "design research mode."

"So here we are in the living room, they pull out their laptop, and I say, 'Could you show me how you check your calendar?' 'Show me how you message with guests?'" Joe recalled. "And in those moments, we see how our perfectly designed interface completely and utterly failed. What we thought took only two or three clicks, people needed ten or twelve clicks [to accomplish]. They were stumbling around, getting lost within our own website." Worst of all for Joe, Brian, and Nate was that up until that fateful weekend in New York, in the first cold months of 2009, they had no idea this was an issue.

"But once we did, it was like a jackpot," Joe said. "We came back with all of our discoveries and designed for them, and our numbers that second week went from $200 a week in fees, which is what we were making for six months and was not sustainable — three guys cannot live off of that in San Francisco — to $400 in one week."

Their numbers *doubled*. Sure enough, it was primarily due to an increase in bookings with the hosts they'd met and taken pictures for in New York. Not coincidentally, once they figured out and solved the photo issue, organic growth began to happen, investors started sniffing around, and Airbnb as we now know it began to take shape.

It is fair to say, in my opinion, that this $30 billion–plus jugger-naut that has redefined hospitality and challenged expectations with regard to travel and tourism around the world is here today in no small measure because of the relentless efforts made by Joe Gebbia, Brian Chesky, and Nathan Blecharczyk to keep it alive. They bootstrapped the business for two solid years, through website re-builds, business model pivots, press inquiries, photo shoots, credit card debt, and mountains of ramen. "Cereal, too," Joe would be quick to add. At first they bootstrapped it because they wanted to, because it was the smart thing to do. Then they bootstrapped it because they *had* to, because it was the *only* thing to do.

Many of the most admired figures in Silicon Valley know the value of bootstrapping and have exhorted aspiring founders to embrace it. Ron Conway, the "Godfather of Silicon Valley," once advised en-trepreneurs that "bootstrapping as long as you can is the best thing for the company because you own the entire company . . . Use your credit cards, do anything you can so that by the time you go to angels you have built a working prototype and have some users. You'll likely be valued higher and will suffer less dilution."

In 2015, Sam Altman, the president of Y Combinator, took to Twitter in defense of bootstrapping. "In our experience at YC," he wrote, "the best companies do amazing things on small amounts of money." He continued, "We especially love companies that can do a lot with little capital. It works much more often than those who do a little with a lot."

Bootstrapping works. But it's also very hard. It takes an uncommon effort to achieve uncommon results. Which is what a successful startup is: uncommon. Don't mistake this for negativity, by the way. I am forever a cautious optimist. I know success is possible. I know that *you* can do this. But I also know that there is one type of business for which bootstrapping never works: the type run by someone who isn't passionate enough about their idea to put in the long days and the endless weeks required; who doesn't care enough to get on that plane to New York or to max out all their credit cards to keep the servers running.

To bootstrap your business right, and to do it well, you need to know what you're facing, what will be expected of you. Can it be scary to rack up that kind of debt while trying to start a business? Sure. But if you ask Jim Koch, it's not nearly as scary (or dangerous) as *not* trying to start your business at all. Does too much ramen and not enough sleep sound like a nightmare? It'll definitely leave you salty, but it's not unbearable. If you have another marketable skill, like Jane Wurwand, or you keep your other job for as long as possible, like Daymond John, you'll always have a soft spot to land if you decide you want to wake up from the dream of entrepreneurship.

These are understandable concerns if you are an apprehensive first-time founder. Remember that cliff you've just jumped off and that plane you're trying to build? Well, the ground comes up at you faster than you think. There's no getting around that. But if the experiences of the Method and Airbnb co-founders teach us anything, it's that if you work fast and smart and hard and together, you can meet the rising challenge of starting a business before it meets you, face-first.

7

Get Your Story Straight

I n December 2019, I had the opportunity to speak to Procter & Gamble's marketing team about storytelling at the company's global headquarters in Cincinnati, Ohio. P&G is a 180-year-old multinational conglomerate that owns more than sixty brands, nearly twenty of which are worth more than a billion dollars each. Judging by numbers alone, P&G has figured a few things out since its founding in 1837.

Before I spoke, I was given a tour of the sprawling downtown campus, which includes a small museum that traces the history of the company and maintains a meticulous archive of all the products that P&G has either created or acquired over the years. Moving through the exhibits, I was amazed to learn the origin stories of so many products that have become household names, most notably Crest Whitestrips and Swiffer.

Crest Whitestrips was the result of a brainstorming session between somebody who worked on Cling Wrap and somebody working in the toothpaste division after they had lunch in the P&G cafeteria one day. Swiffer began as a crude combination of a broomstick attached to a bottle of Mr Clean, with Always maxi pads affixed to the bottom — both of which are P&G products.

What is most amazing to me about these stories, and the stories of dozens of other iconic P&G brands, isn't just that they were the products of internal innovation and collaboration, but that so few consumers know any of those fascinating details. Procter & Gamble is one of the biggest consumer packaged goods companies in the world, and yet very few people would connect them with the word "innovation." They spend more than $1 billion a year in advertising, but neither that word nor any of these origin stories are anywhere to be found in their ads — not in print ads, not on TV, not in radio spots. Instead, P&G advertising tends to focus on utility and effectiveness. It focuses on what the products can do for you, to the virtual exclusion of how the brand relates to you. It's a strategy that works, of course — P&G had nearly $68 billion in sales in 2019 — but it works only to a point, and only so far as the money you spend to get the word out will take you.

So, what if you don't have a billion-dollar ad budget? Or any ad budget at all? Or you just want to spend less and be similarly effective in reaching your target consumers? This, it turns out, is what I could teach Procter & Gamble's marketing team about storytelling: Telling your story is a more cost-effective way to take your advertising beyond usefulness and efficacy and efficiency as topics of conversation. It's like a growth hack that enables consumers to connect to your brand in a deeper, more personal way, which is a big part of how you differentiate and de-commodify your product, create brand loyalty, and set yourself up for long-term success.

While many legacy companies struggle to see the innovation and origin stories right under their noses, it is nevertheless as true for them as it is for young upstart brands that their business is a story — that *every* business is a story. The story, more than anything else, is what connects you and me and everyone out there to the thing you're building. And every defining element of that thing you're building, of that business, helps to tell its story. This goes from the name and the logo, to the function of the product or the style of the service, to the partners who founded it, all the way to the customers who patronize it. The purpose of that story changes with time and with whom it is being told to, but fundamentally its goal is to answer a hundred different variations on one simple question: Why?

Why should I buy your product?
Why should I join this company?
Why should I be excited to work here?
Why should I invest in this company?

These are just a few of the variations identified by Ben Horowitz, the brilliant tech entrepreneur, best-selling author, and co-founder of the venture capital firm Andreessen Horowitz. He described in 2010 how his company evaluates CEOs, whose main job, he contends, is to be "the keeper of the vision and the story."

A few years later, in talking to *Forbes,* Horowitz put the role of the company's story even more succinctly: "The story must explain at a fundamental level why you exist." It is a story you have to tell to your customers, to investors, to employees, and ultimately to yourself. Kind of in that order, in fact — from the bottom up, like the old food pyramid or Maslow's legendary hierarchy of needs.

One of the reasons for this approach seems pretty obvious: in most markets there are already plenty of options to choose from, so you need to give us a really compelling reason why we should choose yours. And in the cases where you're making something no one has ever seen before, when you're creating an entirely new market, it's not always immediately clear what we have been missing. As such, you need to tell us why we need to choose anything new at all.

The other, slightly more complicated reason you need a terrific story is that there are so many other questions one could ask in an effort to understand why you exist, and your current answers don't reveal very much: what you do, where you do it, how you do it, whom you do it for. Those are just discoverable facts. I can search for them on Google. I can buy market research reports. I can hire someone to reverse engineer your product or go through your process. I can read books and articles about all of it.

But the key here is: *Why do you do what you do?* Or, *Why should we care?* I can't know the answers to those questions until you, as the founder, want me to know them, because they exist first in your mind. And like most concepts that are unquantifiable, the answers to these basic questions are usually best understood and best shared with the world through a story.

Whitney Wolfe has a story. She knows it well. To hear her tell it is to get to know her and the history of her dating app, Bumble. It is to know what she is trying to do with her app, why we should *all* care about it, and how it has managed to succeed despite the fact that by the end of 2014, when Bumble was launched, if there was one thing the world didn't need any more of, it was dating apps. There was already Match.com, Plenty of Fish, OkCupid, eHarmony, and Hinge, along with all the niche sites, such as Jdate, BlackPlanet, Christian Mingle, and, way on the other end of the spectrum, SeekingArrangement and Ashley Madison.

And then there was Tinder, the behemoth, which Whitney co-founded in 2012 and had recently left under some of the worst possible circumstances not just for a co-founder but for a woman and a human being. There was both a professional and a romantic split with one of her co-founders, there was a very public sexual harassment lawsuit, and there was an avalanche of despicably hurtful online vitriol aimed directly at her. By the time she left Tinder in early 2014, Whitney wasn't just done with the dating business, she was done, period.

"I was at the very bottom of my barrel," Whitney told me in our 2017 interview. "There were days where I didn't want to live. I didn't want to get out of bed. I wanted to die." Whitney wasn't even twenty-five years old at the time, and the internet had utterly broken her.

All this begs the questions: Why another online business? Why another *dating* app? And why so soon?

Well, part of the agony that Whitney was feeling was this nagging sense that her story wasn't unique. It was much bigger than herself, bigger than Tinder, bigger even than dating as an industry. There was a real problem out there with a lack of online accountability, and whatever she may have gone through — however horrible it might have been — what was even worse to her was that thirteen-year-old girls were seeing all of this on their phones all day, every day.

"And it scared me," she said. "So I sat down and said, 'I can start something right now. And I can change what I hate that I see in the world.'"

Originally, her new idea had nothing to do with dating. It was a female-only social network that she called Merci, where women could use only compliments to respond to one another's posts and messages. "I really wanted to build this platform that was rooted in kindness and positive behavior," she said. "The antidote to what I experienced online."

She'd gotten as far as a fully fleshed-out marketing plan — marketing was Whitney's expertise — when in July 2014 she was approached by Andrey Andreev, the London-based entrepreneur who had built a number of successful companies by this time, including Badoo, the world's most popular dating site outside of the United States. Andrey wanted to hire Whitney to be Badoo's chief marketing officer, which was a nonstarter as far as Whitney was concerned.

"That's just off the table," she told him. "I don't want to touch a dating app. That's not going to be my future. I'm going to start my own business, and I want it to be mission driven, and I want it to be impactful, and I *don't* want it to be in dating."

So she pitched him *her* idea instead. She laid out the whole vision for Merci and answered each of the tough questions you'd expect from a successful entrepreneur and startup investor like Andreev. Whitney remembered that with each answer she gave, it was clear Andreev could sense her passion for her idea and her commitment to its mission, which was heartening.

"You need to build this," he said, "but you need to do it in dating. This has to happen. What you're trying to do *needs* to be done in dating."

I can only imagine how Whitney felt at that moment. She was mere months removed from having her life turned upside down, in part by her very public departure from one dating app, and now the founder of another wanted to hire her but didn't seem to *hear* her. To Whitney's immense credit, though, she took a beat and really considered what Andrey was trying to say.

"I thought to myself, 'Maybe he's got a point. Maybe dating is broken,'" Whitney recounted of her initial meeting with Andrey. "'Maybe connecting is broken beyond just being a young woman talking to a young woman in junior high. Maybe this is something that affects us at all ages.'"

By the end of that first encounter, Whitney and Andrey had a handshake deal. They would build her idea, but as a dating app, and they'd do it together. Within a few weeks, they had a team of fantastic designers assembled, and Whitney had the key functionality that would distinguish her dating app from all the others. This is how she described it:

"I always wanted to text the guy first. But I was never allowed to because society and my friends said no. So I said to the team, 'We're going to reverse engineer this: You're going to mutually match with each other, but women have to send the first message. They have twenty-four hours to do it — which would give them a kind of incentive — and if they don't, the match disappears forever.'"

It was completely different from anything that had existed in the dating space to that point. It now put the ball squarely in the woman's court, whereas before men were expected to be the pursuers, while women were expected to be elusive at best, and supplicants at worst.*

"You're telling men to be overtly aggressive, and you're telling women to be the inverse of that," Whitney explained of the old model she was trying to disrupt. "You're training two human beings to act in opposite directions of each other, and as a society you're setting both up for failure. In effect, you set the men up to be constantly rejected. And you set the women up for abuse."

That is why Bumble needed to exist. That is why we all should care. And that is why Whitney was the perfect person to create the app. The toxic, often destructive dynamic resulting from traditional models of online courtship was exactly what had nearly de-

---

* The core of the Bumble user base is straight, but it bears noting that the app has a large gay user base as well, for whom the "woman first" rule for messaging doesn't apply — anyone can send the first message — but they still have to do it within twenty-four hours, or the match goes away.

stroyed her and what was making so many dating apps such an unpleasant place for many millions of women around the world. It needed to stop.

The essence of this story and the revolutionary nature of what Bumble was trying to do—shifting the sexual power into *women's* hands—are even captured in the app's name. Because Bumble wasn't Whitney's first choice. It was Moxie.

"Like, you've got moxie. You've got courage," she explained. "Because if you made the first move, you'd have moxie."

The problem was, they couldn't secure rights to Moxie. Someone was squatting on the domain and had trademarked every possible version of the name. So Whitney and her colleagues had to go back to the drawing board.

"We had probably a thousand words in the running," Whitney said. "And then one morning Michelle Kennedy, who was a great mentor to me those first couple years, came in to the office ... and happened to call her husband a bumbling idiot, and said in her really adorable British accent, 'What about Bumble?'"

Initially, Whitney hated the idea because of the negative connotations behind the word. But her business partner, Andrey, loved it. And he loved it even more when he searched all the domain registry websites and discovered that it was available—which was a minor miracle in 2014. Then a short while later, Whitney was at the home of family friends (whose daughter would end up being her third hire at Bumble) and asked the matriarch of the family what she thought of the name.

"Oh, like, 'Be the queen bee of Bumble. Find your honey on Bumble,'" this woman said.

"I was like, 'Done!'" Whitney recalled. "Hives and bees and building your hive and queen bee and the women make the first move. It was the perfect branding opportunity."

Beyond the branding, it was also a perfect encapsulation of the problems the app was going to solve for both women *and* men. For women, all the queen bee and hive imagery spoke to the centrality of their role in the dating world. Without a queen bee, a hive collapses. Without bees, the entire ecosystem collapses. That is as true for bees as it is for humans, and it was about time we recognized that fact in the architecture of dating apps that were meant to bring people together but were mostly designed by men. And for men, the implications of the word "bumble" weren't as threatening to their vulnerable egos as the word "moxie," which implied a degree of cowardice that most men would have a hard time getting over. Like it or not, this female-centric dating app would need men for it to work. Fortunately, the biggest problem men faced in the world of dating wasn't courage; it was social competence. Specifically, knowing when a woman was interested in them (or why) and what to say in turn. So, really, "Bumble" *was* perfect.

Bumble, as a name, is inherently part of the company story. But the story of its choosing is also a microcosm of the company story as a whole. It speaks to the power and importance of a good and catchy name. Especially when it comes to conveying your story to customers and investors and employees as you begin to grow. It's equally important for understanding the story yourself, for staying anchored to why you do what you do and, to Ben Horowitz's point, why your company exists.

I ask virtually every founder I interview about the name of their company, and for almost all of them, the question is like a trigger that sends the story of the company's founding practically shooting right out of them. Inevitably, it's a story that unearths the very reasons why the company exists, and sometimes even explains how both the company and the founder have managed to succeed for as long as they have.

Sara Blakely, for example, chose Spanx as the name of her shapewear company for its memorability and relatability. She knew that words with a strong *K* sound were extra resonant with consumers. It was no coincidence, her thinking went, that Coca-Cola and Kodak were two of the most recognizable names in the world for most of the twentieth century. Similarly, "it's a known trade secret among comedians," she told me, "that the *K* sound makes your audience laugh." When she eventually landed on "Spanx" (she changed the last letter to *x* from *ks* at the last second because she'd heard made-up words were better for new products than real ones), the name felt great—

not just because it had the *K* sound but also because it related directly to her product, which was "all about the rear end, and making the rear end look better."

Memorability was key for Spanx because the product itself was something people were rarely going to see. Unlike a shirt or a jacket or shoes, Spanx are hidden to the public when worn, which meant the opportunity to develop broad brand recognition through visible branding on the garments themselves wasn't really there. The name *had* to be sticky. It had to cling to your brain the same way the garments form to their customers' bodies. And "Spanx," to use Sara's words, "was kind of naughty and kind of funny and a little bit risqué" — all of which makes for a memorable name.

Despite some initial confusion, the Airbnb guys went with their shortened name instead of Airbedandbreakfast.com because it offered a direct connection to their origin story. It was a story whose importance they eventually embraced, but whose details they didn't fully appreciate in the beginning. In fact, I think that may have been a big part of the reason they had to bootstrap the business for as long as they did after their first big win at the 2008 Democratic National Convention. Really knowing your story — knowing the *why* — is often the bridge between founding and funding, and it seems as if Joe Gebbia, Brian Chesky, and Nate Blecharczyk didn't quite have the answers to many of those "why" questions when they went out to raise their first chunk of professional money.

When the first twenty potential investors they met with all passed, for instance, it wasn't that the business model wasn't working for them, or even that the investors thought the idea behind Airbnb was weird — which they most certainly did. It was that culturally there was a deeply ingrained narrative that this new idea violated, and for which Joe and Brian had not yet crafted a counternarrative. In short, they needed a *story,* and they didn't have one.

"We've all been taught since we were kids that strangers equal danger," Joe explained. "No one in their right mind would invest in a service where people publicly post images of their most intimate spaces — their bedroom, their bathrooms, the kinds of rooms that they usually close when people come over — and then over the internet they're going to invite complete strangers to sleep in their homes."

This was certainly Paul Graham's position during their interview with the Y Combinator board for a slot in the 2009 winter class. "The very first thing out of Paul Graham's mouth was, 'You mean people actually use this? Well, that's weird,'" Joe recalled during our conversation. Brian, recounting that same moment during a 2015 interview with Reid Hoffman in his Blitzscaling class at Stanford, remembered Graham then asking them a rhetorical question that only a really good story could sufficiently answer: "What's wrong with them?"

"That's not a great way to start an interview of any kind," Joe said. "It kind of went downhill from there."

It went downhill until Joe ran back into the room after their interview and handed Paul a box of their Obama O's, which worked (they got their slot) because Obama O's had a great story behind it, one that explained why Obama O's existed and why Paul and the Y Combinator team should give Joe, Brian, and Nate a shot.

Now, I want to be clear about something here, before these stories start to scare you if you don't have your own story already figured out. Don't worry! You're not always going to have it perfect right out of the gate, like Whitney Wolfe did. Whitney was somewhat unique. She'd had her entire life, her entire personal narrative, deconstructed, litigated, and reconstructed in the press and on social media without her consent, and done so at light speed for weeks if not months. Bumble is the story of her reclaiming her story and building a space for other women to safely reclaim and exercise power over their stories. It's a story that helped turn Merci into Bumble, with more than 20 million registrations to date.

The Airbnb guys, on the other hand, didn't have their story fully developed right away. Personally, I think they had the answers to their big "why" questions right from the beginning — sleeping in someone's house on an air bed, like a sleepover, makes you feel like you're *a part of* the city you're traveling to, whereas staying in a national chain hotel can make you feel *apart from* it — but it took them some time to get it. Once they did, however, once they began to connect more dots, and those dots began to connect to their own stories and to something deeper going on in the culture, the evolution of Airbedandbreakfast.com into Airbnb began in earnest and set them on the unicorn's path.

The stories of Bumble and Airbnb are unique to themselves, but what is true across industries and across time is that *all businesses are stories, and all stories are a process.* They are a mechanism for thinking deeply about yourself, your product or service, your employees, your customers, your market, and the world. They explain each to all the others in a way that facts and figures never can.

Ben Horowitz is right: knowing your story and being able to clearly articulate to the world why you exist is one of your most important challenges as an entrepreneur. Not because it helps you sell more product, or build a cooler brand, or make more money — though all those things are true.

Rather, the basic story that answers the big "why" questions is the one that creates loyal customers, finds the best investors, builds an employee culture that keeps them committed to the venture, and keeps you committed and grinding away when things get really hard and you want to give up (and you will). There are a million reasons for any one of these groups to quit or to say no. Your job is to give them one of the few reasons — to tell them the story — that gets them to keep listening and to say yes.

8

Fund the Business, Part 2: Other People's Money

There's something many entrepreneurs learn quickly as their businesses start to gain traction: with some rare exceptions (Hello, Spanx!), bootstrapping, for all its early effectiveness, will take you only so far. It doesn't matter how hardworking or economical you are, or how well you drive early sales and then flow that revenue back into the business; there will always come a time when you will need something that you can't do yourself and don't have the money to pay for even if you could. That moment comes sooner for some founders than it does for others, but in every case it will require what Daymond John's mother called "OPM" (other people's money). In 1995, after five years of bootstrapping FUBU to varying degrees of success, Daymond had to figure out another way to fulfill their first huge orders out of the makeshift factory he'd cobbled together inside his mother's house.

"OPM doesn't have to be other people's money," his mother told him as he searched for a solution. "It could be other people's manufacturing, mind power, manpower, marketing." Which was an amazing insight then, as it is now, though she definitely understood as well as anyone that in the end it all came down to the money. Daymond needed money to pay for materials, to pay for additional manpower and manufacturing capacity. That's why, in the infamous classified ad she took out on his behalf, Daymond's mother wasn't asking for able-bodied workers or bolts of fabric. "Million dollars in orders. Need financing." *Other people's money.*

Eric Ryan and Adam Lowry needed OPM almost immediately to get Method going, despite doing everything else themselves, because nearly all of their initial $90,000 personal investment was eaten up by costs related to designing, tooling, and manufacturing their distinctive plastic bottles — something they obviously couldn't do themselves.

Jen Rubio and Steph Korey needed other people's money for Away right out of the gate, since they were trying to make a hard-shell, four-wheeled smart bag, for which they would clearly need to go to Asia to find a manufacturer that could prototype it for them. A manufacturer that, like most, preferred to be paid with money, which in 2014 Jen and Steph did not have.

Money is never *not* a complicated subject. On the one hand, it's one of those things we're not supposed to talk about in mixed company. How much you have, how much you make, how much you spend — all of that is off-limits to ask about and usually rude to bring up. Yet on the other hand, we're completely obsessed with it, never more so than in the startup world, where how much early-stage money a company has raised gets thrown out there as though fundraising is a perpetual game of one-upmanship in which run rate has replaced "hello" as a greeting, and burn rate is often easier to find online than a company's physical address.

I'm exaggerating (sort of), but my point is that money is a constant — and constantly changing — consideration in the early days of a business, and because startups have become such a fixture in our culture, the money that flows into them has become an increasing object of our focus as well. We even make popular TV shows about it — *Shark Tank* and *The Profit* foremost among them — and those shows have done a lot to both demystify the topic of money and to confuse it.

The demystification comes with a clearer understanding of what that money will cost. Twenty-five years ago, Daymond John and his mother really had no idea how much financing might set them back. But today, even the most casual observer of the entrepreneurial world understands that for *x* dollars, you give up *y* percent of your company and/or *z* percent royalty. Sometimes that cost is steep. Sometimes it's more favorable. It all depends on the quality of the idea and the story behind it — and on the intense competition to invest that those two factors cultivate.

The confusion arises from the sense these shows create that money is somehow easy to get and that when you have an idea, the first thing you should do is find an angel investor or a venture capital firm and ask for a million dollars. This feeds the notion that there is all this money just sitting out there, waiting to be plucked off the street corner, off TV, off wealthy investors in Midtown Manhattan or out on Sand Hill Road, by anyone with a good idea. And there is some truth to that. There has never been a better time to seek out other people's money. (Investors were sitting on $3.4 trillion in cash at the end of 2019.) But just because it's there doesn't necessarily mean that you can pursue it, or that you should — especially early on, and particularly the large sums of professional money doled out by investors like those on *Shark Tank* and *The Profit*. (I'll talk about professional money in much greater detail in chapter 15.) At this stage of your business, you might actually want to hold off on taking their money for a while. If you don't need to give up 5, 10, 20 percent of your company before you are even sure what it's going to look like, to people who will never care about it as much as you and your partners do, then you shouldn't take this money.

The question then becomes: Where else can you go for OPM? This is where friends and family come into play. Soliciting money from friends and family is sort of like an unofficial step between bootstrapping and scaling up with professional fundraising. It bridges the gap when doing everything yourself can only get you from zero to point-five (to twist a phrase from PayPal co-founder Peter Thiel) and you need money to take you the rest of the way to one.

This is precisely what the Method and Away founders did to solve their early money problems. "We were getting five grand here, ten grand there, from every person that would give us money," Adam Lowry said of the mix of loans and early investment he and Eric

Ryan received from friends and family for Method. "All told, it was maybe a couple hundred thousand dollars we got that way before we were able to raise our first professional money." They ran the business on that for two years. "It was literally five- and ten-thousand-dollar checks," Jen Rubio said of Away. She and Steph Korey raised about $150,000 that way, all of it going into the prototyping process for their first bag.

They are not the only ones who have joined the friends-and-family financing plan, which has a long entrepreneurial history.

In 1962, Gordon and Carole Segal, the founders of Crate & Barrel, decided to open a European housewares store that bought direct from the factory and sold at a normal retail markup, because they'd seen the model work brilliantly in all the wonderful stores they'd visited during their honeymoon in the Caribbean the summer before, and there was nothing like it in the United States. "We had about $10,000 from wedding gifts, and we figured we really needed $20,000," Gordon said. "And there was no such thing as venture capital in those days. There was no such thing as startups. So I spent six months running around to everyone I knew who had any wealth and offering them half the business for $10,000." (Can you believe that? In 1962, you could have had 50 percent of Crate & Barrel for ten grand!) Gordon had no takers, however, except his father, who lent them $7,000 to help open the store out of a dumbwaiter factory in the Old Town neighborhood of Chicago. "It was probably all the money he had," Gordon said of his father's loan. And it was all the money Gordon would get . . . or need. Today, Crate & Barrel has 7,500 employees across more than 120 locations with revenue in excess of $1.5 billion.

In 1979, Ron Shaich, the future CEO of Panera Bread, left his job as regional manager for the Original Cookie Company, a shopping mall–based cookie conglomerate, to start an "urban cookie store" in Boston, where he'd gone to school, that would take advantage of all the foot traffic that downtown city streets get on a daily basis. Ron had $25,000 to get started, but that wasn't nearly enough to open a storefront in a major American city. "I had no credibility. I had no real money. I had no balance sheet to sign a lease," he said. "So I went to my dad and said, 'I want my inheritance, whatever it's going to be. I want the opportunity to use it.'" And his father agreed. He gave Ron $75,000, and with that combined $100,000 Ron opened a 400-square-foot cookie store. He called it the Cookie Jar, and within two years he had folded it into the bakery and café chain we know today as Au Bon Pain.

In 1993, Steve Ells took money from his father, as part loan and part investment, to open the first Chipotle in an old, dilapidated Dolly Madison ice cream store near the University of Denver campus. "It was 850 square feet, the rent was $800 a month, and it was in terrible condition and . . . needed a lot of work," Steve recalled. "So I convinced my father to lend me the money, which ended up being $80,000."

A year later and 1,300 miles to the northwest, in Seattle, Jeff Bezos went to sixty different people in his personal network asking for $50,000 from each of them to help him start an online bookstore. Nearly two-thirds of them said no, primarily because they didn't get the idea behind what would become Amazon, the largest online retailer the world has ever known. But among those who said yes were Bezos's parents and his brother and sister. They may not have fully understood Jeff's idea either, but they knew their son and brother, and that was all they needed to know. (For their faith, each has been made a billionaire. Not a bad return on a $50,000 bet.)*

This is one of the great virtues of taking OPM from friends and family instead of racing straight to private equity or venture capital. Not only is it generally cheaper, but as Eric Ryan put it, it's coming from "people who believe in you more than they necessarily believe in your idea," which makes it easier to change your mind midstream and to iterate your way to the product or service that will eventually become the business, because the money is tied to a bet on *you*, not on a specific formulation of your idea. Ron Shaich's dad thought it was an awful idea for Ron to partner with, and acquire a controlling interest in, Au Bon Pain, from whom Ron had been buying croissants

---

* Bezos's parents would eventually put in $300,000, for what was at the time 6 percent of the company.

and other baked goods so that the Cookie Jar could have something to sell in the morning (nobody bought cookies until lunchtime). "If this is worth having, you're not going to get any of it. If you get any of it, it's not going to be worth having," he said. But Ron could see Au Bon Pain's potential, despite how poorly it was being run, and he was confident he knew how to fix their problems, so his father didn't stand in the way, because the $75,000 he'd lent Ron was an investment in his *son,* not in his cookies.

Now, it isn't lost on me that we've just discussed some big sums of money here. Ten $1,000 checks. Seven thousand dollars in cash. A $75,000 advance on an inheritance. Eighty thousand dollars in rolling investment. It is safe to say that most or at least a lot of us don't know many (or any) people with that kind of money to lend or invest. Indeed, access to other people's money — especially big money — is not the same for everyone and is often connected to individual or societal privilege, which can be anything ranging from family wealth to geographic location to race to business school ties to professional connections.

Ron Shaich went to Harvard Business School. Gordon Segal's family had a retail background, so he had the benefit of their experience as well as a little bit of their money. Adam Lowry and Eric Ryan grew up in one of the most affluent suburbs in America. Jeff Bezos's grandfather was a prominent figure in the early years of the US Atomic Energy Commission and the agency that would eventually become DARPA (Defense Advanced Research Projects Agency). He had helped to cultivate Bezos's interest in technology from a young age during Jeff's summer visits to the family ranch about ninety minutes south of San Antonio, Texas.

That is what privilege can look like. Another way to say it is that some people have distinct, tangible advantages that make it easier for them to pull together enough OPM to get their businesses on solid footing and pointed in the right direction. Recognition of this fact, especially for the entrepreneurs who enjoyed some of those advantages going in, is why I always ask my podcast guests how much they attribute their success to both luck and hard work (a topic we will revisit in chapter 26). Acknowledging privilege and recognizing advantage are essential to understanding the nature of success — both yours and others'.

That does not mean privilege should define or predetermine success, any more than lack of privilege should preclude it. While not everyone has the same privilege of circumstance, everyone has intangible advantages of one kind or another that they can leverage in pursuit of success. Personality is an advantage. Will is an advantage. Likability, unflappability, resilience, having a good memory — those are all advantages that anyone who possesses them can use much the way anyone who possesses privilege uses theirs.

But where does that really leave those of us who may not be lucky enough to have a parent who can write a $10,000 check compared with those whose parents casually carry around $10,000 in cash? It doesn't leave us in the same place, but it does put us in the same race on the same track. Although our access to money differs, the process for securing it is the same, no matter who we are, where we live, how we grew up, or what we're trying to build. In every case, a conversation takes place in which a founder has to describe what they're trying to do and then ask another person for some amount of money — in the form of investment, loan, gift, whatever — to help them get there.

Here's where those early fundraising stories from the privileged and the less-than-privileged start to sound surprisingly alike. To a person, all of these entrepreneurs will tell you that fundraising is brutally hard at every level. It taxes your time, your energy, your ego, and sometimes your relationships. You will have hundreds of conversations. You will have to tell your story hundreds of times and answer ten times as many questions, a lot of them the same, some of them incredibly frustrating, especially from people who you think are supposed to support you or whom you have always called a friend. You are going to need a thick skin, like the heat shield on a space shuttle trying to punch through the incredible resistance of the surrounding atmosphere and not break apart. This is true whether you are blue-blooded or blue-collar, just as it is true that this process starts the same way for everyone — with a conversation, with the people you know.

First a parent, then an uncle, then a family friend, then a mentor, then maybe a kid you went to high school with who also started their own business, and on and on from there, until you've exhausted your total personal network and have, by then hopefully, raised all the money you need. I think about it like a series of concentric circles. You start with the circle of people who are closest to you — the people whose names you don't have to dig to the bottom of your contacts to find, because they're right there in your text messages and the call log on your phone. Maybe you start with a best friend and ask to borrow a few hundred dollars. Does your friend know someone — a relative, possibly — whom you can call for a little more, maybe $500? Does that relative know of someone interested in helping out a startup like yours?

In this way, each person in your inner circle is both a potential resource in and of themselves and also a launching pad to someone in the circle one step removed. In theory, you can move like this out through the concentric circles almost infinitely. In fact, that's kind of how crowdfunding sites like Kickstarter, Indiegogo, and GoFundMe tend to work. They're word-of-mouth mechanisms designed to help innovators and creators just like you get started, by reaching the fifth, sixth, or seventh circle of people whom you could never reasonably expect to know or meet, but whose capital you can use to actually produce the thing you are trying to sell.

Crowdfunding sites are also great for people whose inner circles are a little thin without a lot of people to talk to, or alternatively are quite robust but without a lot of available cash to contribute. Asking people for money is always a difficult, and sometimes uncomfortable, thing to do. Having to do it a hundred times at $20 to $50 a pop isn't just tedious, it's impractical. When are you going to find the time to run the actual business? Crowdfunding consolidates all those small asks into a single conversation broadcast through the loudspeaker we call the internet. In fact, Kickstarter is how Tim Brown first launched Allbirds and how several other companies, such as Oculus, Brooklinen, and the card game Exploding Kittens, initially raised their money.

The lesson here is that despite the sometimes daunting advantages that privilege can confer, this process for raising early money really is available to anyone. Everyone exists at the center of their own set of concentric circles. The built-in advantages of privilege do not change their shape, they only reduce the number of outer circles one might need to explore to reach one's fundraising goals. And that, thankfully, is where we start to find the limits of privilege when it comes to OPM and entrepreneurship — by which I mean, once someone has raised money, even if it was easy for them and there is more where that came from, they still have to do something with it. I can't point to a single example of an entrepreneur I've profiled who raised a bunch of friends-and-family money early on and then merely sat back, resting on their privilege, to watch their business grow organically with no effort.

In fact, just the opposite tends to be the case. Once you've convinced people in your personal network to part with *their* money in support of *your* idea, that's when the pressure to succeed really begins. Understandably, some entrepreneurs don't like that kind of pressure, which is part of what can make the facelessness of crowdfunding and the formality of professional money more appealing pathways. Others use the pressure as fuel. "I found it so motivating," Eric Ryan told me, "because it's one thing to lose our own money or fail, but when you're taking money from people you really care about, you don't want to let them down. It's the best motivation to ensure that no matter how hard things get, you're going to find a path forward."

I also think the pressure of friends-and-family money, especially if you had to wring out that OPM from deep within your concentric circles of contacts, has a way of revealing advantages that maybe you didn't know you had or never thought you could pursue, but that will help you with all the other areas of your business going forward. Because when raising early money is more difficult for you than it might be for someone with the privilege of ready access to capital, you are forced to get better, to *be* better, at everything else. You have to hone your idea until it's razor-sharp. You have to become a much better storyteller, because the farther out into the concentric circles of your network you have to go, where the connections are more tenuous, the less time you have to present your story. You have to get to know your community so much better that, if you do it right, you don't just find a customer base, you also find a home.

Those are advantages that, if you didn't already have them, you can build for yourself as an entrepreneur regardless of privilege. They may be born of the necessity to raise OPM, but they are also tools for making you better. And if you can get better, if you can raise money from friends and family early on to help take your idea from zero to one, all without sacrificing too much of your equity or your vision for the business, then you will be well positioned for success and perfectly situated to grow for a long time to come.

9

Iterate, Iterate, Iterate

Take a look around you right now. At the seat you're sitting on. The shirt you're wearing. The light bulbs illuminating the space you're in. The phone in your pocket. Maybe the earbuds in your ears. Even the cover of this book you're reading or listening to.

If these items have anything in common, it is that none of them looked like they do now when they were first conceived by the people who invented or designed them. And that's because a lot happens between conception and first production for nearly every idea that gets turned into a business. Shape changes. Materials change. Offerings change. Names change. Process changes. Construction methods change. Look and feel and taste change.

As I type these words, I'm wearing a pair of Allbirds wool runner shoes. They're super comfortable. When Tim Brown first conceived of the idea for a simple, clean, logo-less sneaker in 2009, the Merino wool fabric that has been the signature element of Allbirds since their debut in 2014 wasn't even in the picture. The first shoes he produced, in fact, weren't even called Allbirds; they were called TBs, and they were made from canvas and pieces of leather that he shipped from New Zealand to a factory in Indonesia, which produced two versions — high-top and low-top. Fit and comfort weren't really part of the brand vision either. "It wasn't about comfort at that time," Tim said. "It was a design observation about a category that I thought was super complicated and overcrowded and over-logoed."

Then Tim got a whiff, quite literally, of what went into making shoes, especially with leather, and his vision for his shoes began to change. "When I walked into a tannery for the first time," Tim said, "it was an eye-opening experience. I started to understand where these materials were coming from. And what I realized was that the materials that shoes were made out of were not very nice. And I think that opened up the idea of exploring different materials."

One of those materials was wool. "I remember reading a magazine one day about the wool industry in New Zealand," Tim said. "And I was like, 'Gosh, why is wool not used in shoes?' And, 'What if we could do that? That would be hugely interesting.'" Interesting because while the clean design of his shoe, and the story behind it, had resonated with customers enough to sell out virtually the entire 1,000-pair run of TBs at the pop-up shop in Wellington where Tim first sold them publicly (he sold his very first pairs to his teammates on the New Zealand national soccer team), his shoe really wasn't differentiated enough for his taste. "It needed something more both for me and for the product," he said.

So Tim applied to the New Zealand government for a grant from the Wool Research Board — which I swear is an actual thing — to develop a wool textile for the upper part of a shoe. To most people outside of New Zealand, particularly in the United States, this idea would have sounded kind of nuts. Wool is thick and heavy and often scratchy. It's for sweaters and blankets and slippers, maybe, not shoes. But New Zealand's Merino sheep produce an incredibly fine, soft wool with "miraculous properties," as Tim described them. Merino wool wicks away moisture, regulates body temperature, and best of all, as anyone who has ever been caught in the rain wearing a wool sweater can attest, it doesn't smell.

Of course, Tim was not the first person to figure out that Merino wool might be good for clothing. Merino sheep have been around since the twelfth century; in Australia and New Zealand, they've been a staple since the late 1700s. And in recent years, a handful of New Zealand–based clothing manufacturers had begun to develop Merino-blended fabrics, sometimes known as "smart wool," that were becoming increasingly popular.* But in 2009–2010, a similar Merino-based textile did not exist for shoes. "The problem," Tim believed, was that outside of apparel, "wool was being marketed very, very poorly, despite the enormous innovation opportunity." This was the case that Tim made to the Wool Research Board and how he was able to secure the research and development grant that ultimately produced the fabric that would go into the first Allbirds shoes in 2014 and into every other pair since.

There is a name for the creative process that Tim and his cofounder, Joey Zwillinger, went through, from canvas-and-leather TBs in 2009 to Allbirds Merino wool runners in 2014. It's called *iteration* — the incremental evolution of a product or service. It is a phenomenon that is natural to innovation and foundational to the development of products as they come to market and vie for the attention of discerning (and often distracted) consumers.

Typically, there are two phases to the iterative process prior to launch. The first involves tinkering with your idea until it works and you, as its creator, are satisfied with what you have. The second entails exposing the working idea to the public and tweaking the product based on their feedback until it catches on — either with a buyer, a major investor, a retail partner, or a critical mass of your customers.

What makes the Allbirds story somewhat unique is that much of its evolution occurred in that first phase, before the shoes were ever exposed to consumers in any meaningful way. Many of the choices that Tim made — including, but not limited to, his experimentation with Merino wool — were driven by his own goals and preferences. None of his teammates on the New Zealand national team, for example, had complained to him about the fit or the function or the look of those first canvas-and-leather TBs. But Tim didn't like what went

---

* Icebreaker is among the most popular New Zealand smart wool brands.

into making them, and he wasn't all that excited about their sales potential. So he made the switch to wool and then went through 200-plus versions until he found something he loved. That's really what Tim was getting at when he said the shoes needed something more "both for me and for the product."

If all he was doing was making shoes the same toxic way they'd always been made, just without the swoosh or the stripes or the star on the side, how new of an idea was it, really? And how long before that logo-less story ran out of legs? More specifically, from Tim's perspective, what would be the point? The goal, when you're trying to break into an overcrowded market like Tim was, isn't to make Pumas without the tiger; it's to make something no one has ever seen before. Tim and Joey understood that — about the market and about themselves — nearly from the beginning, and they made the lion's share of tweaks to their Allbirds shoe before nearly anyone else had a chance to see it and tell them to do things differently.

As Tim made clear in our conversation, it's important to spend enough time in this first phase to really get comfortable with your product and your story and really get to know the business you're trying to build. Tim, arguably, spent five productive years there. Whitney Wolfe, in contrast, took less than a year to get the first version of Bumble out into the world and onto people's phones, in part because she already knew the business from her time at Tinder and she'd lived every moment of the Bumble story from the day she left Tinder for good. The exact amount of time you spend in the first phase of development isn't as important as making sure you don't get stuck there for too long. Every idea, no matter how great, has a shelf life. If you don't get it off that shelf and out into the world in time, no amount of feedback you get during the second phase of the iterative process can overcome a lack of interest or mitigate first-mover advantage if someone beats you to the punch.

Moving to phase two can be tough for people who don't handle criticism well, or who are dogged by that familiar yet unattainable form of perfectionism that has trapped the next great American novel on the desks or hard drives of countless aspiring writers since forever. Like asking friends and family for money, exposing your idea and all your hard work to feedback can be very uncomfortable, which can make the first phase of internal development feel like a safe space out of which you would rather not poke your head until you're absolutely sure. Except "absolutely sure" doesn't exist.

I would love to tell you a story about an entrepreneur who succeeded in spite of the paralysis of their perfectionism — but I don't have one, because such people generally don't create companies. The creators and innovators whom I meet, if they do struggle with criticism and perfectionism, also understand the importance of allowing their product to be judged by the marketplace, and the opportunity that users' feedback presents to make the product better as a result. They know that they need an *abundance* of feedback to dial in their product. They actively seek it out, in fact. Because while they know what they want to do, and they know why and how they want to do it, they also know that they have no idea if anyone will actually like what they're making. And that's always essential to keep in mind.

Nowhere is this aspect of the iterative process more evident than in the energy bar business. Somehow, over the years, I've managed to interview the creators of three of them — Gary Erickson of Clif Bar, Peter Rahal of RXBar, and Lara Merriken of Lärabar. They are unique characters with similar entrepreneurial journeys, and I think what attracted me to their stories, as someone who loves to cook for other people myself, is just how fraught it can be to come up with a new recipe and then try to get it exactly right so people won't just eat it, but they'll love it, too. You think asking your friends and family for money is hard? Try asking them to taste your food and give you their honest opinion. Try getting them to tell you if it's good, if they like it, *what* they like about it, if there's anything they'd change, if there's anything they'd like more or less of. I can tell you from experience that this can feel like an impossible task — one made even more difficult by the need to discern whose feedback to consider and whose to ignore, and then how to apply that feedback in such a way that it doesn't send you back to the drawing board every time. It is a difficult but necessary process that took Gary Erickson six months, Peter Rahal seven months, and Lara Merriken three *years* to complete.

Each product started with an idea, of course. Gary, an avid cyclist living in Berkeley, California, got his in 1990 on a long, hilly ride through the Bay Area with a good friend. They were planning to do 125 miles, so each of them brought a banana and six PowerBars (also from Berkeley, coincidentally) for fuel. At the time, PowerBars were the only readily available energy bars on the market, so every cyclist ate them — most, grudgingly. "When we were at the top of Mount Hamilton, I'd eaten five of those PowerBars, and I looked at the sixth one and I said, 'No way. I can't do one more. I would rather starve than eat another one of these,'" Gary recalled. Back then, the bars had a consistency somewhere between LaffyTaffy and Now and Laters, without any of the flavor benefits of candied sugar. "The bitter pill," he called them. "I turned to my friend and said, 'I can make a better energy bar than that.'"

A decade later, Lara, a social worker at the time, got the idea for her bar from the bottom of a trail mix bag at the top of a mountain outside Boulder, Colorado, on Memorial Day weekend in 2000. "I was just kind of eating trail mix and thinking of food and raw foods and all of a sudden this light bulb goes off for me," she said. "'Why hasn't somebody made something made of fruit, nuts, and spices — just pure, simple, real foods — but it's portable and convenient and it tastes indulgent like you shouldn't be eating it?'"

In 2012, Peter Rahal came up with the idea for RXBar when, as a hard-core CrossFit enthusiast and an adherent of the Paleo diet (like so many other CrossFitters), he recognized that there was no energy or protein bar out there that met the strictures of that diet. "And the question was, why?" Peter said. "There's this group of people that all do the same activity, that subscribe to the same nutrition values, and yet these gyms are selling water, they're selling T-shirts, but no good-tasting bar that fulfilled the Paleo criteria." Not unlike Tim Brown's sneakers, Peter's idea was to fill that gap in the otherwise crowded energy bar space with something clean and simple.

Interestingly, conceiving of and getting down the rough outlines of the bars' initial recipes — this is what the first phase of their itera-tive process entailed — didn't take any of these creators all that long. Not twenty-four hours after Gary got home from his long ride, for instance, he called his mom, who'd helped him with recipes for the small bakery (Kali's, named after his grandma) he currently owned, and enlisted her help with his energy bar idea. Her response was, "What's an energy bar?" His answer was basically the foundation of the Clif Bar recipe. "It is kind of like that oatmeal–raisin–chocolate chip cookie you make," he began, "but we can't use butter, we can't use sugar, we can't use oil." It was just going to be whole oats, real fruit, and a sweetener made from rice, all of which he would form into a rectangular shape, because "it was not going to be a cookie — it had to be like a bar."

Lara didn't wait a full day to start tinkering either. "I ran down the mountain," she said, "I got out a notebook, and I started writ-ing down ideas. And then when we got back to Denver, I would get ideas from pies and cookies and cakes. And I'd think, 'Okay, how do I take cherry pie and make basically a raw, unprocessed food just in my Cuisinart and make it taste like cherry pie or apple pie or banana bread?'" The recipes came fairly quickly for her after that.

For Peter and his partner, Jared Smith, the initial phase was more of a process. "There was not this moment where it's like, 'Oh, we're going to do it and commit,'" Peter said. "First, we're like, 'Let's go to Whole Foods and tour the market. Let's start playing around with ingredients.' We just kind of did some preliminary market research and started learning." Still, like Gary and Lara, they went into their tour with a clear vision for the product — a minimal-ingredient, Pa-leo-friendly protein bar. "And the general philosophy around the product was that for whatever part of the formula, we wanted to make sure the ingredients were the best possible."

It is precisely at this point in the iterative process that any one of these founders could have frozen in fear of negative feedback and let their idea get stuck in what Hollywood calls development hell. In retrospect, it would be hard to blame any of them if that had hap-pened, because they each faced resistance to their idea from the peo-ple closest to them. Gary's mom didn't even know what an energy bar was. Lara's parents, when she called them to share her idea, thought she was completely out of her mind. "They just thought, 'We've sent her through private high school, USC, she's graduated, she's thirty-two years old . . . Oh my God, what's going on here?'" Lots of people told Peter his Paleo protein bar was a bad idea, though not necessarily with their words. "I'd be very excited about it, and the look on their face was like, *That's a dumb idea,*" Peter said, though he understood their skepticism . . . to a degree. "I mean, the market didn't need another protein bar, that's for sure. But we were just focused, and when we got some feedback, if it was negative, we were like, 'We're just going to do it anyway.'"

By the end of the summer of 2012, Peter was inundating the people at his CrossFit gym with samples. He'd moved into the second iterative phase of the development process. "We'd have logs of this RXBar dough, packed in Tupperware, and we would just get feedback," Peter remembered of those early days — he at his CrossFit gym, Jared at the gym he belonged to. "You just ask a ton of questions: 'Do you like this?' 'Do you not like this?' 'What would you like?' 'Would you pay for this?' We collected tons of data." All of that data went into refining the recipe for their first flavor, coconut chocolate, until mid-March 2013, when they made legitimate sales and collected real revenue for the first time. From there, they were off like a shot, selling online.

Lara's path through the second phase of iteration was appreciably longer than Peter's, since e-commerce solutions for food products were not as common or as popular in 2000 as they were in 2012. For Lara, it was going to be brick-and-mortar or bust. Still, despite the difference in length, the journey itself was the same. "I would make samples. I mean, batch after batch after batch that I would come up with using a Cuisinart* that I'd had for years but never actually used," Lara told me. "And I would do a focus group. I would create my own little survey, and I would ask people, 'What do you eat energy bars for?' 'Why do you like them?' 'Why don't you like them?'

---

* Not surprisingly, Peter Rahal and Jared Smith also used a Cuisinart to come up with their first RXBar recipe.

Then I would give them my concoctions and say, 'Please tell me what you think.'" Which is exactly what they did. "They would give me feedback like, 'I really like the cherry, but I don't taste cherry in every bite,' and I would go back and think, 'I need to add more cherries. You *should* taste cherry in every bite.'" This was her development process for the five flavors — cherry pie, apple pie, banana bread, cashew cookie, and chocolate coconut chew — that she began selling in Denver-area Whole Foods stores in mid-2003.

For Gary's part, a decade before he nearly fell into the opposite of the perfectionist's feedback trap, which can be equally perilous for a new product in development. "We had many failures," Gary said of the six-month period after his now-infamous bike ride. "And at times we tried to talk ourselves into them." They'd tell themselves, "This is great," having grown tired of all the experimentation and the feedback from Gary's cycling friends, which was sometimes good, never great, and often really bad. "I would bring some out to my friends in plastic bags and say, 'Okay, try this but keep it a secret,' and they would be like, 'This is terrible.'" That would send Gary back into the kitchen, despite an overwhelming desire at times to declare his new energy bar "good enough." Finally, after six months of continued sampling, they landed on what they were looking for. "My mom and I just knew," he said, describing the moment when they finalized the first Clif Bar recipe. "Then you take a risk, and you put a package around it, because you are never sure."

Take one last look around you at all the things you observed at the start of this chapter. The people who made those things were just as unsure as Gary Erickson was when he put a wrapper around the first Clif Bar, slapped a price tag on it, and put it up for sale. They made just as many tweaks in the early stages of development as Tim Brown did, based on gut instinct and personal preference, without knowing whether anyone would like them, let alone care. They ignored doubters like Peter Rahal did. And they stayed long enough in the first phase of iteration without staying too long (or forever), so that when they moved into the second phase for consumer feedback — like Lara Merriken did with her focus groups — they were putting their best foot forward. They were sending a version of their idea out into the world that they could stand behind and that could itself stand up to the criticism they were inviting. That is the real recipe for success in the iterative process, and one every creator needs to get right if they want to turn their idea not just into a product, but into a business that is poised for real, sustained growth.

PART II

THE TEST(S)

MOST OF THE ENTREPRENEURS I've interviewed have a healthy fear of failure. They know it's possible at any moment. Even *likely*. When it happens — and believe me it *will* happen — they certainly don't like it. It's not comfortable, and it's definitely not fun. But that never stops them.

Good entrepreneurs — successful ones — have a way of not letting their fear of failure slow them down. They are defined instead by a seemingly inextinguishable belief in their idea — the idea that has pulled them out of their comfort zone and driven them across the unknown to explore new possibilities. They are convinced that, if they can just get there (wherever "there" is), if they can just get their idea off the ground, it will succeed.

If. That's really what entrepreneurs fear at this stage. The uncertainty of whether they will be able to cross that vast space between inspiration and execution, full of tests and traps, twists and turns. A gauntlet that every entrepreneur must pass through, with challenges that are generally the same for everyone, but that take different forms and present in a different order with each trip across the unknown territory of starting a business.

Indeed, every entrepreneurial journey is a new and different story. No two paths are the same. Everyone will proceed through many of the same pivotal points, but your path will inevitably be unique to you, to your idea, and to the time and place through which it passes.

Fortunately, it's never been easier to make this journey than it is right now. So many entrepreneurs have done what you are about to do. You have the chance to prepare for what's coming your way — if you are willing to learn from these unwitting helpers. They've made every mistake. They've fallen into every trap. They've taken every wrong turn. And the good ones — the successful ones — only made those mistakes, fell into those traps, took those wrong turns . . . *once*. Because they borrowed from the entrepreneurs who came before them as well. They heard the stories and learned the lessons. Now it's your turn.

10

Go In Through the Side Door

A funny thing happens when you start to find success with a new business. You suddenly find yourself face-to-face with a host of people who are none too happy to see you. These people have a name. They're called *competitors*. And whether they'll admit it to you or not, many of them will try to do everything within their power to legally — and sometimes not so legally — shut you out. It's a strategy deployed by the big fish in every pond once they notice a new, young fish swimming around and getting bigger by gobbling up the scraps they previously considered too small to care about.

In 1997, as the personal computer business approached 100 million units in annual sales and the dot-com bubble began to grow in earnest, Microsoft was one of the biggest fish in a pond that was about to swamp the world. Late that summer, a Microsoft group vice president named Jeff Raikes sent a now-famous email titled "Go Huskers!" to Warren Buffett, a fellow Nebraska native, describing Microsoft's business in an effort to get him to invest in the company. In the email, Raikes likens the sturdiness and growth potential of Microsoft's operation to that of Coca-Cola and See's Candies (which Buffett had owned since 1972), in no small part because Microsoft's revolutionary flagship product — the Windows operating system —

had created a "toll bridge" that every PC maker would have to cross if they expected consumers to buy their machines.

The graphical user interface that made Windows revolutionary also made it wildly popular, which had the additional effect of creating a "moat," as Raikes described it, between Microsoft and its competitors in the marketplace — one it was able to widen considerably with a 90 percent market share in productivity software applications (Word, Excel, PowerPoint, Access, etc.) that were built on top of Windows and were equally popular. This, in turn, gave Microsoft tremendous "pricing discretion," not just for its applications software but also for the licensing fees the company charged to other computer makers for Microsoft's operating system software.

What Raikes did not say in his email, but what Buffett surely understood from his decades of experience, was that the wider the moat and the longer the toll bridge, the more aggressively Microsoft could wield its pricing discretion in order to cement its growing advantage in the software industry. They could use it as a carrot, by lowering the licensing fee for Windows as an incentive to get their browser and applications software preloaded onto as many new PCs as possible. They could use it as a stick, by withholding volume Windows licensing discounts to punish PC makers that refused their sweetheart deal, or by offering their applications software at cost or below in order to drive competitors such as Lotus, Novell, and Corel (remember them?) out of business.

Microsoft employed each of those strategies to great effect. A year after Raikes's email to Buffett, Microsoft would surpass General Electric as the world's most valuable company and stay in that position for five consecutive years.

Toll bridge. Moat. Pricing discretion. These are euphemisms for the economic term *barriers to entry,* which is itself a kind of euphemism for all the ways existing businesses shut out competitors and make it difficult for new businesses to compete in a given industry. These barriers are not just conscious strategies deployed by old guard blue-chippers; they are also natural forces that rise and shift within a market as competitors enter and exit, grow and shrink, evolve and pivot. They can become the biggest obstacles you will face as a new business looking to grab, secure, and expand your foothold in a market, because they are the mechanism by which you will either be crushed (if your competitors see you coming) or ignored (if the market doesn't).

This is why if, like most new businesses, you aren't doing something *completely* novel or you aren't doing it in a *totally* new way or new place, you should be thinking long and hard about how else you might enter your market besides knocking on the front door and asking for permission to come in. This is something that female and minority entrepreneurs have long had to contend with, whether it means breaking through glass ceilings or breaking down walls built by prejudice. All of which is to say, figuring out how to sneak in through the side door is not new ground you will have to break. A legion of resourceful geniuses have come before you. And what many of them have discovered is that the side door isn't just less heavily guarded, it's often bigger. Or, as Peter Thiel put it in a 2014 lecture at the Stanford Center for Professional Development titled "Competition Is for Losers," "Don't always go through the tiny little door that everyone's trying to rush through. Go around the corner and go through the vast gate that no one's taking."

A year earlier, in Chicago, without fully realizing it, this is precisely what Peter Rahal had begun to do with his idea for a minimalist Paleo protein bar. Peter hadn't started out looking for a side door per se, but he knew that with RXBar he was trying to enter a very busy space. Remember, Peter had already conceded that "the market didn't need another protein bar." It was a conclusion that was more or less inescapable when he and his partner, Jared Smith, did their initial fact-finding tour of Whole Foods. If there was one fact they were sure to find, it was that protein bars were among the most crowded sectors in the entire food business. Long gone were the days when only one main brand existed in this segment, as Gary Erickson had found in the early 1990s when he developed Clif Bar to go up against PowerBar. Even a decade later, ample opportunity was there for someone like Lara Merriken in a way that did not exist for Peter in 2013.

Can you imagine what the shelves of that Chicago Whole Foods looked like when he and Jared walked in? How many linear feet of shelf space were choked with multiple flavors from how many different protein bar manufacturers? Can you envision Peter even being able to secure as much as a hello from a Whole Foods regional buyer the way Lara Merriken did? Especially when the buyer learned what Peter was pitching? *Yet another protein bar?*

Peter knew he wasn't getting into Whole Foods through the front door. Fortunately, that was never his plan. "From the early days, the whole strategy was to make a product that is for CrossFit and for the Paleo consumer, and build it online," he said. "We'd build a web store and sell directly to gyms. Consumers would be coming directly to us." That meant a bar with no grains, no dairy, no peas or bean protein, and no sugar. Nothing quite like it existed.

It was just the kind of advantage that a startup could identify and exploit but a larger competitor couldn't (or wouldn't) see. "A lot of people look at niches, or look at a small segment, and it's not big enough for them," Peter explained. "But we would rather have a CrossFit customer in California than a local Chicago independent grocery store, because in the grocery store we're among the sea of competition. Whereas in a CrossFit gym, we were by ourselves. RXBar was literally engineered and designed for that occasion. It was perfect."

It was his side door. Those niches — CrossFit, Paleo, and direct-to-consumer — which were then on the verge of exploding and truly becoming the kind of vast gate that Peter Thiel was talking about, were the combination that unlocked opportunity for Peter Rahal and allowed RXBar the chance to take root, to stand out, and to grow, before his direct competitors could notice and stamp him out. By that point, those competitors included major multinationals like General Mills and Nestlé, which had acquired Lärabar and PowerBar, respectively, and they could have easily shut him out by erecting any number of barriers to entry into the protein bar market.

For Manoj Bhargava, the founder of 5-hour Energy, his side door into the energy drink market did not take the shape of a small niche, but rather of a small product. In early 2003, a few years removed from his retirement from a plastics business he'd turned around and made profitable, Manoj was attending a natural products trade show outside Los Angeles looking for inventions he might acquire or license in an effort to create a business that would generate an ongoing residual income stream for him in his post-plastics years.

Walking the floor of the show, he stumbled upon a new sixteen-ounce energy drink that produced long-lasting effects he'd never experienced with other energy drinks. "Well, this is amazing," he said to himself, exhausted from a long morning of meetings and now energized enough to continue walking the trade show floor. "I could sell this," he thought. The drink's creators disagreed. They were "science guys with PhDs," while he was "just a lowly business guy." They refused to sell their invention to him or even offer him a license on their formula. When they effectively told him to hit the road, Manoj decided to hit the lab instead and to create his own version of the energy drink that had fueled him up and blown him away.

"I looked at their label and said, 'I can do better than this. How hard can it be? I'll figure it out,'" Manoj said. With the help of scientists from a company he'd founded for the express purpose of finding inventions just like this one, he had a comparable energy drink formula in a matter of months. It would turn out to be the easiest part of the process.

The hard part would be getting his invention into stores. "If I make another drink," Manoj said of his thinking at the time, "I've got to fight for space in the cooler against Red Bull and Monster [Energy]. I've also got to fight Coke, Pepsi, and Budweiser for space. So you're pretty much dead if you want to try that."

He was dead because he would be fighting for a finite amount of space in brick-and-mortar stores, against the competition not just in his own niche but in the entire beverage industry, which is dominated by some of the biggest companies in the world. If you own a 7-Eleven, or you're the general manager of a grocery chain like Kroger or Tesco, are you really going to turn over a Diet Coke, Mountain Dew, or Snapple rack to a new energy drink that no one has ever heard of? Especially when, in 2003, energy drink sales had yet to really spike and there were already two major players — Red Bull and Monster Energy — in the nascent market. Even if you were inclined to give a little guy like Manoj Bhargava a shot, once the regional sales reps and distributors from Coca-Cola and PepsiCo got wind of your decision, they would likely wield their Microsoftesque price discretion against you like a baseball bat, or just pull their products from your store altogether.

Those were the barriers to entry that Manoj was looking at. If he was going to get into this market, he'd have to find some other way. That's when it dawned on him. "If I'm tired," he asked himself, "why am I thirsty also?" By which he meant, why should we have to chug ten to sixteen ounces of a cloyingly sweet liquid in order to get an energy boost? "It would be like Tylenol selling sixteen-ounce bottles," Manoj explained by way of analogy. "I just want to do it quick. I don't want to drink this whole thing," he thought. This is how Manoj arrived at the idea of shrinking his product down from the standard sixteen-ounce drink to a two-ounce shot.

Quickly, everything changed. In less than six months, he'd hired a designer to make his distinctive label, and he'd found a bottler who could produce two-ounce versions of his energy formula. "And at two ounces," he said, "it's really not a drink, it's a delivery system."

This was 5-hour Energy's side door. It wasn't a drink, so it wasn't an immediate threat to Red Bull or Monster Energy. At two ounces, it also didn't need to be refrigerated or given a large, dedicated shelf, so retailers didn't have to worry about space. They understood that the perfect spot for it would be at the cash register, right next to the Slim Jims and pickled eggs!

"It just belonged there," Manoj said. "You could tell it just looked that way, that it should be there." Moreover, because the ingredients that went into 5-hour Energy were actually less about energy and more about focus — "vitamins for the brain," Manoj called them — he could position his product beyond the beverage verticals and outside the grocery or convenience store channels. In fact, the very first place he went with 5-hour Energy in 2004 was the largest *vitamin* store, GNC, which decided to put the product in a thousand of its stores.

GNC turned out to be a genius side door into the energy "drink" market for a couple reasons. The first is obvious — there was much less competition compared with grocery and convenience stores—but the second is more interesting. "It turns out GNC is always looking for new products, because once a product gets mass distribution, GNC is sort of out of it," Manoj explained. "If it's in Walmart, nobody's going to buy it at GNC." Essentially, GNC was an easier route to retail distribution than a place like 7-Eleven or Safeway, and thankfully the tolerance for a slow start was higher as well, because in the first week they sold only 200 bottles. "Which was horrible," Manoj admitted. But they waited it out, manufacturer and retailer together, "and at the end of six months it was selling 10,000 bottles a week." From there Manoj went to drugstores like Walgreens and Rite Aid, which snapped it up, and now 5-hour Energy is near the cash register in most stores basically everywhere.

Today, RXBar, which was acquired by Kellogg's in 2017 for $600 million, is one of the fastest-growing brands in the protein bar space, and 5-hour Energy has a 93 percent share of the energy shot business. It is a market dominance that Manoj has enjoyed from nearly the beginning, with only a brief dip to 67 percent when all his competitors—Coca-Cola, PepsiCo, Monster Energy, Red Bull—flooded the market with their own two-ounce-shot offerings . . . and failed. "Whenever people ask me what product are we like, I say we're WD-40," Manoj said near the end of our conversation, as we talked about 5-hour Energy's phenomenal success. "We *own* the category. We're the guys."

This is the great irony of circumventing the barriers to entry that your competition's apparent monopoly power constructs and then fighting your way in through the side door. If you're successful, you stand a very good chance of achieving market domination of your own. Of digging and widening your own moat and building the toll bridge that crosses it. Of massive, unbelievable success. For many entrepreneurs, that is the goal.

Four days after Jeff Raikes sent his famous "Go Huskers!" email, Warren Buffett responded. His reply contained the normal conversational pleasantries, glowing commentary on Raikes's analysis of his position on investing in Microsoft (Buffett wouldn't), and an envious description of the company's monopoly power: "It's as if you were getting paid for every gallon of water starting in a small stream, but with added amounts received as tributaries turned the stream into an Amazon." At the very beginning of his lecture in 2014, Peter Thiel echoed this sentiment in his own way. "I have a single idée fixe that I am completely obsessed with on the business side," he said in his characteristic, hitched speaking style, "which is that if you're the founder-entrepreneur starting a company, you always want to aim for monopoly, and you always want to avoid competition." You want to be the only one directing traffic and collecting tolls across the widest moat possible.

I mention all this because being really good at going through the side door is an amazing, and sometimes necessary, skill. But it can also be a double-edged sword. It can get you off the ground and set you up for fantastic growth, but it can get you in a lot of trouble, too. Indeed, that tension is present whenever you search for the Raikes-Buffett emails online. They are often held up by aspiring entrepreneurs as brilliant examples of business acumen and strategic analysis, but what many of those people don't realize is that the entire reason they are able to read those emails at all — most often in the form of pdf versions of a printed-out email chain — is because they are part of the public record, submitted as deposition and trial exhibits in a class action antitrust lawsuit brought against Microsoft in the early 2000s by consumers in multiple American states. This email exchange became a key part of the plaintiffs' opening statement in that suit, which was settled not long afterward for more than a billion dollars.

All of which is to say, *Go through the side door, please!* Do everything within your power to find your way into the market where you are likely to have the most success. Just make sure when you get inside and set up shop, you avoid becoming what you fought so hard against in turning your dream of starting your own business into a reality.

11

It's All About Location

I t is a maxim that has defined an industry. *Location, location, location.* In real estate, it is the single most important factor in determining the value of a home. A beautiful four-bedroom house on the top of a hill overlooking San Francisco Bay might run you into the multiple millions of dollars. But take that same house, with the same amount of land, and move it to the bottom of that hill, next to a fire station, and you're looking at a piece of property worth only half as much, if you're lucky.

This kind of raw "apples to apples" comparison is not really what real estate titans are referring to, though, when they talk about the value of a property and the primacy of location. What they are talking about is the *power of location* in the context of the subjective needs and preferences of individual buyers. For parents with young children, a mediocre three-bedroom house in a great school district is better, or more valuable to them, than a great four-bedroom house in a mediocre school district. For retirees looking for their dream beach house, a small place on the sand is better than a large place three blocks away from it.

The same exact phenomenon exists for young businesses trying to find a foothold. Depending on a company's needs, certain locations are simply better than others. For example, if you are making surfboards, maybe Vermont isn't the best place for you. But if you are making snowboards, like the late Jake Burton Carpenter, founder of Burton Snowboards, started to do in 1977, maybe Vermont is just the right place. It's certainly better than the apartment on East Eighty-Sixth Street in Manhattan where Jake was living when he made the first prototypes and realized he needed to move in order for the business to blossom and grow. Interestingly, Ben Cohen and Jerry Greenfield left New York for Vermont that very same year to start Ben & Jerry's, but for another reason. While they were taking a correspondence course in ice cream making, someone opened an ice cream shop near their first proposed location in Sarasota Springs, New York. That was too much competition for Ben and Jerry's tastes, so they moved to Burlington, Vermont.

As the founder of a new company, it's *your* job to figure out where you belong for your business to reach its full potential. Is there some specific place you should be? Like Jake Carpenter in Vermont? Are you in a crowded space you need to get out of, like Ben and Jerry in Sarasota Springs? Or are you just fine right where you are? Like Tobi Lütke, the founder of Shopify, in Ottawa, Ontario.

Now, when you say those words out loud, they don't sound right, do they? Ottawa? Home to what would become one of the largest e-commerce platforms in the world? Shouldn't a company like Shopify be in, say, Silicon Valley? Well, as a matter of fact, that's exactly what every venture capital firm thought when Tobi went out to Sand Hill Road to raise money in 2008.

"No one could possibly be doing anything interesting outside of the valley" was how Tobi described their thinking at the time. And if it wasn't outright condescension he faced, it was general skepticism about the idea of an e-commerce software solution that helped people start online retail businesses. They'd say, "'Didn't we figure out e-commerce in the nineties?' Or 'Did we not figure out that it didn't work in the early 2000s?'" Tobi recalled. He fully understood their hesitancy. After all, "e-commerce and the dot-com emergence and crash was sort of inextricably linked," and here he was riding into town,* trying to raise money, right as another big bubble had just burst.

What those skeptical venture capitalists couldn't see was that their assessment of e-commerce in the early 2000s was only partially right. It hadn't worked . . . *yet*. "There were more online stores in 2001 than there were people who'd ever used a credit card online," Tobi explained. "It's not that people were wrong, just much too early." And so was the technology. The e-commerce experience was severely lacking, both from the shopper side and the merchant side. That was the problem Tobi was trying to solve when he set out to create what would become Shopify, but which began as storefront software for an online snowboard business called Snowdevil that he'd started in 2004 out of his in-laws' garage.

At the time, e-commerce sites were basically just translations of old retail product catalogs into the digital space. There was a static grid of products that might go for dozens of pages. Search functionality was very rudimentary, if it worked at all. Image quality was poor. And it was really hard to pay for things. "What was interesting to us was not to create this sort of anonymous grid of products," Tobi said. "It was to tell stories — something that wrapped good storytelling around products that people are excited about — and that was easy, especially the credit card part."

After four years of refinement and then a shift away from snowboards to software as its core business, the result was Shopify. And to Tobi's surprise, despite their initial skepticism, a number of VC firms wrote term sheets for investment. Some were even the kinds of offers that entrepreneurs today dream about — a benchmark offer from Sequoia Capital, to name just one. But every deal came with a catch. "All the offers were conditional on moving the company to Silicon Valley," Tobi said.

This was a nonstarter for reasons wholly unrelated to the business. "I am fundamentally suspicious of orthodoxy," Tobi said. A

---

* Tobi quite literally rode into town. For his two-week trip to the valley, he bought a bike and rode it to all his meetings.

claim evidenced in his decision a few years earlier to build e-commerce software from scratch, and then to abandon Java for Ruby on Rails as the programming language with which to build it. "I don't react very well to people telling me what to do," Tobi said of the various VC offers he'd received, "so I pretty much tried to figure out a way to not have to move."

That probably sounds like an epic level of stubbornness, considering that for about six months out of the year, Ottawa is not what one might call a fun, easy place to live. It gets very dark and very cold, which makes recruiting key talent to move there more difficult than to a place like Silicon Valley, where the average daily high temperature is a full thirty degrees warmer during those six, hard Canadian fall and winter months.

But as far as Tobi was concerned, Ottawa had a lot of stuff going for it. He'd moved to Canada's capital city from Germany a few years earlier to live with his girlfriend (now wife), Fiona McKean, who had aspirations to become a Canadian diplomat. They lived with her parents rent-free for a full decade (even after success!). He'd already found $400,000 in funding from an angel investor named John Phillips, whose parents happened to live in Ottawa. And beyond that, Ottawa was a place, Tobi believed, that punched far above its weight in intellectual talent. It was, after all, where the best and the brightest in Canada came to devote their talents to government service. Just because most of the VCs he met with couldn't find Ottawa on a map did not mean it was some kind of backwater.

Tobi had another advantage when it came to resisting the demands of his VC suitors: he didn't actually want their money. He wasn't all that interested in scaling Shopify into the kind of billion-dollar back-end behemoth it eventually became. So while VC money would have been nice, at that moment in 2008 it wasn't necessary.

"I think businesses are there to, at some point, make money, but also to be sustainable," he said. "That's what I was hoping for. My intention was to build the world's best twenty-person company."

In fact, the only reason he was talking to any of these VCs at all was because even that number — twenty people — was too big for one of his co-founders, Scott Lake. Up to that point, Scott had been performing many of the functions of a startup CEO and had decided to leave the company to do other things. "Funnily enough, he ended up realizing he's a small-company guy much more so than I," Tobi said, "and I think he also realized that where the software industry was going, most of the people who were CEOs were actually highly technical members of the founding teams." Scott was not technical. He was the business guy, the sales guy, the relationship guy. And Tobi, well, he would always be a programmer first. "I wanted to play with technology. That was what I was good at. That was my identity," he said. In retrospect, this made him oddly suited to run a software company, but in 2008 he had very little interest in doing so, which is the thing that eventually brought him to Silicon Valley. He'd heard from someone that if you got a really good VC to invest in your company, they usually had a big network of people they could pull from to help you find the right CEO, if you needed one.

Tobi definitely felt like he needed a good CEO, and he met with several worthy candidates over late-night drinks on that trip, thanks to introductions from a few of the VCs who would eventually write term sheets for Shopify. But none of the candidates (or the term sheets) were great enough to convince Tobi to move the company from the snowy expanse of eastern Canada to the sunny shores of the western United States.

It's impossible to prove a counterfactual, but I think that Tobi's recalcitrance probably helped Shopify dodge a bullet in the relocation clauses of those initial VC offers. Ottawa gave Tobi the distance he needed to be as creative and unconventional as he wanted to be in building the software that now powers more than 820,000 merchants, who have sold more than $100 billion worth of goods and services in 175 different countries. Had Tobi taken one of those offers in 2008 and agreed to move, it is very likely that the institutional memory of Silicon Valley — which still suffered some PTSD resulting from the role of e-commerce in the dot-com crash — would have rounded off many of the edges on Tobi's plans and may have bent his software into the shape of something less dynamic. This is not to speak ill of moving your business, or of moving it to Silicon Valley; it's just the nature of trying to remake something in an entirely new way. There will always be resistance, and the gravity of money and memory will always pull you toward the familiar. And so you must resist in turn if where you are headed is better, in your estimation, than where they want you to go.

Sometimes, though, you need to give in to the gravity and let it pull you in a new direction, to a different place, toward what Reid Hoffman calls "the heat of the action." For Katrina Lake, unlike for Tobi Lütke, that place *was* Silicon Valley. The move happened for her in early 2011. For the two years prior, she'd been living in Boston and attending Harvard Business School, where she was about to graduate not just with an MBA but with an actual business. She originally called it Rack Habit, but fairly soon after founding the business Katrina changed the name to Stitch Fix because, as she told me, "it was very clear Nordstrom would have sued us for it."*

The idea for Stitch Fix was fairly straightforward. For $20 per month, you would get a box shipped to your home filled with five clothing items that had been hand-selected for you by a stylist based on a personalized survey that you filled out when you signed up. If you bought all five items, you would get a discount, and the $20 "styling fee" would count toward your total. If you didn't want any of the items, you would just send the box back, and all you would be out was the $20 monthly fee.

The idea came to Katrina when she realized that "more and more dollars were moving to e-commerce stores" at the same time a "massive depersonalization of retail was happening," and that if there was one category where that combination of factors would not fly, it was apparel. Clothing purchases are "deeply personal and deeply nuanced and super emotional," she said. Her goal, then, was to re-personalize online clothes shopping — to "deliver a personal experience in apparel and [to] use data and technology to make it scalable and to make it better."

As she got Stitch Fix up and running, Katrina knew that Boston was not the place for this kind of business. It was an apparel company, so obviously it needed to be in New York. That was the cen-

---

* Nordstrom's outlet store franchise is called Nordstrom Rack.

ter of fashion in America. That was where the gravity of her original idea was pulling her. But as the spring of 2011 approached, her perspective changed. "I realized, 'There's no reason we have to be in New York. Lots of brands are in LA, lots of companies are in the Bay Area,'" she explained of her thinking. She also realized that maybe Stitch Fix wasn't actually an apparel company after all, but a technology company.

While it was true that Stitch Fix would be selling clothes, it was the technology that was going to make the business work, and there was only one place in the country in 2011 that had the kind of concentration of technology talent Katrina would need to scale up as quickly as she wanted. That place was Silicon Valley. Almost overnight, the gravity shifted. "The talent is here," she said. "We have many, many data scientists and many, many engineers, and if we wanted to fulfill the vision of using technology to deliver our service, it would have been very difficult to do it elsewhere."

A couple years later, Dropbox CEO Drew Houston, who like Katrina had come up with his idea and founded his company while in school in Boston and then moved to San Francisco to launch it in earnest, gave the commencement address to the graduating class at his alma mater, MIT. Drew spoke directly to this idea of relocating for your business, echoing the advice Reid Hoffman gives to the entrepreneurs he mentors.

"Where you live matters," Drew said in his address. "Whatever you're doing, there's usually only one place where the top people go. You should go there. Don't settle for anything else ... If the real action is happening somewhere else, move."

It's not unreasonable to imagine that hundreds of thousands of people have moved to Silicon Valley from all over the world to start businesses since the turn of the millennia for this very reason. Apoorva Mehta, the founder of Instacart, did so after quitting his job at Amazon in 2010. "As I read more and more about entrepreneurship, I started to find all these prolific entrepreneurs and investors had something in common, which was that all of them were in Silicon Valley," he said. "And to me it was like, if you're playing soccer, it's probably a good idea for you to be in Brazil; or if you're in acting, it's probably a good idea for you to be in Hollywood. So, you know, why not move to San Francisco?"

This is not a new phenomenon, of course. And it doesn't just apply to the valley. It's what compelled Jane Wurwand to move halfway around the world in 1983, from Cape Town, South Africa, to Los Angeles, to break into the skin care game. (It was the only place with a meaningful concentration of skin care salons.) Six years earlier, it was why the legendary magazine publisher Jann Wenner actually *left* San Francisco and moved the entire *Rolling Stone* operation to New York City. "It was kind of a no-brainer that that's what we would do," he told me. "If you want all the resources of talent, they were available in New York. That's where the industry was."

There are situations, however, when you want to go where the industry is *not*. Ben Cohen and Jerry Greenfield opened their business in Burlington, Vermont, because, in Ben's words, "there wasn't much ice cream there." The brilliant songwriters and producers Antonio "L.A." Reid and Kenny "Babyface" Edmonds formed LaFace Records in 1989 in Los Angeles, then left for reasons that they didn't entirely understand in the moment, but that became crystal clear when they hung out their shingle in Atlanta, Georgia. "We would just hold auditions looking for talent," Reid said of those first days in Atlanta, "and before long the talent just came running, because we were the only shop in town."

Almost twenty years later, Sadie Lincoln left California as well, except she went north, up to Portland, Oregon, to found a studio fitness business called Barre3, built around the use of the ballet barre and utilizing small isometric movements derived from ballet. Today, barre workouts are incredibly popular. There are a number of popular brands, including Barre3, with thousands of studios in medium-sized to big cities all over the world. But in 2007, when Sadie and her husband, Chris, and their two young children moved, the barre craze had not yet found Portland. Like many trends and boutique fitness concepts — yoga, Pilates, indoor cycling, HIIT (high-intensity interval training) — it was concentrated in the big coastal cities like New York and San Francisco, where she worked. The experience in these places had also become somewhat standardized, based on the expectations of a rather homogeneous customer base. Portland offered Sadie a new type of fitness audience and a clean slate on all fronts.

"We moved to Portland as a conscious decision where there was no barre around us," Sadie said. "I loved using the ballet barre. I loved the isometric work and the small movements and the music. Everything else, we detached from the fitness industry, from yoga, from any traditional ballet heritage, and decided instead to just approach it with fresh eyes."

Sadie wanted to remake the barre experience into something more holistic and self-directed, which ran counter to the tendency of barre brands from New York and LA at the time, which sought to systematize their workouts. "I wanted to create a studio that instead of being 'the answer' or being a methodology, I just wanted it to be an exercise experience," she said. "At the very beginning of class, every instructor will start by saying, 'Welcome to Barre3. I give you full permission to do something different than I say. Your only job is to listen, not to me but to yourself. I'm your guide. I'm going to give you a platform here. We're going to turn the music on. I'm going to show you how to align your body. And then I want you to make it your own.'"

In talking to Sadie, you get the sense that only in Portland could an approach like hers take root the way it did and then grow nationwide to "more than 140 franchise studios all powered by female entrepreneurs." In fact, that is the sense I got from each of the founders I've profiled in this chapter regarding the importance of location in the growth of their businesses: "only in _____."

That is, only in Ottawa could Shopify get to become Shopify, without Silicon Valley doubters meddling with Tobi Lütke's software. Only in the Bay Area could Stitch Fix find its footing as a technology business in order to fulfill its mission of re-personalizing apparel sales online. And only in Beverly Hills, or New York, or Burlington, or Atlanta, or Portland could these other amazing businesses find the growth they were looking for as well.

Whether it's actually true or not, in the minds of these founders, there was *one* ideal place for them to start and grow their business. But it just so happens that there were *three* different ways to get to that place: some had to move in order to break into their industries; some had to move in order to break *out* of them; and some were perfectly situated right where they were. Your job is to figure out which camp your business belongs in.

12

Get Attention, Part 1: Building Buzz

Kleenex. Google. Coke. Xerox. Band-Aid. Popsicle. Chap-Stick. Jet Ski. Q-tips. Scotch tape. Post-it. These classic brands have achieved such ubiquity in our culture that they are becoming genericized and sometimes turned into verbs. When you need to blow your nose, you grab a Kleenex, not a tissue. When you need to find an address, you google it. When your lips are dry, you apply ChapStick, not lip balm. They have become such a part of our daily lives that a lot of people don't even realize they are brands. Inevitably, we forget that at some point in the past, someone actually created these things and put them out into a world that had never heard of them before and had no idea what they were.

The fact that any brand could achieve this kind of legendary, all-world status is a miraculous feat. That it could survive at all is itself a small miracle. Do you want to hear some crazy statistics? Every year, roughly 850,000 new businesses are established in the United States. Of them, 80 percent will make it to their first anniversary. Most of those will be non-employer businesses, meaning it's just one person, in the proverbial garage, trying to make their dream come true.

The numbers are even crazier when we drill down a little more and look at a single business category such as mobile apps. Across the five biggest app stores, there are now well over 5 million apps available for download. In 2018, those apps produced nearly 200 billion individual downloads and $365 billion in revenue. In 2019, while I was writing this book, more than 1,000 new apps were added *every single day* just to the iOS app store.

That's the good news. Mobile apps have become part of a flourishing marketplace with massive potential that remains to be tapped in places like China, India, and Brazil, among several other countries. And on the general business front, there is an appetite for new things. There are places continually opening up at the table for those who have the courage to present their ideas to the world. There is, in so many words, more than ample opportunity.

Now the not-so-good news. Nearly 800,000 existing businesses close their doors every year. And while 80 percent of new businesses make it through one year, by year five or six survival is a fifty-fifty proposition. A coin flip. And the app market? Well, it is subject to a power law so steep it makes the streets of San Francisco, where many of the biggest apps have been developed, seem like gentle inclines. The top five apps, for example, account for 85 percent of all in-app time spent by users on their mobile devices. Which means that all the other 5 million–plus apps are competing for some portion of the remaining 15 percent of users' in-app time. Not great.

What I have learned, though, is that the difference between the apps at the top of the power curve and those near the bottom — or the businesses that make it past the five-year mark versus those that can only get to one year — rarely has much to do with the quality of the idea, or the passion of the entrepreneur, or even the size of the market.

More often than not, the success of a new business depends on its ability to get attention — specifically, *its ability to build buzz and to engineer word of mouth.* While these two concepts are often used interchangeably, I actually think they are distinct phenomena that should be treated differently if a founder wants to be effective in attracting attention and growing their business.

The first step is building buzz, which is somewhat self-explanatory.* It's about getting a nontrivial number of people talking about your product out in the culture. It's about creating a general awareness that your company exists and that there's something cool or interesting or new (or all of the above) about what you're doing.

But just because building buzz is self-explanatory doesn't mean it's easy or simple. A lot of companies are bad at it, in fact, because their industries are, by their nature, not particularly exciting. This was one of the big obstacles that the Method guys had to overcome in order to break through. I mean, how do you get people excited about soap? By Eric Ryan's own admission, the reason he hid all his research under his bed was because they were going into a category that was "so low interest and so boring" and that he himself thought was dorky. Dullness aside, the beauty of buzz — and the reason I think of it as the first phase of getting attention — is that you can often start to build buzz before you've even launched your business, long before the world has a chance to make up its mind about you or your product.

One industry that is great at building buzz that way is Hollywood. When a studio wants to get behind a film, there are few operations better in attracting the public's attention. In 2009, for example, one of the most talked-about films of the spring was the R-rated buddy road trip comedy *The Hangover.* For months leading up to the film's release, Warner Bros. blanketed American cities with billboards and bus stop signage featuring hilarious pictures of the main characters — most famously, Ed Helms's character, disheveled and confused, sporting a missing front tooth, and Zach Galifianakis's character, in sunglasses, carrying an infant in a BabyBjörn. After that, the trailers started to come out, each with an increasing amount of unbelievable craziness, culminating in a scene inside a destroyed Las Vegas hotel room featuring Mike Tyson and a pet tiger.

By the time the film debuted on June 2, everyone was talking about *The Hangover,* and a great many of them put their money where their mouth was that first weekend. *The Hangover* was the

---

* The second step, engineering word of mouth, is the topic of the next chapter.

number one film at the box office the first and second weekends after its release. It amassed more than $70 million in ticket sales the first week alone, and it went on to a virtually unheard-of (for comedies) six-month run in theaters. All of it built on buzz created by the studio through a tsunami of major paid advertising that only increased as it became clear the movie was set to perform well.

Obviously, most startups don't have access to the kind of money the Warner Bros. marketing department was able to spread around for *The Hangover* in 2009, but the principles involved in building buzz are still the same. It's only the *tactics* that need to shift. Barely a year later, in fact, the founders of Instagram, Kevin Systrom and Mike Krieger, figured out a way to get people talking about their photo-sharing app prior to its launch — not through public billboards but through private invitations.

"One of the things we had was 100 invites for people to try Instagram out before we launched through the Apple Store," Mike Krieger explained to me. "And we had this intuition that if you're going to throw a party, which is kind of what an app launch really is, you want people to sort of know how they should act and who else is there, so we had to figure out how are we going to use these hundred people?" Essentially, they had to determine who would be best suited to telling the world about their new photo-sharing app.

They decided to spread the invitations out among two groups: journalists and designers. Journalists are a no-brainer, right? They're writers with platforms that reach thousands and sometimes millions of people. But designers? Wouldn't photographers make more sense? Not really, according to Mike. "We figured photographers might not instantly take to Instagram because they want super high resolution when they have other constraints," he said, "and designers love photography, but it's not their main job." Basically, professional photographers are kind of snobby about photos, and Instagram, which was developed to democratize the ability to take cool photos, allowed designers to pretend to be photographers.

Kevin and Mike tapped into their network of Bay Area–based journalists whom they'd gotten to know over the previous couple years while trying to launch their first idea, a check-in app called

Burbn. Then, to find designers, they went to a site called Dribbble. "It's a place where designers go and show off their best work," Mike said. "So we picked the ten top designers and we emailed them. Some ignored us, which is fine, but some wrote back and said, 'Sure I will try your app.'"

It turned out to be an ideal combination for spreading the word about Instagram. On the one hand, Kevin and Mike could leverage the audiences of writers who held some degree of authority on the subject of technology. And on the other hand, they had a group of highly qualified users who were, in their own way, talking about the app to the world through their images.

"It was great because coming into the app on day one, we had a page that showed the most popular photos across the community," Mike said of the earliest users' experience seeing the designers' photos, "and they were like, 'Wow, you could take that on the phone?'"

The response from the market was immediate. "The first twenty-four hours we had 25,000 people signed up around the world," Kevin said. Shortly thereafter they took $8 million in financing on a roughly $30 million valuation. Within a year, they had 10 million registered users, and investors were showing up at their offices unsolicited to help them grow even further.

In effect, what Kevin and Mike were able to do by recruiting designers and journalists was to play a game of show-and-tell. The designers showed people that there was something really amazing they could do with just the phone in their pocket, and the journalists told prospective users exactly what that something was. It was the perfect combination of demonstration and explanation, which I think is the recipe for building the kind of buzz you need in order to stand out — regardless of whether you have an app or a consumer packaged goods business or a clothing line or a brick-and-mortar retail store. In short, you need to show people what you've got, and you need to tell them what it is.

Depending on your relationships and your resources, you may have greater access to one group than to the other — demonstrators or explainers, showers or tellers — and even then your access might be limited. But fortunately it doesn't always take a massive groundswell to get the buzz going. Sometimes it's just a matter of being in the right place or finding that one right person.

For Randy Hetrick, the former Navy SEAL and the creator of the TRX Suspension Training system, that place was the IDEA World Convention in San Diego, and the person was future NFL Hall of Fame quarterback Drew Brees.

The IDEA World Convention brings together more than 10,000 health and fitness professionals from around the world every year. In 2006, armed with dozens of Cordura nylon training straps that he'd developed while deployed overseas as a Navy SEAL and then incubated into a startup during his years at Stanford business school, Randy set up a ten-by-ten-foot booth on the convention floor, rigged and anchored a fake door over which he hung his TRX Suspension Training straps, and for the next three days proceeded to do demonstrations and give instruction to every personal trainer and gym owner who stopped by the booth.

"It was a big moment," Randy explained, "because these trainers are a skeptical lot, and if they think this is really a great thing, then all right, now I'm cooking with some gas." If they don't like it, however, if they think it's dumb or dangerous or ineffective, then that gas Randy would like to be cooking with might turn into a bomb that could very well blow up everything he'd been trying to build since he first came up with the idea for TRX.

This is the tricky part about buzz. There's the good kind and the bad kind. The kind that can build you up or the kind that can burn you down. That's why demonstration *and* explanation are so important, particularly in a case like Randy's. Imagine if he tried to explain the TRX system to someone using only words. The system consists of two heavy-duty adjustable nylon straps with handles on the end that you can hang over a door frame or a bar and use to do all sorts of bodyweight exercises — pull-ups, push-ups, dips, rows, planks. If you're lucky enough to have one of those rare minds that can visualize what Randy is describing, it might all sound too good to be true.

But if you can look at the straps, and you can see someone like Randy *demonstrating* them while he explains how they work, it's a different story. Or at least it was for the legion of fitness profession-als who caught wind of this new training system on the floor of the IDEA World Convention in 2006.

By the end of the first day, Randy sold out his entire stock of TRX straps. That night he called his office to have his assistant ship every-thing they had left in their shop up in the Bay Area down to his hotel in San Diego. By the second day of the show, the interest in TRX had only grown, and Randy was giving out IOUs to trainers who'd heard the buzz floating around the convention floor, had come to see the straps in action, and didn't want to wait to lock up their own set. "I was basically selling paper futures," Randy recalled. "Thank good-ness the product arrived on the third day and the people could come and exchange their paper for straps."

Not long after, likely due to the buzz generated at the conven-tion and to the exposure he received from some of the elite personal trainers there, TRX started to find its way into the hands of some athletes. Foremost among them was Drew Brees, who was coming off a rotator cuff injury to his throwing arm that threatened to end his career. The injury *did* end his time with his first pro team, the San Diego Chargers, when they tried to lowball him in free agency.

"He was doing rehab, and he fell in love with the Suspension Trainer," Randy said. Then, in the spring of 2006, Brees signed with the New Orleans Saints and reached out to Randy. "He said, 'Hey, Randy, give me a half dozen of these, and I'll take them with me. I'll see if I can get the Saints to start training on them.'"

It was an amazing gesture, but the real opportunity for Randy and TRX came when *Sports Illustrated* decided to do a feature story on Brees's comeback. "Drew made sure that the picture they featured was him training on the Suspension Trainer," Randy said. "And all of a sudden, all the strength and conditioning coaches and the ath-letes who read *Sports Illustrated* got their eyes on this crazy strap and thought, 'Well, maybe we ought to have a couple of those.'"

By 2007, the buzz around TRX had spread from Navy SEAL team rooms at forward operating bases around the globe, to classrooms at Stanford business school, to the convention floor of one of the larg-est fitness expos in the world, to the pages of the most important sports publication in the United States. At that point, Randy's main concern was no longer getting attention but meeting demand.

And that is the goal, right? It is not just to get attention for its own sake. The purpose of building buzz is to convert it into product demand, to generate sales. The media, both mainstream and social, are a big part of that conversion process. Randy Hetrick and the Instagram guys certainly relied on media outlets to spread the word about their products, as have many of the entrepreneurs we've met so far. Lisa Price got a shout-out on Oprah Winfrey's talk show. Daymond John and his partners went on *Video Music Box* with Ralph McDaniels. The Airbnb guys went on CNN during the 2008 Democratic National Convention.

Even Gary Erickson used traditional media to build buzz for his Clif Bar back in the early nineties, albeit in a characteristically untraditional manner that almost backfired. He took out ads in cycling magazines calling out the only other real player in the market, PowerBar. "The headline was 'It's Your Body, You Decide,'" he said. The ads asked the reader whether they wanted refined ingredients or whole ingredients in their energy bars. It even included pictures of both sets of ingredients. "That caused us to be sued immediately," Gary said, "but it created this buzz in the bicycle industry where people said, 'Hey, have you heard of Clif bar?'"

If there's one entrepreneur I've spoken with who really understands how to leverage all forms of media to build buzz, drive demand, and generate sales, it's Jen Rubio. Before founding Away, she was the first social media manager for the online eyewear retailer Warby Parker and would eventually run all of their social media by the time she left. Early on, back in 2011, she did things as simple as reply to every message, positive or negative, on the company's Twitter, Facebook, Tumblr, and Instagram feeds (which had just launched when she arrived at Warby Parker), in an effort to create a sense of constant conversation and a growing, vibrant community. When customers posted pictures of themselves in each of the five eyeglass frames they ordered as part of Warby Parker's home try-on program, she'd repost them on Warby's official Tumblr and Facebook pages and encourage the community to vote on their favorite. "We'd basically crowdsource what frames people should buy," she recalled, "and we built a really loyal, really engaged community that just kept growing and growing."

Jen had found a way to convert social media buzz into online buying decisions. She had also seen firsthand what can happen when you get attention from traditional media. A few months before she joined the company — in fact, before Warby Parker even existed as a company — the founders hired a PR firm to get them some prelaunch press. They targeted *Vogue* and *GQ*. "We really wanted to be in these premier magazines as a stamp of approval," Warby Parker co-founder Dave Gilboa said, "but we were really pitching them as exclusive launch partners." Their pitch worked. Before they even had their e-commerce site live, *GQ* ran a piece, that called Warby Parker the Netflix of glasses. The result was tens of thousands of units sold. "Within a four-week period, we sold out of our best-selling styles and we had a wait list of 20,000 customers," Dave said.

But what Jen Rubio took from that experience, and what she applied to the launch of her own business a few years later, was an understanding that "nobody cares what a brand has to say about itself." With the initial round of friends-and-family money Jen and her partner, Steph Korey, raised, they could have poured whatever they didn't put into prototype manufacturing into advertising and marketing. But instead, they took a page from the Warby playbook and hired a PR firm.

"We knew one of the big things that would set us apart was if we got these other outlets that people trusted, whether it was press or influencers, to tell our story for us," Jen explained. This was the strategy that guided their prelaunch attempts to get into the holiday gift-buying guides of big magazines like *GQ* and *Vogue*. When that didn't work because they got started too late — the magazines had already made their picks, and their suitcases wouldn't be ready until February of the following year anyway — it inspired Jen and Steph to create a small, glossy, four-color coffee-table book about the world of travel that featured exotic travel stories about and photos of forty tastemakers. They would print only 2,000 copies of the book, the number of suitcases in Away's first production run, and price it at

$225, the retail price of Away's first suitcase. Each book was essentially a coupon redeemable for one free Away suitcase.

"When the books got delivered in these huge boxes," Jen recalled, "Steph and I looked at each other and we were like, 'This is either a great idea or we're going to have these books in this office for eternity.'"

The idea to publish an expensive travel book as a way to get attention for a company that sells suitcases was certainly a gamble, but it was one built on a smart strategy for building buzz. "With the tastemakers in the book or with the editors that we reached out to through the PR agency or the social media influencers that I would send messages to asking them to post about us," Jen said, "all of our efforts in the beginning were trying to get *other* people to simply talk about us — so that we didn't have to talk about ourselves as much."

The gamble worked. On November 9, 2015, Jen and Steph woke up to a feature on *Vogue*'s website about a new travel brand called Away. By the end of the day, multiple outlets had picked up the *Vogue* story, and Jen and Steph had sold hundreds of their $225 travel books. Within a couple weeks, they'd sold out the entire 2,000-book print run, which meant they'd sold out their very first production run of suitcases. That's nearly half a million dollars in revenue generated from a coordinated buzz involving traditional media, social media, tastemakers, and the founders' personal networks.

It's funny, when Randy Hetrick told me the story of Drew Brees getting his TRX straps into *Sports Illustrated,* I could feel a visceral sense of relief wash over him, even years later. It gave me an even deeper appreciation for how hard it can be for someone with a new idea to find a seat at the table. It was a feeling he articulated in his next words: "You know, for somebody who's starting a venture, and particularly if you've got a product for which there isn't precedent, the big challenge is obscurity — trying to get out of obscurity and get up on the radar."

It got me thinking about that old philosophical thought experiment: If a tree falls in the forest and there's no one to hear it, does it make a sound?

I think there is a business analog to that: If a company opens its doors and no one hears about it, does it ever really exist? Or is it just one of the 170,000 new businesses that year that didn't make it to its first birthday and whose existence you can only infer from a table of numbers in a Bureau of Labor Statistics report?

The answer, I believe, is *Of course it existed!* If you took that leap off the cliff while attempting to build your own airplane on the way down, you deserve to be known. But as the builder of that plane, it's also your job to be the creator of the buzz from that plane's engines.

It's your job to make sure that the sound of your doors opening reaches past your front steps and far enough out into the world for potential customers to hear it. It's your job to get attention for the product or the service you are bringing to market.

It's usually not easy, and you are going to need help from all forms of media to make it happen, because like Jen Rubio said, nobody wants to hear you talk about yourself. But it's doable, particularly when you are able to build buzz among many *possible* customers while at the same time engineering word of mouth among your *ideal* customers.

13

Get Attention, Part 2:
Engineering Word of Mouth

I n 2012, amidst an explosion of social networking platforms, smartphones, and big data, the statistician Nate Silver published a book titled *The Signal and the Noise,* about the difficulty of developing accurate predictions. Up until that point, "signal-to-noise ratio" was a term used primarily by scientists and engineers to describe the power of a desired bit of information in relationship to its surroundings. After the success of Silver's book, however, the phrase morphed into convenient shorthand for nonscientists to talk about problems of communication and value and relevance. In other words, with all the information coming at us today, what should we listen to? What is worth remembering? What is actually important or reliable?

Out of all this noise, where (and what) is the signal?

This is a problem that nearly every founder has to solve. How do you cut through the endless clutter of everyday life? How do you stand out from the competition? How do you get consumers to pay attention to you and your product? How do you break out from the noise and *become* the signal?

As we saw in chapter 12, building buzz is a big, important step in that direction — in fine-tuning your frequency and amplifying the sound — but it's not the only step. There is another, arguably bigger one to be taken. I'm talking about creating *word of mouth*.

Building buzz is about leveraging specific relationships (taste-makers, media contacts) and resources (OPM, expertise) to get your name out there in front of as many people as possible. It's about bill-boards, blog posts, podcast interviews, and celebrity shout-outs. It's creating what the investor and best-selling author Tim Ferriss calls a "surround sound effect." It's the sense that you are everywhere, when in reality you're just getting your name out in the handful of places where your core customers spend their time. "I would cre-ate the perception, and to some extent, the reality that I was ubiq-uitous, inescapable," Tim told an audience during a Q&A session at the headquarters of a product design firm called ZURB in 2011. "Tim Ferriss is everywhere. No, actually he's just on TechCrunch, Giz-modo, and Mashable, but that's okay."

Engineering word of mouth is about converting all that wonder-ful name recognition you've just achieved from the buzz into sales. It's about getting your product into people's hands so they can then put its name in the ears of all their friends. This is how we fueled the growth of the *How I Built This* podcast and how we *continued* to grow to reach nearly 3 million people each week. Our listeners tell their friends. And by the way ... we encourage them to do so! Because word of mouth is not a billboard or an article or an interview. It's a dialogue. A conversation. It's a text message from one friend to an-other telling them, "You've gotta try this."

"There's a hidden power to that simple phrase ... It's like 'open sesame,'" Reid Hoffman said on an episode of his podcast, *Masters of Scale,* titled "Why Customer Love Is All You Need." "All the money and all of the marketing savvy in the world cannot sustain a success-ful product's growth in the long run. You need more than customers' attention. You need their unflagging devotion."

Indeed, the difference between buzz and word of mouth is the difference between taking a big step toward brand awareness and then making a quantum leap toward customer acquisition and long-term fandom.

Remember the example of *The Hangover* in chapter 12? It rode almost entirely on early buzz to $45 million at the box office during its first weekend. But it was the wave of enthusiastic personal endorsements starting with that first weekend of moviegoers that propelled the film to its ultimate success. Friends told friends, who told more friends. They went to the theaters in groups, often multiple times. *The Hangover* finished its first week at $70 million, landed at number one for a second weekend in a row, and then went on to complete its unheard-of (for modern comedies) six-month theatrical run that netted more than $275 million at the box office in the United States alone.

Two years before *The Hangover* came out, during the announcement of a new Facebook user-centered advertising program, Mark Zuckerberg told an assembled group of tech journalists and advertisers that "nothing influences people more than a recommendation from a trusted friend."

The Hangover franchise would prove Zuckerberg correct over the next several years. It developed such a loyal fan base that today the first two films in the series are two of the top ten highest-grossing R-rated films of all time, with more than $1 billion in ticket sales between them worldwide.

"A trusted referral is the Holy Grail," Zuckerberg said in describing what is, effectively, the true currency of word-of-mouth marketing.

One need only talk to a founder whose business has benefited from the spread of that currency, someone who has sipped from the Holy Grail, to understand the value and power of word of mouth. Someone like Jerry Murrell, who, in 1986, decided to open a burger joint in Arlington, Virginia, with his wife and four boys that they called Five Guys.

Today, Five Guys is one of the most popular and beloved fast-casual chains in the country with more than 1,500 stores worldwide. But the first thing to know about Five Guys is that it absolutely should not have worked. The 1980s was a golden age of expansion for fast food. At the same time, 1986 was the slowest economic year in the United States since the recession four years earlier. And Jerry, well, he was already a serial failed entrepreneur, having joined the ranks of that unfortunate 20 percent whose big ideas don't last much more than a year.

"I tried a few businesses," he said of his early ventures in the mid-1970s and early 1980s. "I was a financial planner. I started a company in the oil business in Texas. I tried to start a water business, of all things. My wife and I went into the real estate business. We were experts at buying real high. I really didn't know what I was doing."

So obviously the natural next step was to open a hamburger shop just down the road from the Pentagon and Arlington National Cemetery, "where nobody can see it," as Jerry described the place. I'm being facetious, but that's actually how he and his wife, Janie, saw things at the time. This little, out-of-the-way, hole-in-the-wall burger stand . . . *it was a good idea!*

"Something was telling us it was the right thing to do," he said, "and for some reason we all seemed to be on board with it." So they took $35,000 from their children's college fund, fixed up some old equipment, found a place with really low rent, and put the rest of the money into opening its doors. Their thinking was, "If we can put the store where it's hard to find, but we can get people coming there, then we know we've got something."

It sounds crazy. The first thing the owner of a new store should do is to find a storefront with the highest visibility possible, the most foot traffic. That's Retail 101. It's fundamental. Like building buzz but with brick-and-mortar.

In retrospect, however, this was a shrewd, if also lucky, choice. Had they been on a more highly trafficked main road, not only would Jerry and Janie have been competing with the massive fast-food chains that dominated that kind of real estate, but they'd also never really have known whether diners in those critical early days had stumbled upon Five Guys by accident or actively sought it out based on early buzz and word of mouth. By making Five Guys harder to find, Jerry had actually set up the conditions to more accurately determine whether or not the word was spreading, and if so, how fast.

He did not have to wait long. "When we first opened up, at eleven o'clock, there was no business at all until quarter to twelve. Then one person finally walked in. And by 12:30, we were almost packed," he said.

The next day it was more of the same. And the day after, and the day after. Right away it was clear to Jerry what was happening: people were leaving Five Guys, going home or back to work, and telling their friends and family about this new place down the road, a little off the beaten path, that they absolutely had to try if they liked great burgers and fries. "That's the only way they would have found out about it," he said, reflecting on those first fragile weeks when they had no money for advertising and marketing, only for product and payroll.

Luckily, Five Guys made money from its very first day. They were even paying their sons a good starting wage (for 1986) to work after school and on weekends alongside a couple early hires. Before long, Jerry was lining up investors to open a second store—a scenario that was at least as unlikely and as unexpected as their early success. When Jerry and Janie went to banks for a loan to open the first store, every banker they met with thought they were out of their minds. When they went back to those same banks and told them they wanted to open a *second* store, there was even less support.

"They laughed at us," Jerry said.

But that didn't matter, because they already had a lot of people who, as Jerry put it, "just wanted to throw money at us," including the parents of a number of his sons' friends. They had heard from their kids how well Five Guys was doing, and they wanted to get behind it. Word of mouth hadn't just spread about the burgers; it had begun to spread about the business as well.

"Eventually, we got about 150 or 200 people who were willing to give us money," Jerry said. All told, they raised $150,000 from those investors to open the second Five Guys location in a similarly small space—this one in a run-down strip mall in Alexandria, Virginia— and from there it was off to the races.

Jerry's story is not unlike that of Carley Roney and David Liu, who ten years later, in 1996, co-founded The Knot with two of their friends from NYU film school. Originally funded by AOL as a portal to provide wedding content for its members, The Knot broke away from AOL in July 1997, when Carley and David launched Theknot .com on its own, as a full-service wedding planning destination. By then, they already had a quarter million monthly visitors to their little corner of the AOL universe, and they were adding 300 members every day. All within a year.

"Once you found us, you wanted to tell anyone you knew who was getting married about us," Carley said. "People were very loyal and excited about the brand, and so we were growing in that way like wildfire."

By "in that way," she meant by word of mouth. "Word of mouth was the only way we were marketing," Carley said. Her co-founder and now husband, David, put an even finer point on it: "We didn't spend any money on advertising."

It turns out they didn't need to. The following year, 1998, The Knot clocked $1 million in revenue. The year after that, QVC put in $15 million to help the site expand its suite of products. Within three years, the growth trajectory of The Knot was unmistakably up and to the right, largely propelled by word of mouth.

Ten years after The Knot hit its stride, Alli Webb experienced the same kind of growth with her blowout business (which would become Drybar) before she even had a bar to do the drying in. She started it in 2008 as an in-home service called Straight-at-Home by posting on a Yahoo! "mommy" group called Peachhead, which acted as an online resource for about 5,000 moms in the Los Angeles area. "I said, 'I'm a longtime stylist. I'm thinking about starting a mobile blow-dry business where I'd charge thirty-five or forty dollars. Would anybody out there be interested?'" Alli told me.

Moms were more than interested. "I was flooded with emails," Alli said. Those emails quickly turned into bookings, which then turned into trusted referrals that extended outside the Peachhead mommy community. "I got really busy really fast, and it was very word-of-mouth," she said. "I'd go and do one mom, and then she would tell like six of her friends. And all of a sudden, they would call me. I got to the point where I was saying no more than I was saying yes." With a single forum post, Alli Webb hung out a shingle, built her own buzz, and set in motion a word-of-mouth marketing machine that would culminate in the opening of the first four Drybar locations less than two years later, in 2010, and eclipse $20 million in annual revenue across twenty-five locations two years after that.

That's three sets of amazing founders in three wildly different industries across three different decades, each of them managing to drive sales and spur growth with no gimmicks and no huge ad spends —just the word of people who used their product and loved it. Amazing! That's the dream, right? You make something, you give it to someone, they love it and tell all their friends, who tell their friends, and before you know it, you have 1,500 locations like Jerry and Janie Murrell, or 250,000 monthly users like Carley Roney and David Liu, or $20 million in revenue like Alli Webb.

Okay, but how does one do this?

I expect that's the question you're asking right now, having just heard these stories. It's the same question I had when we first launched *How I Built This* in the fall of 2016. I understood that starting a podcast with NPR would generate a certain amount of buzz that would lift the show from the start. I knew that the news would travel — *Hey, did you hear Guy Raz is starting some kind of business podcast about entrepreneurship?* — and that a decent number of NPR listeners and fans of *TED Radio Hour* would check out at least the first episode or two.

But I also knew that we would hit a ceiling eventually if we depended only on the buzz that we built prior to launch. I'd seen it with *TED Radio Hour* back in early 2013. People loved TED Talks. People were starting to really love podcasts. Put those two things together, and you had a recipe for a very respectable listenership right out of the gate. Except the download numbers for *TED Radio Hour,* as respectable as they were, stayed somewhat flat for a while. It wasn't until a few weeks into the show, when people began telling their friends about the podcast and recommending that they listen, that the download numbers started shifting up and across the y- and x-axes of the growth chart. We needed to replicate that word-of-mouth spread for *How I Built This* if it was going to achieve the potential we all believed it had.

So back to the big question: How? We know that word of mouth is important, but how do we create it? How do we engineer it so more people buy our burgers, visit our website, come to our salon, or, in my case, download our new podcast?

I wish I could tell you that there is some kind of formula for creating word of mouth, or that there is an easy growth hack to accelerating its spread. But what I have found in my own experience and from listening to the experiences of entrepreneurs across the spectrum is that there is only one reliable way to engineer word of mouth: *you have to make a really good product.*

Actually, that's not precisely true. It can't just be really good. It has to be *so good* that someone *has to* recommend it. And because nobody is going to recommend something ordinary, it has to be new and special and leave people with something they can easily share with their friends by way of their recommendation.

That's what I think about when my team and I are putting together every episode of *How I Built This*. What about this founder's story is unique? Where are those "wow" moments I talked about earlier that will make this episode truly special and shareable — and a reliable record of a journey that will ultimately end up on the person's Wikipedia page?* I approach our work on the podcast in this manner not just because I want our listeners to love it, but also because I don't want to waste their time.

Think about it: There are sixteen waking hours in every day. Of those sixteen hours, you will spend eight at work or at school, one to two getting ready and commuting back and forth, another one to two eating and drinking, and another one to two running errands or doing household chores. Assuming you don't have children, that leaves two to four hours of discretionary time, which I know feels very generous when we think about our daily lives but is still not a lot. So every Monday morning when we release a new episode of *How I Built This* into the world, what I am essentially asking listeners for is forty-five to sixty minutes, or nearly 25 percent of their precious daily free time. That's a huge responsibility! One that, if I shirk it, means I am also squandering an opportunity to make a new fan who might be

---

* This happens more often than you might think.

inclined to tell their partner or their co-worker or their best friend about the story they just heard on this podcast they just discovered.

Consciously or not, this is a calculation that every successful founder has made in designing and building their business. They figured out a way to do something new, something special, something *great*. Something that got people talking. And then spreading the word.

Carley Roney and David Liu built, in their words, "the world's coolest wedding magazine mixed with an online community." Then, when they realized that "the thing brides seemed to be really vexed about was the whole registry process," they added an online gift registry, which, like e-commerce itself, was completely new in 1997. They alleviated a huge stressor for brides-to-be and gave them a forum to share information with others working their way through the "wedding industrial complex."

In contrast, there was nothing new about the service Alli Webb was trying to provide with Drybar. She'd been going to her friends' houses for years to style their hair for parties, weddings, and other important events. But what made her idea special was that it solved a very specific problem that every one of her friends seemed to have: when Alli wasn't around and they needed a blowout, they either had to go to their expensive cut-and-color salon, where they'd get pressured into things they didn't need, or trudge down to a discount chain that would inevitably do a mediocre job.

"There really are two bad choices out there, and that's it," Alli thought at the time. There was no middle path: salon-quality styling at a reasonable price. That was what made Drybar great, what made it special and new. Making a woman look amazing without draining her checking account was all Alli had to do to get a huge portion of her first clients to tell all their friends about her service.

On the surface, there was nothing new about burgers and fries either. In fact, their ubiquity in the American diet was only increasing in 1986 when Jerry and Janie Murrell started Five Guys. The year before, McDonald's had opened a record 597 new stores, bringing their total store count to nearly *9,000*. Wendy's had booked record annual revenue on the heels of its famous "Where's the Beef?" campaign, and Carl's Jr. had finally begun franchising stores. Fast food was on the way up. So what did Jerry do? He went the other way. He slowed things down. He opened a place where the burgers were three or four times as expensive and took that much longer to prepare.

"We used to have a sign in one of our stores that said 'If you're in a hurry, there are a lot of really good burger places near here,'" Jerry recalled. Everyone told him he was crazy for putting that sign up, "but it helped," he said. It helped because it was an open proclamation to customers that Five Guys was doing something different than the other guys, something unique.

What Jerry and Janie were doing was using the absolute best ingredients they could find to make the tastiest burgers and fries possible. Not the cheapest, not the fastest, not the most complex. Just the best. And even more special, they let their kids decide what that actually meant.

"The thinking was that they're going to pick the best product if they got to pick what they liked," Jerry said. So they bought the most expensive pickles. They bought buns from the best little bakery in Arlington at the time. They sourced the mayonnaise from a supplier in New York who was impossible to deal with and whom their first purchasing agent begged them to abandon. But they stuck with that supplier because his mayonnaise stuck to the bun and the other ingredients better than the alternatives. They used peanut oil for their french fries, which was the most expensive of all the cooking oil options, but it also produced the tastiest fries.

And the potatoes they used for those french fries? Well, they sourced those from a little farm in Rigby, Idaho, because that's where Thrasher's in Ocean City, Maryland, got their potatoes for their fries. Thrasher's was a little boardwalk french fry stand that Jerry and his kids discovered when they first moved to the Washington, DC, area. "There must have been twenty places selling boardwalk fries," Jerry said, "but only one place had a long line, and that was Thrasher's. So [I realized] their potatoes must be good."

Jerry and Janie's commitment to using the best ingredients produced the tastiest burgers and fries, which produced immediate fans in the people who had not experienced anything in the DC area like what Five Guys was offering. Yes, burgers and fries weren't new, but this level of quality sure was. That's what made them special, remarkable, and ultimately recommendable to anyone who loved a good burger. Just as Alli's blowouts were to any woman who loved to look great and not break the bank. Just as Carley and David's online bridal registry and wedding planning community was to anyone who was getting married and unsure of where else to turn.

Walt Disney is often quoted as saying, "Whatever you do, do it well. Do it so well that when people see you do it, they will want to come back and see you do it again, and they will want to bring others and show them how well you do what you do." That, to me, is the unifying characteristic of every founder I've met who counts positive word of mouth among the principal reasons for their success. Each of them made something really great, really special. They were so good that they became the signal that broke out from the noise of their competition and reached farther than they could have ever imagined.

14

Survive the Crucible

There will come a day well into the entrepreneurial process when you'll think about quitting. This is normal and something almost everyone I've interviewed thought about at some point — even if only fleetingly.

You won't want to quit, you will have made many amazing strides, but you will look out at the landscape, at the path laid out immediately before you, and it will seem obvious that the easiest thing to do is to quit. Some people will even tell you that quitting is the *smartest* thing to do, that it is what any right-thinking person would do. Of course, what those people are forgetting is that almost no one starts their own business if they're in their right mind, so really what good is this advice anyway?

In fact, the advice does have some utility — not as advice, mind you, but as a signal that you have officially entered the crucible of your journey. You've got the plane built and the engine fired up, but you're struggling to gain altitude, and you're not sure why. It is here that you will have a choice to make: Turn back or push forward. Eject or find more power. It has the feel of a do-or-die moment.

The poet Robert Frost would say to push forward. You've probably seen his famous quote that decorates countless inspirational mugs, posters, and accounts of Instagram influencers: "The best way out is always through." Frost wrote this line in his 1915 poem "A Servant to Servants," about a woman who runs a boardinghouse on a lake with her husband, and who has grown tired "from doing things over and over that just won't stay done." She's begun to indulge fantasies of escaping into nature—she wants to "drop everything and live out on the ground"—but her husband, Len, "looks on the bright side of everything" and says "one steady pull more ought to do it . . . the best way out is always through." A sentiment she ultimately agrees with, if only because she, too, "can see no way out but through."

You may not be there yet, but as I've learned from the founders I've interviewed, one day this sentiment will resonate deeply with you. I imagine every successful founder, at one point or another, has related to both characters in Frost's poem. When they couldn't seem to make any headway—when the work wouldn't stay done—they may have wanted to throw it all away and go live in a shack in the woods. But when they looked at all they'd built, how far they'd come, and all the people who counted on them, they decided to recommit to "one steady pull more," because that was going to be the pull that would finally get them out and through.

This is where Gary Hirshberg was for much of the 1980s as he and his partner, Samuel Kaymen, struggled to get their company, Stonyfield Farm, out of the red and into the black. From the very beginning, Stonyfield was the crème de la crème of yogurt, quite literally. It was the number one plain, cream-on-top, whole milk yogurt in every market that stocked it pretty much from the day Gary and Sam started getting retail placement. Yet no matter what they did, they couldn't seem to turn a profit.

At first this was because they had only one product—six-packs of plain, whole milk quarts—which they sold more or less at cost in order to get their foot in the door at Harwood's Market, the local grocery store in Wilton, New Hampshire. This brought in revenue right away, but never enough to get ahead. "The product was selling through," Gary said, "but any money that came in we used to pay for grain to feed the cows or to buy lubrication, equipment, fuel, wood, whatever." Typical startup costs for a yogurt business, I guess you'd call them.

Five months in, the duo had done $50,000 in sales but were $75,000 in debt. They'd run out of cash and couldn't keep up with the demand for their product, which continued to grow. "The Harwood's people called and said, 'Gosh, you know this is good, it's selling,'" Gary remembered, "so I did what any self-respecting entrepreneur does: I called my mother, and I borrowed $30,000."

And he would continue borrowing money, from his mother and his wife's mother and literally hundreds of others, numerous times, for various reasons, to the tune of more than $2 million by the time it was all said and done.

Their second year in business, 1984, Gary and Sam found a way to crack into other grocery chains and natural food co-ops in New England, and they were producing 360 cases of yogurt a week and doing $250,000 in sales. But by summer they were nearly broke again. Gary's solution was to raise $500,000 to expand their plant so they could move beyond plain quarts into small, individual serving cups and flavored yogurts. Having enough money to simply pay their bills wasn't going to get Gary and Sam out of this hole they continually found themselves in. They had to *grow* their way out of it. (Very Frostian, right?) So that Thanksgiving, Gary started his fundraising by borrowing $50,000 from his future mother-in-law, Doris, whom Meg, his future wife, had just introduced him to for the first time that weekend!

The following year, Stonyfield sales increased again, to $500,000, and to meet demand they started sourcing milk from outside dairies (a decision that, paradoxically, involved selling their own cows). But their operation was still week-to-week. "I always had payroll on Thursday mornings, and by this point it was about a $5,500 payroll," Gary said, "and I never had cash in the bank the night before." So on numerous occasions, he would sneak out of bed in the middle of the night, walk down the hall to his office, and call his mother-in-law to see if he might be able to borrow another couple thousand dollars to make ends meet for the week. It got so bad, and became such a regular occurrence, that eventually Meg caught on to what was happening and stepped in. "One night I heard the *click-click* of call waiting on my mother in law's phone," Gary recounted, "and Meg was calling from the house phone to say 'Mom, don't do this.'"

If you're Gary Hirshberg and you're two or three years into this business, with a product that everyone loves but that you can't seem to get sufficient lift from, and your spouse basically throws up her hands and says "Stop the insanity!" how do you *not* stop? Especially when you agree with her.

"She was living a nightmare," Gary said. "She saw how crazy it was. We had chimney fires, we had the well pump go out, the power go out, we were on this hilltop farm a long way from anywhere. It was insane."

And yet, Gary would keep going, and things would only get more insane. A year later, with Stonyfield yogurt's popularity still on the rise, they were doing more than a million dollars in sales, they were buying milk from a dozen different local suppliers, and they'd reached the absolute limit of the production capacity of the farm they'd raised $500,000 to expand. So they contracted with a dairy over the border in western Massachusetts that had unfilled capacity to take over production. And for a year and a half, things went great. "We've got paved roads, regular power, and we really began to grow," Gary said. Sales increased from $1.1 million to $1.7 million. "We thought we were coming out of the woods."

Then the famous stock market crash of October 1987 happened. Black Monday. The Thursday before, the bank called Gary to tell him that the Small Business Administration was pulling their loan guarantees for the dairy in Massachusetts and asked him if he wanted to buy the dairy. Things were good, but they weren't "buy a dairy over the phone" good. Gary politely declined, and on Monday, as the bottom was falling out of the stock market, the bank put the Massachusetts dairy into receivership and slammed a padlock on the front door with an entire run of Gary's cups, lids, fruit, and yogurt inside. Then the state demanded $100,000 from Gary and Sam in outstanding co-packer fees to get it out.

Now is when you quit, right?

Not Gary. He goes back to the well. He asks his investors — which include his mother and mother-in-law — for even more money. But not just the $100,000 to get his stuff out of hock, which he needs within hours so the fruit and yogurt mix don't spoil. He also asks for an *additional* $100,000 to get the old plant at Stonyfield Farm back up and running so he and Sam can take over production.

"What could we do?" Gary asked rhetorically. "We took a look at the old yogurt works up on the hilltop farm where the roosters were now living and said, 'Son of a gun, we've got to come back here.'"

Which is exactly what they do, despite having now grown more than 100 percent beyond the capacity of the plant. "In order to keep up, we have to produce twenty-four hours a day, seven days a week," Gary said. "Every other night, Samuel or I had to make yogurt, and this continued for twenty months."

Twenty months!

It's like the crash put them in a time machine and sent them back two years. Not just because Gary and Sam were back to making yogurt with their own two hands again, but they were also starting to burn through cash like in the old days, too. "Twenty-five thousand dollars a week on top of the $200,000 that we had borrowed." By Christmas, they were $600,000 in debt. By Christmas of the following year, that number had ballooned to nearly $2 million. By Christmas of 1989, they were $2.7 million in the hole, with nearly 300 very nervous individual investors starting to ask questions. And in the middle of this tailspin — with more than a million dollars of his mother-in-law's money that "she could never afford to lose"; with Meg pregnant with their first son and at her wits' end with all the ups and downs — he and Sam spent three months negotiating with a new dairy in Vermont to take over production and to solve all their capacity problems, only to have the dairy change the deal at the very last second and basically try to steal their business out from under them. News of which Gary had to deliver to his wife upon his return home from their meeting-cum-ambush — after driving two hours at night in an early spring blizzard and making that day's batch of yogurt once they got there.

Okay, now *has* to be when you quit. What right-thinking person would continue to endure this parade of horrible events, especially with a baby on the way?

"I knew it was over," Gary said of the realization that they would have to sign this poison pill of a deal. "This was the darkest of the dark hours. We're burning $25,000 a week. We're taking money we cannot ever pay back. We have no solution."

In the startup world, there is a name for this flat, desperate, prof-itless in-between place that Gary Hirshberg had spent a decade bat-tling through and now found himself swallowed up by. It's called the "trough of sorrow" — a term coined by Paul Graham to describe the period young companies find themselves in as a result of a lack of product-market fit. This is when, as Marc Andreessen described it in his 2007 Guide to Startups series,* "the customers aren't quite get-ting value out of the product, word of mouth isn't spreading, usage isn't growing that fast, press reviews are kind of 'blah,' the sales cycle takes too long, and lots of deals never close."

This is where Airbnb found itself after the Democratic National Convention in 2008, for example. They'd signed up 800 homes in a matter of four weeks, they got a bunch of bookings, and then, as Joe Gebbia remembered, "the convention ended, and all of those numbers came crashing back down." It was demoralizing to Joe and his co-founders, Brian Chesky and Nate Blecharczyk, because they thought they'd figured everything out and were in prime position to raise money and really grow this startup. But all their numbers trending back toward zero seemed to validate the skepticism of a siz-able portion of the venture capital world that didn't get their idea. When only ten of the first twenty investors they emailed with their pitch deck responded, and when none of those respondents chose to invest, I don't think anyone would have blamed the guys if they'd de-cided then and there to pull the rip cord on this crazy home-sharing rental concept. Just as no one would have blamed Gary Hirshberg and Samuel Kaymen if they had chosen to call it a day on yogurt as

---

* The title of part 4 of this series is, not coincidentally, "The Only Thing That Matters."

they drove back to the farm through whiteout conditions on that cold April night in 1988.

Even so, neither set of founders gave up. They continued to push forward, to fight for altitude, until they found a solution to their problems. Gary and Sam happened to find theirs right there on the ride home from Vermont. "I turned to Samuel," Gary recalled, "and I said, 'Just for the fun of it, what would be the cheapest yogurt plant we could build somewhere that would actually cover our capacity?' And he said, 'You know, I was thinking the same thing.' So he flicked on the dome light in the car, pulled out his pad, and we started designing a yogurt plant."

Gary and Sam got back around 11 p.m. that night. Gary helped Sam make the day's yogurt, then Gary went home to give Meg the news. "She wakes up and says, 'So is the deal signed?' And I said, 'No, that is not going to happen . . . but we've got a much better idea!'"

Gary slept alone in his office that night, but he wasn't wrong. Building their own plant, one that could meet and adapt to their changing capacity needs, was a great idea. It was the piece of their entrepreneurial puzzle that had been missing this entire time. A piece that would take eighteen months and $597,000 (with an 85 percent loan guarantee from the New Hampshire SBA) to build.

By the end of 1989, Stonyfield Farm was operating out of its new facility in Londonderry, New Hampshire, where it is still headquartered today. That year, the company lost $1.4 million, but it was on $3.4 million in sales, with trend lines that had already started to turn around. The next year, revenue nearly doubled, and Stonyfield lost only $900,000. Then the following year, 1992, sales climbed past $10 million, and the company actually made money for the first time in its history.

Like Stonyfield, Airbnb's problem wasn't the founders' idea (there was a market for this service); it was their execution. The problem was twofold: First, many people who were listing their homes were posting crappy pictures, which made the homes look ugly, if not also a little sketchy. Second, renters were uncomfortable paying listers in cash when they arrived to check in. Handing someone a wad of cash for allowing you to stay in their home *is* a little weird. I get it. So did

Joe and Brian and Nate. They quickly added a payment system to the Airbnb website and then hit the road to teach some of their earliest power users how to take and post good photos of their homes.

The results were fairly immediate. The indicators for every relevant factor that Marc Andreessen identified as evidence of product-market fit began to turn toward the positive. They saw an increase in repeat customers and referrals; people couldn't stop talking about the company; site visits, user signups, and bookings went through the roof; they got a whole new round of press coverage; and not too much later, they started signing meaningful term sheets with big-time investors.

That's how integral product-market fit can be to the success of a young business, and how simple it can be to get to product-market fit. Just one or two things on the margins can change everything, both for the user experience and for the long-term prospects of the business itself. "When you get right down to it, you can ignore almost everything else," Andreessen said, if you just fix these things.

Stonyfield fixed one thing: they built their own yogurt plant. That was really all it took to get them through the trough of sorrow, into product-market fit, and onto a rocket ship of growth. They turned a profit in 1992, they did $44 million in sales in 1995 and $78 million in 1998, and they ended the decade by hitting $100 million in total revenue.

Airbnb made two tweaks — pictures and payments — and in a matter of only a few years, they went from three guys with a weird idea that only seemed to work when a city ran out of hotel rooms, to billionaires at the head of a tech unicorn that was threatening to disrupt the entire hospitality industry.

When I talk to founders like Gary Hirshberg and Joe Gebbia, I'm always fascinated by the decisions they made when they were in this crucible period. But what I'm most intrigued by is *how* they knew what to do. If you ask them, they'll tell you they didn't know; they were just doing whatever made sense in the moment. Of the available options in front of them, they chose the least bad ones. But I think there's more to it than that.

When I was a Nieman Fellow in 2008, trying to navigate my own crucible of career advancement in journalism (earlier that year, I had been told by a powerful executive that I didn't have the chops to be a radio host), I sat in on a leadership class at the Kennedy School of Government taught by a professor named Ronald Heifetz. At one point in the class, as he talked about how leaders can effect meaningful change in their organizations, he sketched out his now-famous ballroom metaphor of the dance floor and the balcony.

The idea is that when you're down on the dance floor, your focus tends to be on your partner and on not colliding with other dancers spinning around you, which can often leave you with the impression that the ballroom is a crowded, chaotic environment to which you must be prepared to react. But if you remove yourself, find your way up to the balcony, and look down on the dance floor, the view is completely different, often in ways you never could have expected. Sometimes the floor isn't nearly as crowded as it felt at ground level. Other times it gets crowded, but only in a particular set of circumstances. Inevitably, patterns emerge, and before long behavior that at first felt chaotic now seems predictable.

This is Heifetz's strategy for facing the challenges of leadership through crisis, through times of struggle and uncertainty, whether you play sports or command an army or run a business. To know what to do, you need to have a *true understanding* of your situation. And, as Heifetz has written, "the only way you can gain both a clearer view of reality and some perspective on the bigger picture is by distancing yourself from the fray." The trick is in taking that perspective back down to the dance floor with you and then applying it to the challenges that sent you up to the balcony in the first place.

And make no mistake, it is a trick, because your instinct when you're caught up in the struggle is to resist removing yourself from the action. You'll need to have just enough wherewithal to let someone or something take you there.

The Airbnb guys had Paul Graham at Y Combinator. He's the one who made them zoom out and recognize that their biggest pool of users was in New York City, and if they were going to solve their growth problems, the solution was likely there, not in Silicon Valley. Gary Hirshberg and Samuel Kaymen didn't have a Paul Graham, but what they did have was the entrepreneurial version of a near-death experience that took them out of their bodies and forced them to reckon with the carcass of a business that the Vermont dairy had left bloodied and dying on a conference room floor after changing the terms of the deal that was supposed to save Stonyfield. Only then was there enough distance from the daily grind, from the weekly payroll anxiety, to recognize the space that was there for them to build their own plant and to solve their own capacity problems.

When that day comes for you, when you think seriously about quitting for the first time, getting some true perspective is going to be the thing that gives you the courage to push forward.

At the end of "A Servant to Servants," Robert Frost's boardinghouse heroine finally admits, to herself and to the visitor with whom she is having this conversation, that she's not going to give it all up and run away to live in the woods. She can't. She doesn't have it in her. It's not who she is.

"Bless you, of course, you're keeping me from work," she says. "But the thing of it is, I need to *be* kept. There's work enough to do —there's always that."

This, to me, is what unifies every successful founder who has survived the crucible of growth, who has endured through the trough of sorrow and fought for product-market fit, and who has chosen not to quit but to push forward. All of them have done whatever it takes to stay alive, to make it another day, to get their product on shelves, to get customers in the door, to get vendors paid, to get investors to write checks. All in the hope that, as they stand on the balcony and survey the dance floor below, whatever they realize they have to do today, or they might have to do tomorrow, is that one steady pull more that will finally get them out and through.

15

Fund the Business, Part 3: Professional Money

Not every founder can build a unicorn. Nor should they need to. There's nothing wrong, for example, with running a small business with a few employees that you bootstrap until you retire and either hand down or sell off. Not only is it not wrong, it's actually the norm.

The vast majority of American small businesses have fewer than twenty employees (if they have any employees at all) and generate annual revenues somewhere between $300,000 and $2 million. Indeed, most of the entrepreneurs I've met over the years aimed at just this kind of success. They weren't particularly focused on all the things that come with scaling a business, such as limitless growth, total market disruption, and raising loads of professional money.

But if scale *is* your goal and bank loans and cash flow can't get you there, you will, at some point, find yourself engaging with the venture capital world. There are only so many ways to get a resource-intensive business off the ground, after all. This can be a daunting prospect for many entrepreneurs, since venture capital has a reputation as being a closed world that operates in small pockets on both coasts (Silicon Valley and Midtown Manhattan) with unwritten rules and unfamiliar terminology that feels impenetrable to anyone accustomed to speaking in plain, clear language.

There are angels and seed rounds; cap tables and exits; Series A, B, and C dilution and preferred shares; burn rate and run rate. There are VCs and PE guys; FINRA and NASD and the SEC. There's vesting, investing, and just plain vests. So many vests! It's enough to make a founder's head spin. And that's kind of the point. All these fuzzy, poorly defined terms are left deliberately vague in order to create and maintain opacity, lest you discover the one thing about VCs they don't want you to know: that they're human, just like the rest of us. And just like you and me, they aren't seers or superheroes. In fact, the most successful ones are usually the luckiest ones — lucky to have access to promising businesses early on, and lucky to have access to so much money that they can make *a lot* of bad bets and still find success in the end.

To put it simply, VCs — even the most experienced ones — get it wrong more than they get it right. I mention this not to sow doubt in your mind, not to scare you, but rather to prepare you. Because this chapter isn't actually about *how to raise* professional money; it's about *how to think about raising* professional money once you've determined that you might need it. It's about understanding the world of professional money and the mind-set of professional investors, from the perspective of those who've been through the process, so that you know what to expect when you walk in the room, for better or for worse.

Like Jenn Hyman who, in 2009, went out to raise a $1.75 million seed round for an online designer dress rental business she called Rent the Runway, where women could browse dresses that might cost thousands of dollars to buy, but that they could rent for a fraction of the cost. A dress would then show up at a customer's home, she'd wear it for whatever occasion had brought her to the site to begin with, and then she'd ship the dress back when she was done with it. It was like Zipcar meets Netflix meets Zappos, with what would eventually become the country's largest dry-cleaning service on the back end.

Today, Rent the Runway has more than 1,200 employees and does more than $100 million in revenue, but in 2009 the responses

Jenn and her co-founder, Jennifer Fleiss, got from investors were less than encouraging, sometimes even startling.

"We had several different very condescending conversations," Jenn told me, "one in which a partner at a very prestigious firm took my hand into his and said, 'This is so adorable. You're going to get to wear such pretty dresses. This must be so fun for you.'"

They did not engage with this investor or his firm ever again, but the exchange was the most egregiously arrogant and dismissive example of a whole set of responses they received from the predominantly male venture capital class.

"Most investors said, 'Let me talk to my wife,' 'Let me talk to my daughter,' or 'Let me talk to my admin.' Those were the three target customers that we would hear about," Jenn said. On the surface, that sounds like a reasonable response, right? What do a bunch of men in their forties and fifties know about dresses? Probably nothing, but they *are* supposed to know about business, and they were ignoring that part of the equation in their responses to Jenn and Jennifer, as if the business model or the business plan were irrelevant. As if the business-worthiness of Jenn's idea had already been foreclosed by the potential investors' lack of familiarity with the underlying product. Not only that, in deferring to the women in their lives, these investors weren't even consulting the right demographic cohorts.

"Let me tell you why each [of the 'target customers'] is problematic," Jenn said. "Number one, the wife of a venture capitalist is a multimillionaire. She can afford to buy any dress she wants, so she is not my target customer, right? The daughter of a venture capitalist in most cases is about twelve, because most venture capitalists are, when they're in the prime of their careers, in the forty-five-to-fifty range. So their daughter is not a great target either. And the admins who work in the venture capital industry, because it's such a prestigious job, are often women who are in their fifties and sixties — again, not women who were in my target demo."

If an investor didn't have experience with the product and didn't know anyone in the target demo, it seemed as if the idea wasn't for them — or, worse, it wasn't an idea worth pursuing at all. After enough of these conversations, Jenn and Jennifer began preempting investor responses to their pitch altogether. "We showed them videos and invited them to some of our pop-ups to show them who the customer was so that they really got a sense for who we were catering to," Jenn said.

The pop-ups were revelatory. They were what convinced Jenn in the early going that this idea had legs, and they were ultimately what got the idea to click with a good number of investors. "You saw the facial expressions of women change," Jenn said of her experience witnessing pop-up customers try on her dresses. "They threw their shoulders back, they tussled their hair, and they walked with a new sense of confidence." Seeing this, enough of the know-it-all investors who knew nothing about her customers finally knew enough to engage with Rent the Runway as a *business* proposition. That's when capital for the seed round finally started to trickle in.

This didn't open the floodgates of professional money, however. There was still plenty of skepticism about these two twentysomethings and their repository of "pretty dresses." It wasn't until their story ended up in the *New York Times* business section, with their picture on the front page above the fold, that things changed. A hundred thousand people signed up for the site. They met their first-year sales projections in a matter of weeks. And wouldn't you know it, they had "a clamoring of venture capital investors coming in to the office pitching us on Series A," as Jenn described it. "We had gone from a very undesirable investment to people showing up at the elevator in our building to meet with us unannounced because they wanted to pounce on the deal."

To be clear, while there are frustrating and nauseating elements of sexism and chauvinism in Jenn Hyman's story, the way professional money came to her is not uncommon. Venture capitalists know money, but they don't always know *your* business better than you do, and sometimes they don't know your industry better than you do either. So many founders have told me that they've had to spoon-feed and connect all the dots for potential investors in order to show them the opportunity staring them in the face.

Not every investor is like this, of course, even when they don't quite "get it." And not every founder has had to deal with what Jenn Hyman endured, even when they are female and in the apparel space. Take Tyler Haney, for example, the founder of the athleisure company Outdoor Voices, based in Austin, Texas. When she went out to raise an initial seed round in 2014, the scrutiny she faced from (primarily male) investors was not cynical snark about girls playing dress-up, rather it was legitimate skepticism about whether the market had room for a brand like this.

"Pretty consistently, I'd get an email back or in the session it'd be like, 'But we have Under Armour and we have Nike. Why do we need another activewear brand?'" Tyler told me. "What I started to piece together was that I was in offices with men, and these traditional activewear brands had been built by men and really catered to the competitive athlete. And what I started to recognize was, me, over here pitching this activewear brand around play and freeing fitness from performance, didn't make sense to these folks that had grown up as competitive athletes."

She couldn't keep going into these male-dominated offices and having the same conversations. They weren't going to get her anywhere. So what Tyler did was get out ahead of being shunted to secretaries and daughters by confused investors, the way Jenn Hyman had. She went directly to their female support staff and to their girlfriends and wives before she even came in for her meetings.

"I started sending product to the women in the offices, and the wives of some of these investors," Tyler described. "And I started to find that by getting the product onto the women in the offices and the wives, I started to [encounter investors] that were willing to hear me out and understood that this could be something real. I started to get more time with them."

The first investor to bite was Peter Boyce, from a big VC firm headquartered in Cambridge, Massachusetts, called General Catalyst. "He saw the product, saw the pitch," Tyler said. "I had gotten product on his girlfriend, Natalia. She loved it, and he said, 'I love this concept. I want to back it.'" General Catalyst ended up leading the $1.1 million seed round, which Tyler then used to hire three additional employees, open an office, and, of course, make more product.

Jenn Hyman's and Tyler Haney's experiences raising their first chunks of professional money occurred five years apart and were widely different in style as well as in substance, but they were very similar to the extent to which the professional investors they encountered had an outsized influence on their funding prospects, regardless of their subject matter expertise or their business experience. Some of that influence, while frustrating to live through, ultimately turned out to be incredibly helpful. Sometimes, though, for some people, it isn't.

This came into sharp relief for me when I interviewed Tristan Walker onstage in Washington, DC, in September 2019. Tristan is the founder of the eponymously named Walker & Company, which makes health and beauty products for people of color. Much as Lisa Price recognized an unmet need in the skin care market for African American women in the early 1990s when she created Carol's Daughter, Tristan recognized, in 2013, that men of color, especially African American men, were similarly underserved when it came to their shaving needs. There were no products in the market that addressed their unique problems — in particular, razor bumps — that were not also old, tired, and segmented out into the "ethnic beauty" aisle, which in fact was nothing more than a dusty, disregarded shelf in most stores.

Tristan's idea was to create a suite of beautifully designed and packaged products that bundled everything a man of color would need for the ideal shaving experience: a safety razor, a packet of blades, a brush, shaving cream, and pre- and post-shave oils. He called his product line Bevel and figured he needed to raise $2.4 million of professional money to get it off the ground, since this was not something — what with the manufacturing costs for both the hard and soft goods — he could reasonably bootstrap or go to friends and family for help with, without it becoming an unwieldy mess.

Unlike Jenn Hyman, though, Tristan knew what to expect. He knew the VC world intimately, from the inside. He'd spent the previous few years in Silicon Valley, attending the Stanford Graduate School of Business, interning at Twitter, working in business development as one of the first employees at the location check-in app

Foursquare, and then leaving to join the venture capital firm Andreessen Horowitz as an entrepreneur in residence, where his entire job was to develop and evaluate new ideas. "This was around the time that a lot of the e-commerce companies started to pop up," he said. "I was listening to their pitches. I understood the kind of companies that got funded, the types that didn't. It was just great timing to start something like this." Tristan even had the blessing and guidance of Ben Horowitz himself, who'd given him two important pieces of advice during his time at the firm: First, Horowitz told him, "what usually look like good ideas are bad ideas, and what look like bad ideas are good ideas, because the problem with good ideas is that everyone tries to do them, and as a result, there's no value to be created there." Second, he said, "you need to do the thing that you believe you are the best person in the world to do, where you have a unique proposition, given your story, to solve a problem." Accordingly, Horowitz encouraged Tristan to abandon a few of his earliest ideas — one to revolutionize freight, another tackling childhood obesity with play — and instead to pursue this thing he was uniquely experienced to execute.

It was under these conditions that Bevel was born and Tristan began his trek up and down Sand Hill Road to raise money. By every metric professional investors use to evaluate opportunities, Tristan's idea scored highly. "VCs say they want founders who they've worked with in the past, who have pedigree and experience, who have a blue ocean opportunity," Tristan said. "And with this it was check, check, check, check." He laid out the market for them: "Folks of color spend more money on every single category of health and beauty than anyone else." He laid out the opportunity: "Folks of color, especially black folks, are the most culturally influential group on the planet." Then he laid out the vision for how his products would solve this urgent problem that affected 80 percent of people of color and 30 percent of the rest of the population. The entire time thinking that Bevel was as sure a thing as one could expect to find in the crowded health and beauty segment. "If you're a VC who talks about this white space, blue ocean stuff, why wouldn't you invest in this?" he said.

Tristan met with sixty investors. All but three said no, and it

took a long time to find those three. Fifty-seven professional investors turned him down — a Stanford-pedigreed venture capital vet-
eran with experience operating inside two early major tech startups,
who knew exactly what kind of rationale these firms used to place
their bets. It was the kind of consistent rejection that could have
been completely demoralizing. It could have made Tristan question
everything he was doing and doubt all of his instincts. But he didn't,
for a few reasons.

"I knew there were sixty more investors right behind those sixty,"
he said, "and if they weren't going to invest in my idea, I knew they
weren't going to fund somebody else's version of it either." His point
being that the problem wasn't the idea; the problem was that investors didn't think there *was* a problem. "It wasn't until they started to
push back that I realized they just didn't get it," he said. "I was trying
to explain to these VCs that people are different, and it wasn't even
registering." Tristan was creating a line of products to address a set
of issues they didn't have or couldn't see, so therefore they must not
be real or at least not big enough to be worth their time and money.
Which, paradoxically, was the other reason he never doubted himself. "Silicon Valley, particularly venture capitalists who have never
operated before, have this interesting worldview that they're always
right," he told our bemused audience, "but the job of the venture
capital investor is to be wrong 90 percent of the time. That is literally their job. And I knew this bad idea was good as hell."

Now, there are probably some things Tristan could have done differently or better when he met with investors to make the process
move more smoothly. Maybe his pitch deck could have been better
— his first version *was* in PowerPoint and it *did* use clip art — or he
could have spoken more directly to their self-interests. "I sold the
hope and the dream," he said. But maybe he should have just talked
dollars and cents. "My growth chart was up and to the right," he
noted. Maybe he could have talked slower or faster, more or less. Or
maybe there was nothing he could have done. Maybe he did everything right. Who knows? I certainly don't. And like I said, that's not
what this chapter is about. It's about understanding how to think
about venture capital.

The first thing to understand is that raising venture capital is about making a promise. A promise that you have a product or a service that people will pay money for, that you have a plan to reach as many of those people as possible, and that in exchange for lots of money, you will bust your butt to reach them.

The next thing to understand is that good investors know the promise you are making to them is just that — a promise. They know you can't make any guarantees. You can do everything right, but if the world shifts under your feet, there's nothing you can do about it. Venture capital is by its nature a gamble — it's right there in the name — and every gamble comes with the risk of heavy losses. Professional investors know and accept this fact, which is why they also do everything they can to mitigate the risk before writing very large checks.

One of the principal ways they do this, especially if they are unfamiliar with your industry, is to ask lots and lots of questions:

How do you expect to scale this?
Where is the growth going to come from?
Who is the customer for this?
Doesn't something like this already exist?
How will you get costs down?
Where will you manufacture?
Where will you be based?
What's your marketing strategy?
Why does anyone need this?
Why would anyone do this?*

Melanie Perkins, the co-founder of the Australian online graphic design platform Canva, encountered countless of these types of questions from the more than 100 investors she pitched over a three-month period in 2012. She traveled from Perth to San Francisco, then to Maui (for a kitesurfing excursion masquerading as a tech conference run by the investor Bill Tai, whom Melanie had met at another conference in Perth), then to any number of places in be-

* Remember, this was essentially the question the Airbnb founders got from nearly every investor.

tween. Anywhere there was an event with investors present, Melanie found her way there.

For almost the entire time Melanie was in the United States trying to raise money to build out and launch Canva, her efforts were fruitless, at least as far as getting anyone to write a check was concerned. They were not without merit, though, because with each rejection she learned a little more.

"It was really beneficial because we got so many different questions and comments," Melanie said, "and it meant that we really had to know what we were doing and really refine our strategy." Every single day, after she'd pitch an investor who would invariably pass, she'd go back and revise the pitch deck to reflect what she'd learned from the questions that had been asked of her.

"Every time we got a really hard question, that would go right to the front of the pitch deck," Melanie recalled. "So the hardest questions were answered right at the front."

Eventually, investors ran out of questions whose answers didn't already appear in the front of Melanie's pitch. Before long, those answers were able to allay the doubts and concerns of investors who maybe didn't fully understand Canva's business, but who recognized the opportunity that was beginning to emerge with design and publishing tools moving online. By the time Melanie's tourist visa expired and she had to return to Australia, she'd raised $750,000 and would eventually oversubscribe her $1.5 million seed round. All, I think Melanie would say, because she was able to come up with an answer to every question a skeptical, risk-sensitive investor might have.

As an entrepreneur, you have to expect these questions. You have to know that you are going to face them. Jenn Hyman did. Tristan Walker did, too. And you have to be prepared to manage the fact that when you are faced with what feels like an inquisition with no right answers, it is only natural that the doubt pouring out of investors will begin to creep into your brain and make you start to wonder, "Am I the crazy one here? Maybe this idea really is silly. Maybe there is no way it can work."

This is a daily fight when you're raising money. And if your goal is to scale your business, as I talked about at the beginning of this chapter, then you need to fight extra hard to reject each of these nagging, self-doubting thoughts. If, however, you find that you aren't all that concerned with becoming the biggest you can possibly be, then the resolution of this fight could very well be walking away altogether.

It's Tristan's greatest regret in the building of Walker & Company that he took professional money at all. The things he had to endure in the seed stage were tough enough — comparisons to the Chris Rock movie *Good Hair,* confident assertions that the problem he thought he was solving wasn't really a problem at all — but when he went back to Sand Hill Road to scale the company a couple years later and really take it big, that's where the real frustration occurred. He could not, no matter what he said or did, raise more than $30 million. That sounds like a lot, but at a time when VCs were throwing hundreds of millions of dollars at far less worthy companies — as well as at competitors like Harry's, which started the same year as Walker & Company — $30 million felt like the ultimate vote of no confidence. Without more money, Tristan wouldn't be able to invest in marketing, product development, research, and, of course, production. He would have to find another way to grow his company.

All Tristan could do was remember that "if there was anyone qualified to do this idea, [it was] me"; that he had the best "bad" idea in the space; that he was uniquely positioned to execute it; and that he knew more about his business and his market than the VCs did. They knew money, but he knew his business. Fortunately, there was one other thing he could do in support of his long-term vision for the company. In December 2018, he sold Walker & Company to Procter & Gamble for much less money than he might have gotten on the open market.

As part of the deal, Tristan moved the company to Atlanta, became the first African American CEO of a Procter & Gamble portfolio company in its 180-year history, and in the process severely limited the return the VC firms that had invested in his Series A got on their money. This was Tristan's attempt to grow the company on his terms, to take a step back in order to move forward with more confidence down the road, and to show future entrepreneurs — especially those of color — that while VCs might have all the power over the money, that doesn't mean they are necessarily wiser than you or that they are always right. You can be right, too, whether you choose to take their money or not.

16

Protect What You've Built

I've lived in cities most of my life. But on the rare occasions when I've used a wheelbarrow, more than once I've had the experience of catching the tire on an uneven edge and having the whole thing topple over. Have you ever pushed a full wheelbarrow over a curb or down a step, only to have it bounce and tip and send the load flying in the air? It's so frustrating!

What if there was a better way? What if, instead of a wheel on the front of your wheelbarrow, there was a *ball?* And what if that ball rotated 360 degrees for increased maneuverability and was attached to the front of a redesigned barrow that allowed for easy hauling and unparalleled stability? Well, look no further, because the Ballbarrow is here! Trust me, it will change your life, much the way it should have changed the life of its inventor, James Dyson, who, thanks to an opportunistic sales manager, a fickle board of directors, and a failed lawsuit, ended up with nothing to show for nearly a decade of hard work.

Today, James Dyson is best known for the bagless cyclonic vacuum cleaner that bears his name. It has made him one of the richest men and largest landowners in the United Kingdom. But in the early 1970s, long before he spent five years in his coach house — which was really more of a glorified toolshed — building more than 5,000 prototypes of the vacuum cleaner that would make him a household name, Dyson bought the old farm on which that coach house sits and which inspired the invention at the heart of his very first business — the Ballbarrow.

"I was fixing up the house and doing a garden," he told me, "and I noticed the deficiencies of metal wheelbarrows with narrow wheels. They're very unstable. The legs sink into soft ground. The wheels sink into soft ground. So as I used one, I started to redesign it."

The product he eventually took to market solved every problem he encountered as he went about renovating his new home, but it came with some problems of its own. Namely, hardware stores and garden centers didn't want to carry it. "They felt it looked very strange," he said, and beyond that, "not many people buy wheelbarrows. So it's a very small market."

Think for a moment: How many wheelbarrows have you purchased in your lifetime? One, *maybe* two. Exactly. James's solution to that was to sell directly to consumers through advertisements in local newspapers. "[The ad] was always next to incontinence pants or the baldness cures," he said, "but I started to get quite a lot of business. People actually sent checks."

So many checks, in fact, that within a few years, his Ballbarrow had 50 percent of the UK market, for whatever that was worth, which was apparently not enough, because he still wasn't making any money, and he needed to take on investors as a result.

He formed a company with a group of investors. They called it Kirk-Dyson, a fifty-fifty partnership. As part of the funding process, James also assigned the patent for the Ballbarrow to the company. This was, and continues to be, standard practice in most industries. The problem for James was that when they ran out of money again and additional investors came on board, his ownership stake was diluted down to 30 percent, which meant he effectively no longer owned the patent on the very product that he'd designed and that sat at the center of the entire business. It was owned instead by whoever controlled the other 70 percent of the shares in the company.

To make matters worse, when they decided to expand into the US market in hopes of clawing their way toward profitability, the sales manager tasked with securing a partnership decided to sell the design to an American plastics company so the firm could manufacture and sell the Ballbarrow under the machine's own name. Naturally, James sued to protect his intellectual property. Except it wasn't his property anymore, even though his name is on the patent. He lost every suit, along with hundreds of thousands of dollars in lawyers' fees. After he returned to the United Kingdom following another legal defeat in an American court in 1979, the board of directors fired him from his own company.

James would not make this mistake a second time. Several years later, Amway copied his Dual Cyclone vacuum design and made their own version called the CMS1000. A decade after that, Hoover did the same thing and didn't even bother to hide it. They called their machine the Triple Vortex Cleaner. Very original. In both instances, James was prepared. This time, he owned the business and controlled the underlying patent for his invention. And this time, when he sued for infringement, he won. After five years fighting Amway in US court, they settled and Amway became a joint licensee that sold Dyson vacuums. Hoover lost at trial in the UK High Court, and then again on appeal. In 2002, after a three-year battle, Hoover settled with Dyson out of court for £6 million, which, at that time, was the largest court-ordered award ever granted in a UK patent suit.

Over the years, James seems to have gone back and forth on how he feels about his experience with the Ballbarrow. In 1994, he said it was a "terrible mistake." In his autobiography three years later, he said, "It was like giving birth, and then losing the child." But with time and multiple successful patent defenses, he was much more sanguine about the whole thing. (A few billion dollars can do that for a person.) When we talked in 2018, he said, "Sometimes one needs to go through these rites of passage to understand the importance of ownership of intellectual property, the importance of having a majority share in your own company, or even all the shares."

He is right, of course (and who are we to argue with someone who owns more property than the queen of England?), but it's also not that simple when it comes to protecting what you've built. Owning and controlling your intellectual property is one thing; defending it in court is another. Sure, in some instances, the decision to sue to protect your property is self-evident, as it was for Randy Hetrick in 2010 when he found his TRX Suspension Trainer drowning online in a sea of Chinese counterfeits. "They were devouring my business," he told me. "If you looked for TRX on Amazon, for instance, you would be served up our product alongside a bunch of others that were a quarter or a fifth the price, because of course they didn't have to spend any money to develop the market. It puts huge pressure on the entire business model."

It got so bad with the knockoffs in 2014 and 2015 that TRX actually experienced negative growth. Randy *had* to sue. So he identified one of the largest infringers and filed a patent and trademark suit in federal court. It took three years and $2.5 million, but eventually TRX won a unanimous verdict and a jury award of $6.8 million in damages. "It validated all of our trademarks and our key patents," Randy explained, "and our business almost immediately leapt up by 40 percent."

Clearly, Randy made the right decision in bringing a lawsuit in defense of his intellectual property. But if there's one thing I have learned about intellectual property from interviewing so many entrepreneurs, it's that knowing when *not* to sue is just as important as knowing when to do so. And knowing *why* you're suing is even more important than that.

This was a lesson that Curt Jones learned the hard way with his ice cream company, Dippin' Dots, founded in 1988. If you haven't been to a sports stadium, a concert arena, a mall, or an amusement park in the past twenty years, you may not know that Dippin' Dots are colorful bead-sized ice cream balls created by dripping a flavored ice cream mixture into liquid nitrogen, freezing them instantly. They are delicious the way any ice cream is delicious, and they are fun kind of the way Pop Rocks are fun. My kids love them.

By the mid-1990s, children across the United States and abroad loved them, too. Curt had shifted the business into a wholesaler-dealership model, which by then had helped the Dippin' Dots brand spread beyond brick-and-mortar retail and small stands in places like Opryland, in Nashville, Tennessee, where they got their start. It also helped the Dippin' Dots business make money for the first time. "You were always spending what you made," Curt said about the beginnings of the business, "but we were starting to generate some income through wholesale. Within five years or so, we reached a million dollars in sales on a wholesale level."

As part of the dealership license, a dealer would buy a large, branded storage freezer along with product on a revolving basis. The product would arrive packaged as five 1-gallon heat-sealed bags of ice cream packed into an old milk crate, which would in turn be packed into an insulated container filled with dry ice. Dealers also had the right to use the Dippin' Dots logo for their cups, bags, and related packaging and marketing items. All of which should have been fine, except "it wasn't a very tight contract, and we started losing control of the brand a little bit toward the late nineties," Curt said. Dealers were producing all sorts of things with the Dippin' Dots name, but with different colors and in different sizes. It was kind of a "hodge-podge," as Curt put it.

Other dealers who were leveraging the brand appropriately were making good money with Dippin' Dots but were complaining that it was impossible for them to build equity in their businesses and make improvements because they were only signed to a one-year contract. This led Curt to shift to a franchise model in 1999, which gave dealers greater security with a five-year contract and a five-year renewal, but required them to pay Curt a royalty on sales (instead of simply the flat fee that comes with wholesale) and allowed Curt to include "more stipulations as to how to use the Dippin' Dots logo," among other things. It was a win-win proposition—one that quadrupled Dippin' Dots' annual sales revenue over the next six years for the 105 (of 113) dealers who made the transition to franchises.

The eight who didn't sign the franchise contract had other plans related to something that had been going on in the background for a few years. Curt had been locked in a patent infringement lawsuit with a man named Thomas Mosey, out of Dallas, Texas, since 1996, after Mosey decided to start making his own "dot ice cream" using liquid nitrogen and called it Dots of Fun. Dippin' Dots' slogan was "Ice Cream of the Future." Mosey's slogan for Dots of Fun? "Tomorrow's Ice Cream . . . Today."

Based on the patent for his ice cream that Curt had filed in 1992, Dippin' Dots was able to secure an injunction against Dots of Fun in 1996, which put the competitive situation on the back burner for a while. But in 1999, just as Dippin' Dots was making the transition to a franchise company, a special master in the patent case ruled that if Dots of Fun put a regular chunk of ice cream in the cup with its dots, its product would no longer infringe.

That's when the "ringleader" of the eight holdout dealers, as Curt called him, reached out to Mosey in search of a better deal. "They went to him and said, 'Hey, we think you can make ice cream based on this new ruling,'" Curt said, "and that's exactly what happened. He started making ice cream again and changed the name to Mini Melts."

This was only the beginning of Curt Jones's long nightmare. He would fight Thomas Mosey in court for another six or seven years. He sued Mosey and Mini Melts for $16 million. Mosey countersued for $10 million, challenging the validity of Curt's patent in the process. I will spare you the details of what would become a long, protracted court battle, but in the end neither side won a judgment, Curt's patent was invalidated on the basis of fraud, and because of that, he ended up having to pay Mosey's attorney's fees in addition to his own. A bill that came to a whopping $10 million, not including the $750,000 he had to spend to appeal the fraud finding and to clear his name.

Had you ever heard of Mini Melts before reading this? Have you ever had a cup of Mini Melts ice cream? Did you know they are still around? If so, you are in the minority, in America anyway. What about Dippin' Dots? Had you heard of them? Have you seen one of their stands? Have you had a cup? If you have young kids, I suspect the answer to at least one of those questions is yes, not only because the ice cream is good but also because the brand is really strong.

As Curt acknowledged in our interview, the decision to go after Thomas Mosey and Dots of Fun/Mini Melts — even though it was justified on principle — turned out to be a big miscalculation. Even if the courts hadn't blown apart Curt's patent claims, the value in Dippin' Dots was not really in the intellectual property; it was in the *brand*. It was no coincidence that the dealers who were most successful in the beginning were the ones who leaned into the branding. Nor is it a surprise that once the company moved over to a franchise model and made the branding requirements more strict, the entire enterprise took off. When kids go to baseball games or amusement parks, they don't want "dot ice cream," they want Dippin' Dots. You simply can't buy that kind of brand equity. You can't copy or sue your way to it either, as Mosey would discover eventually.

Obviously, Curt could not have predicted all of this when he first filed suit in 1996. At that time, his position and his intent made total sense. "We felt like [Mosey] was infringing a valid patent," Curt said. "All we really wanted the guy to do was to stop what he was doing." Perfectly reasonable. But then the landscape changed. Between the time the initial injunction became circumventable in 1999 and the litigation concluded in 2006, Dippin' Dots grew by leaps and bounds. By then, one competitor flagrantly exploiting Curt's patent didn't seem to be affecting Dippin' Dots much at all. And its sturdiness as a business, I would argue, was due almost entirely to its strength as a brand. A *leading* brand, no less.

This is what differentiates Randy Hetrick's decision to sue from Curt's. While Curt was defending his intellectual property just like Randy was, and rightfully so, he ended up exposing the thing he actually built — the brand, the business — to an existential risk instead of defending it from an existential threat, as Randy did. With the best of intentions, Curt lost sight of *why* he was suing and what actually needed protection.

Now here's the key: Curt still could have weathered this storm and survived what in hindsight was a strategic misstep. In 2006, the year the lawsuit concluded, Dippin' Dots had its best year to date, doing $47 million in sales. Except then the world around him started to unravel. Milk prices went up by 34 percent. Fuel prices went up. Even liquid nitrogen prices increased by 10 percent. "All of a sudden, on almost the same sales we had the year before, we went from a net of two or three million dollars in profits to a loss," Curt said. On top of that, they now carried a $13 or $14 million debt load — twice the amount of debt they normally carried, thanks to the lawyers' fees they still had to pay. Then the global financial crisis hit, just as that note came due. The local bank Curt had been working with for years gave Dippin' Dots a three-month extension to figure out a way to either pay off or restructure the debt.

But during those three months, the financial crisis got appreciably worse, and in that environment, with everything going upside down, the bank decided to tighten its purse strings and close what used to be an open, helping hand into a fist, with which it punched Curt right in the gut. Not unlike what happened to Gary Hirshberg and Stonyfield Farm in the wake of the 1987 stock market crash, the day Dippin' Dots' extension expired and the payment was due, Curt's bank sent an email informing him that he was in default and that therefore all his other loans with the bank were also in default.

Curt fought for the next three years. He fought creditors. He fought the market as sales declined. People didn't buy as much novelty ice cream when they had to worry about their own loans defaulting. He paid what he could to the bank, often at exorbitant credit-card–style interest rates. He did whatever he could to keep the company alive. "We could've walked away and been okay," Curt said, "but I grew up on a farm in the second-poorest county in the state of Illinois. In that area, if you weren't farming, you could be a teacher or you could work at the prison, but not much else. We had 200 employees. We provided 200 jobs for that area. So when things got bad, we put a lot of our personal assets back into the business to keep it alive. I guess we were thinking, 'We've just got to get through this, and everything's going to be better.'"

For a while, it seemed like it would. "We had actually survived from late 2007, during some of the hardest times with the recession and low sales [through 2010]," he said. "In 2011, we actually felt like we were going to dig our way out of this." And then the bank put them into foreclosure, which forced Curt and Dippin' Dots to file for Chapter 11 bankruptcy — something, as an old-school guy who paid his debts as a matter of pride and principle, Curt thought he would never do.

It was then that the company really began to slip away from Curt, much the way Ballbarrow gradually slipped away from James Dyson. Three days after Dippin' Dots filed for bankruptcy protection, a father-son duo named Mark and Scott Fischer reached out to express interest in coming aboard as investors. They owned a family oil concern called Chaparral Energy, and they were planning on divesting from it a bit and putting some of that money to work in other places. To Curt, who had never imagined himself in bankruptcy, who had been getting badgered by the bank for years to sell, the Fischers coming in as fifty-fifty partners was very attractive.

If only it were that simple.

"There would've been a lot of positive reasons to just stick with what I was doing," Curt said of continuing through the restructuring process that comes with Chapter 11, "but this seemed like not only would the Fischers come in and be partners, they talked about putting more money into the company, growing it faster. They said a lot of the right things."

Before long, many of those right things went wrong. "My deal with them kept getting worse and worse. Instead of being a fifty-fifty partner, they took more of the ownership because they were going to be taking on some of the financial risk," Curt recalled of the Fischers' rationale at the time. "And so over about a six-month period, I ended up with really no ownership in the deal. They basically bought the company for the debt and kept me on as CEO for three years." At the end of the three-year agreement, which included ownership earn-back provisions for Curt, Dippin' Dots' new owners chose not to renew the deal. Curt was officially out.

It's incredibly difficult to protect what you've built from outside threats. It's even harder when the threats come from the inside, from partners who gain your trust with promises of assistance at times when you need it most, because they can often feel like guardian angels, like saviors. And how do you defend against someone who has come to save you? Curt didn't know. "Had I gone through the restructuring process, I probably would've had a very good chance of coming out with my company," he said. But remember: *They said a lot of the right things.* And unfortunately, none of those things ended up including him.

As uncertain as the business world can be, one surefire way to know you've built something great that is primed to grow and scale is when your competitors start either copying you or suing you, sometimes both. Or like Jenn Hyman in good times, and Curt Jones in bad ones, when investors come knocking on your door unsolicited, ready to write a check. In both of those instances, as the founder you need to be able to get up on the balcony and look down on the dance floor to know what needs to be protected and how best to protect it. You need to know when to pull the trigger and when to holster the weapons at your disposal. It's not an easy thing to know or to do, but neither is building a great business. And if you can figure that out, you can figure this out, too.

17

When Catastrophe Strikes

Heading into 1982, the pharmaceutical giant Johnson & Johnson was on track for a great year. Profits were up more than 16 percent from the year before, even as the country began to slide into a recession. A multibillion-dollar, multinational conglomerate with more than 140 companies in its portfolio and at least that many products on the market, Johnson & Johnson was thriving in no small part because of the performance of one product: the over-the-counter pain reliever Tylenol. In 1981, after several years of steady promotion, Tylenol had managed to capture more than one-third of the analgesic market and more than $500 million in sales, accounting for nearly 20 percent of Johnson & Johnson's total profits. Executives within the company saw no immediate end to its growth potential. They expected Tylenol to have 50 percent of the market within five years.

Then, in the fall of 1982, seven people in the Chicago area mysteriously died within a few days of one another. An investigation soon found that the common denominator among the victims was the recent use of Tylenol products sold in capsule form. Testing and tracking of the Tylenol bottles revealed that they had been tampered with by someone who had purchased a number of bottles from area drugstores and grocery stores, had opened up some of the

capsules, and had then laced the acetaminophen inside with cya-
nide.

News of the poisoning set off a panic. Law enforcement agencies
rode the streets of metro Chicago warning residents through loud-
speakers not to use the Tylenol in their medicine cabinets. Within
two days, the mayor of Chicago was urging people to turn their Tylenol in to their local police and fire departments. Two days after that,
she banned Tylenol from the city's stores altogether. Other cities
and states quickly followed suit. The story led the news every day for
six weeks. Tylenol sales dropped by as much as 80 percent. It was an
unqualified disaster for Johnson & Johnson.

What followed, however, was a masterwork of leadership and crisis management by Johnson & Johnson's CEO, James Burke, that is
still taught in business schools nearly forty years later.

Within days, Burke recalled all Tylenol capsule products nationwide — 31 million bottles in total. In addition, he announced that
Johnson & Johnson would replace all Tylenol capsules returned by
customers with the safer tablet form, free of charge. Within a month,
Burke unveiled Johnson & Johnson's plan to return Tylenol's capsule products to store shelves, but now in new, "triple-seal" tamper-
proof packaging that included a glued box, a plastic neck seal, a foil
seal under the cap, and a printed warning to return the product if the
foil seal was broken upon opening. This tamper-proof packaging was
the first of its kind on the market. One of the big reasons the story remained in the news for six weeks was that Burke was in constant, almost daily, contact with the news directors of every major national
media outlet to make sure the public had all the most up-to-date information.

Today, these steps taken by Burke seem like standard practice
in the face of such corporate calamities. But in 1982, they were anything but common. "Before 1982, nobody ever recalled anything,"
one public relations executive who advised Johnson & Johnson during the crisis told the *New York Times* in a 2002 anniversary piece
subtitled "The Recall That Started Them All." In fact, Burke faced
more resistance to a recall from outside his own boardroom. Both

the FDA and the FBI were against the idea. "The FBI didn't want us to do it," Burke told *Fortune* in November 1982, "because it would say to whomever did this, 'Hey, I'm winning, I can bring a major corporation to its knees.' And the FDA argued it might cause more public anxiety than it would relieve."

Still, Burke moved forward. His resoluteness down this path was costly. By the time it was all over, Johnson & Johnson had spent $100 million on the recall and the relaunch with tamper-proof packaging. Their net income for the first quarter after the poisoning was off more than 25 percent. By the end of the year, Tylenol's share of the market had plummeted from a high of 37 percent all the way down to 7 percent. "There were many people in the company who felt there was no possible way to save the brand, that it was the end of Tylenol," Burke said.

Of course, that would not end up being the case. The fact that Tylenol rebounded was not in itself remarkable; what was astounding was the speed with which the recovery occurred. Within two months, Johnson & Johnson's stock price had returned to pre-poisoning highs. Within eight months, Tylenol had recovered 85 percent of its previous share of the pain reliever market, and by the end of 1983, Tylenol had recaptured nearly all of it.

Credit for Tylenol's miraculous recovery sits entirely with James Burke and his ability to act quickly, decisively, transparently, and in a manner consistent with the values of the company, which had been baked into the Johnson & Johnson credo pretty much since its founding in the late 1880s: "We believe our first responsibility is to the patients, doctors and nurses, to mothers and fathers and all others who use our products and services."

"The credo made it very clear ... exactly what we were all about," Burke said of those first days immediately after the seven tragic deaths. "It gave me the ammunition I needed to persuade shareholders and others to spend the $100 million on the recall." It also allowed him to build trust with consumers — whom "the credo is all about," Burke said — as Johnson & Johnson worked through the crisis over several months.

Trust was at the core of everything Burke did. He trusted his team inside Johnson & Johnson to do the right thing, and he trusted the public to respond accordingly. Trust was how they were able to build Tylenol into such a "big and important franchise," Burke believed. Trust was "an operative word" in his everyday life. It embodied "almost everything you can strive for that will help you to succeed."

Time would prove James Burke right, but even he knew that Johnson & Johnson was in a privileged position when it came to absorbing the financial hit and reputational damage incurred from this fatal product tampering. "Often our society rails against bigness," Burke said at the time, "but this has been an example where size helps. If Tylenol had been a separate company, the decisions would have been much tougher."

That is what makes Jeni Britton Bauer's choices in April 2015 so noteworthy.

In 2015, Jeni's Splendid Ice Creams had been in business for nearly thirteen years. It was by then very well-known around central Ohio, where Jeni is from. Its revenue was a mere fraction of that of a business like Tylenol, but it was meaningfully profitable — surprisingly so, some might say — for a business of its size, profile, and character. Jeni and her three partners had a half dozen scoop shops. They sold to high-end grocery stores and did a brisk mail-order business. But what set them apart, and what made their success so remarkable, was Jeni's almost maniacal focus on quality. She was obsessive about how and where she sourced ingredients. She spent countless hours experimenting with the molecular structure of the milk proteins to make sure her ice cream had a very specific mouthfeel. She paid dogged attention to all the little things that cost a lot of money and cut into the margins of a business in an industry that had not experienced any kind of artisanal renaissance since Ben & Jerry's in the late 1970s and so was subject to commoditization and constant downward pressure on price. Still, Jeni persisted in her quest for perfect ice cream flavors and in 2011 wrote a cookbook about them that received national attention. Her company landed back on the national map once more in March 2015 when it launched a series of ice creams based on colors from the Henri Matisse *Cut-Outs* show at the Museum of Modern Art in New York City, while at the same time opening its first store in Los Angeles — its most competitive market and the farthest from its headquarters in Columbus, Ohio, to date.

"We were riding high," Jeni said, "and then one day we get this bomb dropped on us. A pint of ice cream in Lincoln, Nebraska, tested positive for listeria."

Listeria is a foodborne bacteria that can cause fever, muscle aches, nausea, and diarrhea, and can be fatal to immunosuppressed individuals such as the elderly, the chronically sick, and pregnant women. Its presence in your product is not the news you ever want to get, especially when it feels like your business has turned a corner, when it has survived that crucible of early growing pains, built a recognizable brand, and seems primed for long-term success.

"It was the call none of us could have imagined," Jeni said.

Immediately, she found herself in the same position James Burke had found himself in thirty-three years earlier. The day the news broke that the deaths in Chicago were linked to Tylenol, Burke and his team huddled at Johnson & Johnson's New Brunswick, New Jersey, headquarters to decide their next moves. The day Jeni's partner, John Lowe, the company's CEO, got the call about the contaminated pint of ice cream in Lincoln, the Jeni's team huddled in their headquarters to decide what they would do.

"We had to make a lot of decisions very quickly over a very short period of time," Jeni said, reminiscent of James Burke's thinking. "Nobody was sick that we knew of yet, but we needed to prevent an outbreak. We had to decide what we were going to do."

They chose to shut down production and to recall everything, which initially they didn't even know how to do, because if something like this has never happened to you before, why would you?

"We figured out how to do it, we filed paperwork and got approval from the FDA, and within hours we had 265 tons of ice cream that had been out in the world coming back to us," she said. Which meant, with no ice cream out in the world and no way of making new ice cream until they found the source of the listeria, they would have to close all their stores, too.

In 1982, Tylenol's sales dropped by 80 percent, but not to zero, because they had other non-capsule products they could sell. But in 2015, ice cream was it for Jeni's. Their sales went to zero in an instant. While their stores were closed and their machines were quiet, they lost $150,000 per day.

"At that point, the clock starts ticking," Jeni said. Ticking down, toward zero. "We have 600 employees who now have nothing to do — including me, actually. We started to look around, realizing that that was it, there wasn't anything left."

But, in fact, there *was* something left: the loyal community that Jeni; her husband, Charly Bauer; her brother-in-law, Tom Bauer; and their CEO, John Lowe, had built over the previous decade.

"We raised our company *as* a community and *with* our community, slowly," Jeni said. They were a staple of the North Market food hall, where Jeni's Splendid Ice Creams was founded, for three years before they opened their first stand-alone scoop shop in 2005. They opened three additional shops in the next three years, all in or around Columbus. They didn't expand outside the Columbus area until 2011, and even then it was only to Cleveland, less than 150 miles away. Jeni's belonged to Columbus.* Jeni and her company were one of theirs.

"There was a lot of trust built into that," Jeni said. "And that's what saved us."

There's that word again: "trust." James Burke had to build trust with consumers on the fly, in real time, as he managed the Tylenol poisoning crisis. Jeni Britton Bauer had smartly baked trust into her brand, which soon gave her the confidence that, as long as she

---

* I interviewed Jeni Britton Bauer live onstage in Columbus. Her introduction to the stage produced one of the loudest roars from the audience of any live episode we've ever done.

made good decisions, things would never get as bad as they otherwise could.

The first indication of her customers' trust in her came almost immediately, when they started to paste notes of encouragement on the closed front doors of local Jeni's stores. "We had these wonderful people who would put Post-it notes up at the stores, and they were so beautiful," Jeni recounted during our conversation in early 2018, less than three years removed from the listeria contamination. "We were just like, 'You know what? We're fighting for *that*.'"

Eventually, they discovered the source of the listeria. It was coming from a hairline crack in a wall behind a piece of equipment in their 2,000-square-foot manufacturing facility. Jeni's team quickly fixed the problem and prepared to resume production at the previous level. But like James Burke, merely fixing the problem wasn't enough for Jeni Britton Bauer. This was a woman, after all, who did not just *make* ice cream; she *reinvented* it. She did not settle for canned peaches to make her peach cobbler ice cream (my personal favorite, and one I will drive miles to get a scoop of if I'm anywhere near a Jeni's scoop shop); she scoured the country for the best peach purveyors she could find.

Whereas Burke introduced triple-seal tamper-proof packaging to all Tylenol products, Jeni published an open letter on the company blog at the end of August 2015. The letter outlined every single thing that had happened; described their ice cream–making process so consumers knew how the whole thing worked; announced the hiring of a new quality control leader, whom she described as a "Food Safety Jedi"; and revealed that, as part of their newly instituted listeria control program, they'd done "almost 200 swabs every day for two months — almost *1,000 times* beyond the industry recommendation — in order to understand where the Listeria was coming from and eliminate it."

It was the ultimate gesture in transparency, but also an act of faith, one anchored in mutual trust. It was not unlike the trust in the public that drove James Burke's openness with the news media, which was not only uncharacteristic for the time but also out of character for Johnson & Johnson, which had a reputation for keeping the media at arm's length when it came to any information they considered sensitive.

No matter what their natural tendencies might have been, both Jeni and James knew that their decisions in these moments of crisis were pivotal, because such a moment can often be an inflection point in the trajectory of a business, for better or for worse.

Jeni described this moment in an NBC News story as one that "lives on in my memory as a sort of before and after moment. With crisis — when there is a before and after — you go forward in a whole different way than you were before." Precisely *how*, or if, you go forward depends very much on how quick, decisive, and transparent you are in responding to the moment itself.

James Burke and Jeni Britton Bauer were paragons of quick, decisive, transparent leadership in the face of their respective crises. Leadership that saved their businesses in the short run and set them on a path to sustained growth in the long run. Today, Tylenol is a billion-dollar business by itself; Jeni's Splendid Ice Creams has more than thirty stores and is doing $40 million in sales annually.

One need only look at a company whose leaders took the opposite approach, who tried to hide or delay or obfuscate in the face of catastrophic problems, to understand what can happen to a company and the community around it when effective leadership is absent.

Beginning in 1996, personal injury attorneys and traffic safety consultants had become aware of a spike in rollover accidents — thirty in total at that point, some fatal — involving the failure of Firestone ATX tires installed on Ford Explorer SUVs. At prolonged highway speeds and high road surface temperatures, tread would separate from the tires' sidewalls and in some instances send the SUVs into a roll.

Under James Burke's leadership, the immediate recall of all Tylenol capsules in 1982 occurred within days. Jeni Britton Bauer pulled pints of her ice cream off shelves within *hours* and closed the company's stores just as quickly. But the recall of Firestone ATX tires did not happen for another *four years,* and even then it took an investigation by federal regulators, opened in February 2000, to spur the leaders of Ford and Bridgestone Firestone into action.

Fault for the initial failure to act does not sit with Ford or Firestone. Lawyers preparing to bring suit on behalf of accident victims in those first years, 1996 and early 1997 in particular, were trying not to tip their hand to Ford, about the stability of their Explorers, or to Firestone, about the integrity of their tires, so they withheld relevant information from federal regulators, whose investigations would have alerted the automaker and the tire manufacturer to their plans. Moreover, they did not trust regulators to investigate in good faith. They worried that regulators would conduct open-and-shut inquiries — as they had done in the past and that had concluded with no finding of fault — which would neuter the financial potential of the lawyers' claims if any of their cases came to trial.

Still, by the end of 1997, one plaintiff's attorney said, the "series of lawsuits he filed involving tire-related deaths should have alerted Ford and Firestone to the problem." If that didn't do it, then the warranty claims that had begun to accumulate on ATX tires by 1998 should have alerted Firestone. And by 1999, Ford didn't need to be "alerted," because some of the company's key leaders had already been informed of Firestone tire failures on Explorers that had been sold in a number of international markets.

And yet, nothing happened. Actually, that's not true: tire accidents continued to happen, and fatalities continued to stack up. When the National Highway Traffic Safety Administration (NHTSA) finally launched the first investigation into this issue in early 2000, they reviewed reports on more than *200* tire-related deaths. Almost 95 percent of them occurred *after* 1996. Even then, it took another six months for Ford and Firestone to agree to a mass recall of what remained of the nearly 14.5 million affected tires that were still out on the road. It took that long because leaders within both companies were spending most of that time arguing over whose fault those accidents were, and therefore who was liable for the pain and suffering of the victims, rather than taking appropriate steps to end *future* pain and suffering as quickly as possible.

Ford blamed Firestone for faulty tire construction. Firestone blamed Ford for, among other things, poor roof design, excessive oversteer, and setting factory tire pressure standards too low. Ford suggested 26 psi; Firestone recommended 30 psi.

Ultimately, who was actually to blame mattered only to the victims, and the families of the victims, of the tire-related accidents. What is more relevant for the purposes of understanding how to lead your company through a crisis, is getting a complete picture of what happens when there is a void in leadership.

In the case of Ford and Firestone, the picture is bleak. By the end of 2001, when the investigation concluded and the recalls were complete, more than 270 people had died and 800 had been injured in tire-related rollover accidents. Ford would post a $5.5 billion loss for that year, and Bridgestone Firestone would undergo a corporate restructuring that would cost the company $2 billion. As part of these losses and shake-ups, Ford would end up replacing its CEO, Bridgestone Firestone's CEO and president would both resign, and Firestone would close its plant in Decatur, Illinois, where all the faulty tires had been manufactured, costing the company $200 million and costing 1,500 people their jobs.

Eventually, the companies would combine to settle thousands of claims and lawsuits for well over a billion dollars, and Bridgestone Firestone would sever their 100-year working relationship with Ford. In his letter to Ford CEO Jacques Nasser (six months prior to his ouster) announcing the dissolution of their partnership, new Bridgestone CEO John Lampe expressed a sentiment that should, by now, sound familiar: "Business relationships, like personal ones, are built upon trust and mutual respect. We have come to the conclusion that we can no longer supply tires to Ford since the basic foundation of our relationship has been seriously eroded."

There is that word again: "trust."

Now, if only these leaders had shown the same level of trust and respect to the public — to their customers — as they were demanding from their business partner, maybe fewer people would have died and more people would still have had their jobs. Regardless, it is unmistakably clear that when catastrophe strikes a business

—whether it's a storied multinational conglomerate that has been around 100 years or a scrappy upstart just getting its footing at the national level—the only reliable way through that critical "before and after" moment that Jeni Britton Bauer described is through quick, decisive, transparent action that puts people first and public perception second.

18

The Art of the Pivot

Modern evolutionary theory has been dominated by two competing schools of thought. There are the gradualists, who, like Charles Darwin, believe that large species-level change occurs as a result of the slow, gradual accumulation of smaller changes over long periods of time. And there are the punctualists, who believe in the "punctuated equilibrium" hypothesis — popularized by Niles Eldredge and Stephen Jay Gould in the early 1970s — which argues that species-level change occurs rapidly, in short bursts, with long stable periods in between.

The reality is that both schools are probably right. Evolution can happen slowly *or* it can happen quickly, and sometimes both kinds of change occur within the lineage of the same species. In fact, we seem to have understood the fundamental truth of this idea as part of the human experience far longer than we've understood the particulars of evolution itself.

In 1926, forty-five years before the idea of punctuated equilibrium was first articulated, Ernest Hemingway put these words casually into the mouth of Mike Campbell, one of his secondary characters in *The Sun Also Rises,* when he was asked how he went bankrupt. "Two ways," Mike said. "Gradually and then suddenly."

Eighty-five years later, inspired by the Hemingway line, John

Green wrote in *The Fault in Our Stars:* "I fell in love the way you fall asleep; slowly, and then all at once."

That same year, the Nobel Prize–winning economist and psychologist Daniel Kahneman published his iconic book, *Thinking, Fast and Slow,* whose central premise is that the human mind operates on two interdependent systems of thought: one that is slow, calculating, logical, and deliberate; another that is fast, impulsive, and sudden.

Evolution. Wealth. Love. Sleep. Thoughts.

These are all subject to the gradual, then sudden, nature of change. So, too, is business. And when that change occurs — either to a market or an industry, to consumer tastes or even just to the weather, as it did for Stacy Madison of Stacy's Pita Chips — an affected founder has to be fully prepared to pivot in response if they want their business to survive and grow.

On the streets of downtown Boston in 1996, Stacy Madison and her co-founder, Mark Andrus, were riding the leading edge of the wrap sandwich wave that would crash onto America's lunchtime shores in the early 2000s. They sold healthy, made-to-order roll-up pita sandwiches, out of a repurposed, refurbished hot dog cart that they named Stacy's D'Lites. At the time, "pita roll-ups were all over the place," Stacy said, "but there were very few options. A chicken Caesar was about the extent of what you got. We had about a dozen sandwiches you could order, all with more upscale food choices."

This and the rise of corporate email combined to make them an immediate word-of-mouth success in Boston. "We were right on the edge of the financial district, and somebody would go back to their building and they'd email their office, and then that office would tell another office," Stacy recalled, "and eventually, there was a line twenty people deep all through lunch."

In an effort to make standing in those long lines more bearable, Stacy started cutting up their leftover pitas at the end of each day and then baking the pieces into different-flavored chips (cinnamon sugar and parmesan garlic to start) that she would hand out for free to customers while they waited for their sandwiches.

"Initially, it was just a way to retain our customer base, but people loved it," Stacy said. "It was kind of like a happy hour, where they didn't mind waiting for their sandwich because they got to munch on these delicious, free pita chips." Before long, people were asking Stacy how they might get some of her chips for parties or office meetings. Some suggested she should start producing the chips for sale, as their own individual stand-alone product, which she did, but only on a scale consistent with the volume of the food cart: in baggies tied with gold ribbon and sold for a dollar at the register with the sandwiches.

The chips weren't going to make them rich, Stacy thought at the time, but that wasn't the point. "It kept them coming back," she said of this evolution of their offerings and its impact on her customers, "because now they could also buy some for later in the afternoon or for a snack."

As all of this was happening, fall arrived. The weather began to change.

"It gets a little cold in New England in September and October," Stacy said in the understatement of the year, "and that was when we decided that we would have to do something else."

She didn't mean something else *as a business,* at least not initially. Things had gone well for Stacy's D'Lites in 1996, which was their first year in business. They'd made $25,000, which doesn't sound like a lot, but for a two-person food cart open five days a week, with sweltering summers and frigid winters further limiting a consistent flow of customers, $25,000 counted as real success. What Stacy meant was *somewhere* else to run their business out of — specifically, an indoor location.

Stacy and Mark didn't need anything huge, by any means. They just wanted a space big enough to make sandwiches and to bake pita chips and that would allow them to serve their downtown clientele comfortably year-round. So they started working with a realtor who, when Stacy told them what they were looking for, basically laughed in their faces.

"If you want a tiny little indoor location near where you are," the realtor said, "you can get in line behind Au Bon Pain and Dunkin' Donuts." What Stacy didn't know was that as the weather got cold that year and the ground began to harden, it also began to shift as the commercial real estate market for small storefronts in big cities was heating up. The wave Stacy and Mark were riding wasn't just sandwich wraps, the realtor's response was telling them; it was grab-and-go food service generally, and it was the big chains that were behind it, pushing the wave ashore. "At the time, Starbucks was coming into the world," Stacy explained, "and everybody wanted those little spaces."

As fall turned to winter, their real estate search didn't get any easier. Spots downtown close to where they'd established themselves outdoors were getting snapped up quickly or were out of their price range. They went down the road a ways on a possible deal for a café inside Macy's department stores — she cleverly dubbed it "Stacy's at Macy's" — but it was a much bigger project than they originally intended to undertake, and it began to fall apart as Macy's corporate in New York made things too complicated.

So, in January 1997, Stacy and Mark incorporated the pita chip company and started to figure out what would be required to bring the chips to market. At the same time, they ran Stacy's D'Lites and continued to search for small, inside locations. They ran both businesses for a full year — making pita sandwiches to order out of their retrofitted hot dog cart on weekdays and spending the rest of their time working on perfecting the chip recipe, designing the packaging, securing all the necessary licensing, and getting the product into stores.

Eventually, they realized that they had to choose one pathway or the other. "It was just getting to be too much to do both," Stacy said.

They chose pita chips for a few reasons. "Come winter, it's really rough being out there in the cold," Stacy said, "and we could get bigger, faster, if we were able to sell these chips to some stores [rather] than if we tried to expand on one, two, or three locations of the food cart."

This was true not just because the capital required to build out a brick-and-mortar retail business is much greater than it is for a consumer packaged goods business. But also because, in 1997, by shifting to an all-natural snack food with "nothing in them," as Stacy described her preservative-free chips, she was able to hop from one wave (grab-and-go food) that was about to swallow her up to another wave (natural foods) that was just starting to gather significant momentum. It was the same wave, actually, that Gary Hirshberg rode to $100 million in sales with Stonyfield Farm.

"People were all into natural foods, and that's just what we were innately doing," Stacy said. "So when we first started, we were selling to little gourmet food stores and then to the natural food markets." The exact same markets as Stonyfield Farm, as a matter of fact — New England's Whole Foods antecedent, Bread & Circus, which had about a half dozen stores at the time.

"I walked into Bread and Circus in downtown Boston, and I said, 'Hi, I'm Stacy. These are my chips, and I'd love for you to give them a try,'" Stacy recounted. The manager loved them; then he ordered them for his store and brought them to the attention of Bread & Circus headquarters, which placed orders for all the other stores.

By 2001, Stacy's Pita Chips was doing $1 million in revenue. By 2003, the chips were in Costco and Sam's Club. And by 2005, less than a decade after Stacy and Mark opened up their little sandwich cart on the edge of Boston's financial district, they sold $65 million worth of the same chips they used to give away. Stacy's Pita Chips was officially acquired — reportedly for $250 million — by PepsiCo early the following year.

Stacy and Mark's first few years are a study in both the gradualness and suddenness of change. One moment they felt like they were ahead of the curve in a growing movement, and the next it seemed like their ambitions were going to get flattened by massive competitors intent on capturing as much of their respective markets as quickly as possible by gobbling up the only kind of retail spaces Stacy and Mark could afford.

Their pivot from pita sandwiches to Stacy's Pita Chips is a textbook example of a response to that change in the market, made both out of necessity and with an eye toward opportunity. That seems to be the recipe for every successful pivot — not just the recognition that you can't keep doing what you're doing if you want to grow or survive, but also identifying something else to do and/or some other place to do it.

That's how it was for Justin Kan, Emmett Shear, and Twitch, the livestreaming video platform that got its start in March 2007 as Justin.tv, a single 24-7 live feed of its creators' lives. Like Stacy's D'Lites, Justin.tv found success right away, but on a much larger scale. The creators got a ton of national press for starting the "life-casting" revolution, which quickly drew hundreds of thousands, then millions of unique monthly users. But by that summer, the on-going, constant exposure had started to drive Justin insane, so he had to stop. Fortunately, Justin.tv's CEO, Emmett Shear, said, "lots of other people wanted to stream live, and the technology we built to support the live video stream was actually broadly useful, so we pivoted to being a service that anyone could use."

The result was rapid growth. By April of the following year, they had 30,000 broadcaster accounts and multiple categories for users to search and explore. Justin.tv evolved along these lines for the next few years, adding millions of users and dozens of channels as they went.

By 2011, though, the founders had "capped out growth and didn't know what to do next," Shear recounted in a talk at a Brainstorm Tech dinner put on by *Fortune* magazine in early 2019. At the same time, they realized that one of their video categories — Gaming — was drawing more users than all of the others combined. That was no surprise to Shear. "The only content on Justin.tv that I watched was the gaming content, because that's the only thing that I actu-ally enjoyed," he told the Brainstorm Tech audience. So they decided to spin it off into a sister site called Twitch.tv and, not unlike Stacy Madison and Mark Andrus with their chips business, to run both in parallel. They did that until 2014, when Twitch finally got so massive that they pivoted *again,* this time shifting the entire company over to Twitch, rebranding it as Twitch Interactive, and shutting down Justin.tv completely.

To be clear, they didn't shutter Justin.tv because it was failing. Far from it. It was just not succeeding at the same level as Twitch, nor was it growing at the rate or to the size that Twitch was growing. This is by far the most interesting aspect — and, I think, one of the most important characteristics — of so many of the pivot stories that

I have heard from founders directly or that have become business school and Silicon Valley lore. Rarely, it seems, do companies pivot from failure to success. They don't go from a bad idea to a good idea. Rather, they go from a good idea to a great one.

Even Instagram, one of the most famous pivot stories, wasn't the result of its predecessor, a check-in app called Burbn, failing or being a bad idea. It had a small user base, sure, but its founders had raised $500,000 in venture capital, and the app did have a feature (photos, of course) that everyone liked using. The problem for Kevin Systrom and Mike Krieger was simply that Burbn wasn't good *enough* or growing fast *enough*. And, as Justin.tv experienced with gaming content at almost the exact same moment, people loved a particular feature of the app more than the app itself. That is what inspired their pivot.

Same story with Jane Wurwand and Dermalogica. Her skin care school, the International Dermal Institute, was never failing. "I had full classes with wait lists," Jane said. "People were flying from San Francisco, they were flying from Phoenix, they were coming from Nevada. They were meeting each other, they were rooming together, they were forming friendships." The idea was working. Her problem, as Tristan Walker would say, is that "*you* don't scale." Jane was only one person, and the Dermal Institute was only one location, so the growth potential for the business was inherently limited.

A skin care line, on the other hand, had virtually unlimited potential, because at that time in America, "there was nothing in the salon industry," and everything her students were using when they returned to their salons were products from Europe. That gap in the market — American-made skin care products — was "the big opportunity," Jane said, that triggered an immediate pivot and changed her business virtually overnight.

What makes all of these pivots so impressive to me is that they also represented an evolution in the mind-set of the entrepreneurs who made them. So much of getting to this point has been about doing whatever it takes, often alone, to turn the dream into a reality; it's been about nurturing the seed of the idea in your mind, protecting it from doubters or competitors, in the hope that one day it will blossom into a real business. And what Stacy and Mark, Kevin and Mike, and Jane confronted in their respective pivotal moments was the realization that the work they did to grow their *ideas* was fundamentally *different from* the work they now had to do to grow their *businesses.*

That was the case for Stewart Butterfield in 2012, when he made the excruciating decision to shut down a massively multiplayer online game called Glitch. He'd been developing the game for a few years with the help of venture capital and a team of engineers, designers, and coders — all of which, money and manpower alike, he'd secured on the strength of his reputation as the successful co-founder of the online photo-sharing service Flickr, which had been acquired by Yahoo! in 2005. That was in itself a pivot from Stewart's *first* attempt at designing an online game in 2002 — a never-ending massively multiplayer online game he called . . . wait for it . . . Game Neverending.

As it was for Emmett Shear, gaming was Stewart's true passion, and like Justin.tv in its time, Game Neverending was incredibly innovative for the early days of Web 2.0. Ten years later, Stewart's ambitions for Glitch were the same. "It was completely different than anything that anyone had ever seen before," Stewart said. "It was much more open-ended and cooperative. The look was kind of like Dr. Seuss meets Monty Python meets modern-day graphic novels, where we really tried to encourage individual creativity."

Their encouragement was effective. A population of dedicated gamers — in the thousands, Stewart estimated — loved Glitch right from the beginning, even its earliest iterations in 2009–2010. "We had a bunch of really positive early indications, so we charged people money," he said. "The average person was paying $70 a year."

They also got hundreds of thousands of people to sign up to try the game. This, paradoxically, is where those early positive indications started to tip negative, because a significant portion of the interest in their game was actually just a product of an increased fascination with online games in general. "Simultaneously and totally independent of us, FarmVille and Zynga and all of these casual games became a huge thing," Stewart said. The upside was that online games "became a thing that investors really believed in. It was suddenly worth billions and billions of dollars," which meant that securing VC money was no sweat for the gaming entrepreneur and creator of Flickr. He raised $17.5 million without too much trouble. The downside was that with this surge in interest for online gaming, the *kinds* of games that were finding massive sustained success were much more down the middle than Glitch.

"It was really hard for us to get people even to go through the first few minutes of the game because it was just so different and so weird," Stewart said. "Most people who tried it were like, 'What the hell is this?' and they would leave after three minutes." Their solid sales funnel had turned into what's commonly called a "leaky bucket." And the leaky bucket wasn't working. This is how the funnel was supposed to work: "First people hear about your thing, then they go to the website, then they sign up, then they play the game a little bit. In each of those stages, some people fall out of the process — that's why it's called the funnel — but then some end up paying you."

But with Glitch's leaky bucket, people were falling out of the top of the funnel before they even got close to a place in the process where they could pay if they wanted to. "Not enough of them made it all the way through," Stewart said. "It was always the next thing that was going to fix it — the next game dynamic we added, the next bit of customization. But as we continued to try those things, we never found the magic formula that would make them stick with it."

By 2012, Stewart realized Glitch wasn't going to work. "It was never going to become the kind of business that would justify $17.5 million of venture capital investment," he said pointedly. So one night he drafted a letter to his co-founders and to the Glitch board of directors to inform them of his decision. The next morning he went in to the office and called an all-hands meeting. "Before I could even get the first half of the first sentence out, I was crying," he said. "Almost everyone in the room I had personally convinced they should come work at this company, that they should accept our stock options, that they should believe in the project, that they should believe in me. There was a real sense that I had failed all these people."

Unlike Stacy Madison and Mark Andrus, who read the writing on the wall and made their move before their fate was sealed by the

Dunkin' Donuts and Starbucks of the world; or Jane Wurwand, who saw a gap in the market that she was uniquely suited to move into; or even Kevin Systrom and Mike Krieger, who knew photos were what made Burbn interesting, not the check-in functionality, Stewart Butterfield had no idea what, if anything, he had left to show for himself after he ended Glitch besides millions of frames of game-specific animation and hundreds of hours of original music intended to accompany it. What could he possibly do with any of that stuff?

It took him about a week to figure out what they really had.

"So the interesting thing about Glitch," Stewart said, "was that while it wasn't successful as a business, we were extraordinarily productive because of this system for internal communication that we had developed." This system didn't have a name. They never discussed it as something separate from the communication that occurred on it. "We didn't even think about it as a thing," Stewart said. It was just something they'd built for their own purposes, around the concept of a channel, that was "an inversion of the typical interoffice communication," that gave any employee access to the entire history of the company's workflow-related conversations, regardless of when they joined the company. Something that was not possible with standard email-based communication systems where, when you joined a company, you basically started at in-box zero.

"It was only once we decided to shut down the game that we realized we would never work without a system like this again and thought maybe other people would like it, too," Stewart observed.

This system, or idea, would become Slack, which today is a multibillion-dollar cloud-based collaboration software business. But at the time, it was difficult for Stewart and his team to pitch this concept to prospective enterprise customers because they didn't really understand how this idea was, at its core, an organic pivot. They thought it was just this ancillary thing over to the side, connected to their original business but unrelated to it philosophically. It's understandable. How do you construct a through line between a complicated online game and a piece of enterprise middleware?

The truth was, they didn't need to construct it, because it was already there in the form of the true motivating force behind everything Stewart Butterfield had done, beginning all the way back in 2002, in Vancouver, British Columbia, where he got his start. "There were two massively multiplayer games," Stewart said of Game Neverending and Glitch, "and there was massively multiplayer photo-sharing with Flickr. Slack is just massively multiplayer communications at work."

That was the real seed of the ideas Stewart pursued: massively multiplayer collaborative systems. Every pivot he ever made had that seed at its core. It's also what kept the Glitch founding team together and what eventually drew so many of the employees who faced layoffs at Glitch back into the fold. "I just like making software, and I like doing it with these other people," Stewart said. "They all like making software as well. And the more we worked, the more we realized this all actually totally makes sense."

It takes an immense amount of emotional maturity, no matter how old you are, to recognize that the business you are leading is bigger and more important than the idea (*your* idea!) on which that business was originally built. It takes humility to accept that the idea itself maybe isn't what you thought it was, or that it has evolved gradually, then suddenly, away from what you intended it to become while you were busy managing the business growing on top of it.

And it takes real courage to make that move away from the familiar and toward the new — especially in those instances where your good idea is starting to look not so good, and it doesn't appear as if you have anywhere to go or anything even remotely related to your business to take with you.

PART III

THE DESTINATION

IN MANY WAYS, the scariest part of entrepreneurship is success. It's reaching your destination, your objective. Because that's when the work really starts. When you've got to decide: What now? What next? Do you keep moving and do it again? Do you stick around? Do you build? *What* do you build? How big? With what? And why? Getting here was difficult enough. The anxiety that comes with the responsibility of continued success isn't making things any easier. Why continue to put yourself through all this?

These questions are difficult to answer. And the answers are often hard to get exactly right. Because in the beginning, all you're worried about is trying to survive. You're not aiming for perfection; you're just hoping to avoid pitfalls. You're not thinking about legacy; you're just focused on lasting one more day in your quest across the unknown.

Eventually, though, these questions will become paramount if you want to build a business that stands the test of time. Something more than just a vessel for the idea that drove you in the beginning. Something that reflects your mission and your values, that honors all the work you put in, and that treats the people who helped you get here well.

Figuring out your answers to these questions is also what will make you *feel* successful, no matter what your next move is: whether you stay and build and lead, whether you go, whether you move on and try to repeat your success in another area. If you're not doing it for reasons that are authentically yours, if you've lost sight of what inspired you from those very first days, then the long, arduous entrepreneurial journey you just endured might very well fill you with regret. Like promise unfulfilled.

Forget feeling successful. You can feel like a downright failure when you get to the right place for the wrong reasons, no matter how much money you have. That's because the path to true entrepreneurial success is not strictly about profit; it's also about finding and fulfilling a deeper purpose. That has been the destination all along. Knowing that, and recognizing when you've reached it, is when the rewards truly begin to accrue.

19

It Can't Be All About the Money

O ver the course of little more than a week in March 2008, the fifth-largest investment bank in the United States, Bear Stearns, finally collapsed under the weight of its massive bets on mortgage-backed securities. Six months later, the *fourth-largest* investment bank in the country, Lehman Brothers, filed for bankruptcy for similar reasons. It was a move that is generally understood to be the falling domino that tipped markets officially into recession and the world into financial crisis.

We cannot point to naive imprudence or delusional exuberance as explanations for these collapses in the same way we might for more recent failures like the blood-testing company Theranos or the e-commerce startup Fab. Bear Stearns was not a young, overzealous giant like the modern-day tech unicorns that operate with mantras such as "Move fast and break things." Bear Stearns was founded in 1923. Lehman Brothers had been around in some form for more than 150 years. In many ways, you could argue that they helped finance the building of America into the strongest, wealthiest nation the world has ever known, that there was a real purpose behind the services they offered. During the real estate bubble of the early 2000s, however, both firms struggled in vain to resist the pull of mortgage-backed securities on the secondary market — a market so choked with greed that commentators in the aftermath of the subprime mortgage crisis took to calling it a casino because they could find no other purpose for it. The participants acted more like gamblers than investors or money managers — taking bigger risks in search of bigger paydays, regardless of what it took to place those bets, which in this case meant getting lenders to increase the number of mortgages they granted to increasingly uncreditworthy borrowers, just so they had more chips to play with.

Between them, Bear Stearns and Lehman Brothers had survived the American Civil War, the Great Depression, both World Wars, and dozens of financial panics. They had helped hundreds of companies and made thousands of millionaires. Yet neither of these venerable firms, in the end, could survive their own greed.

The Beatles told us that money can't buy you love. Rousseau taught us that money doesn't buy you happiness. The Bible warns us that the love of money is the root of all evil. And these casualties of the subprime mortgage crisis showed us that money can't be the primary motivating force behind our businesses.

A company that is successful and resilient and that acts as a force for good in the world long after you're gone has a larger purpose — *a mission* — at its center. One that you, as founder, are responsible for identifying and articulating from the very beginning, then guarding during times of plenty and leaning on during times of difficulty.

Founders who approach their businesses with a "mission first" focus tend to be better equipped to handle the lure of unrestrained and manic growth that has damaged or even sunk so many companies with early potential. But having a defined mission is even more valuable when money is scarce or growth is anemic — especially for younger companies — because it gives them a reason to keep on fighting. In contrast, if they are operating with a "money first" mind-set, money's absence makes it so much easier to abandon what they're doing and to pivot before they should, to give up on their original idea at the first sign of trouble, or to just plain old quit.

Jenn Hyman didn't endure the sexism, chauvinism, and outright harassment she experienced at the hands of male venture capitalists because she wanted to get rich with Rent the Runway. She is double Harvard (undergraduate and business school). When she was a twenty-two-year-old junior analyst at Starwood Hotels and Resorts right out of college, she came up with the idea for a honeymoon registry that the company still uses and has even expanded. She was the director of business development at the IMG talent management agency. She is a superstar. If all she wanted was to be a millionaire, there would have been a hundred easier ways for her to get there than by going through a gauntlet of forty-to-fifty-year-old rich men who didn't understand women's fashion, women's relationship to their wardrobes, or women, period. Jenn could have easily quit when she hit that withering wall of condescension. She could have agreed with whatever each venture capitalist told her that her business should be if she thought it would get her the money she was trying to raise.

But that's not why Jenn Hyman was in those rooms. She was there for a purpose, *with* a purpose. "Clothes make you feel a certain way about yourself," she said in explaining what drives this idea. "You put on an amazing outfit in the morning, and it makes you feel powerful or beautiful or sexy or relaxed or however you want to feel that day, and your entire day can change." She'd felt that transformative effect from her own experience, but she saw it again and again in women during a number of pop-up shops she and her co-founder, Jennifer Fleiss, put on to test their assumptions and to see how the model for Rent the Runway would work in real time.

"I saw the emotional effect that wearing something that made these women feel self-confident had on their demeanor, on their body language, and on how they felt about themselves," Jenn said. "In the pop-up, I saw girls stripping down, trying on these amazing dresses, and feeling beautiful. They walked with a new sense of confidence, and I really thought this could be a business that isn't just about offering women a rational or smart choice, but it also can be a business that delivers something emotional, making women feel beautiful every single day."

That's the *mission* of Rent the Runway. Knowing that what she and Jennifer were trying to build — a company that made women just like them feel strong and empowered and beautiful — gave her the drive and the will to fight through the indignities of all those investor pitch meetings and to actually reach out to some of those VCs and invite them to pop-ups so they could understand for themselves what she already knew. And they did. Jenn sold more than a couple VCs not just on the business model but also on the business's larger mission.

More than just stoking the flames of a fighting spirit when things aren't going your way, the mission is what gives your business, and you, direction. It helps you identify opportunities. It helps you categorize and prioritize the field of choices in any situation, from those that advance the interests of the business to those that subvert it or hold it back. This is perhaps the most important thing that a mission does for a young company, because with everything swirling around you — whether it's product development, funding, hiring, or marketing — it's very easy to lose your sense of direction both individually as a founder and collectively as the business. Once you lose your sense of direction, the chances of keeping hold of any sense of mission become slim. After all, if you don't know where you're going, it's hard to know why you're going there.

In 2019, I was invited to speak to the folks at Drinkworks, a joint venture between Keurig Dr Pepper and Anheuser-Busch based in the Boston area. They make a machine that is, functionally speaking, a Keurig for cocktails. If you want a Moscow Mule, for example, the machine tells you what size glass to use and how much ice to put in the glass. Then you pop in the pod, fill the reservoir with water, press the button, and out comes a perfectly mixed Moscow Mule at the perfect temperature. It really is a very slick piece of engineering.

When I met the team, they were in the early stages of navigating the crucible of growth. They had all their patents filed, they had a full product line, and they'd built a ton of buzz. Their demo video went viral, they got a billion impressions of earned media, they were on the *Today* show, and Jimmy Fallon talked about them on *The Tonight Show*. But they were struggling to get real traction in the marketplace, because spirits are such a highly regulated industry with rules that change from state to state, and at the time you could buy their machine only if you lived in Florida or Missouri. Everyone had heard about this thing they were working on, but nobody could buy one, not even people in the state where their company was based. That is not a great place to be as a new company. It can start to feel pretty hopeless as regulatory red tape continues to suffocate your potential.

So at the end of my talk to the assembled Drinkworkers, I said, "Let me ask you all a question: What is your mission? When you come in to the office every morning, what are you trying to do?"

The first person to speak up said that their mission was to work as a team and to make the best quality product they could.

The next person said that they were very mission-oriented and that they were all there to make the best beverage maker in the world, one that would add value to the consumer.

Neither response got the blood flowing, either for me or for their co-workers. I received no follow-on responses. Nobody piggybacked on their answers. The energy in the room just sort of flattened.

I said, "Okay, what about this: Our mission is to create a product that facilitates gatherings. A product that makes it easy to throw a party, to create community in your own kitchen, in your own living room. Whether you're a two-income household out in suburbia or you're young and live in the city and you don't have space for a traditional bar setup. Drinkworks is for your home, what the water cooler is for your office — the gathering place around which conversations are held, connections are made, and community is built. Oh, and it also makes perfect cocktails."

Now, you might think that sounds like a bunch of branding nonsense. And, admittedly, some of it I did pull out of thin air as I was talking. But a lot of it was stuff I arrived at days before, as I prepared to speak to the team. Sure, they make a machine that makes cocktails. Simple enough. But *why* they make that machine is different from *what* they make. The same way that renting designer fashion is *what* Jenn Hyman does at Rent the Runway, but the *why* of it is because she wants to empower her customers to feel strong and beautiful.

So what does Drinkworks really do? And why? Those were the

questions I tried to answer for myself, and they were at the heart of the question I posed to them about their mission. The intention being that they needed to arrive at an answer that would offer them constant direction as they navigate the byzantine bureaucracies of individual state governments that stand between their product and full market penetration.

Andy Puddicombe, a former Buddhist monk from the southwest of England, had the opposite of the Drinkworks problem. Where Drinkworks had its product figured out but struggled with where to go with it, Andy's mission — to demystify meditation and make it accessible to as many people as possible — never changed. From the moment he turned in his robes in 2004, after an unlikely and unexpected stint teaching meditation in Moscow, he knew exactly where he was going. He just didn't know that it would take him eight years and multiple twists and turns to get there with the creation of the popular meditation app Headspace.

The mission behind Headspace took its earliest shape during Andy's Moscow years, while he waited for a spot to open up in a four-year meditation retreat at a monastery in Scotland. "I wanted to make a long-term commitment to better understanding my mind," Andy said, but in the meantime he found himself in this whole different experience, learning what it meant to teach meditation.

In the beginning, Andy's approach was very by the book. "I was teaching in a very orthodox way," he said. "But the more I got to know people who would come to these sessions we'd have at the center, we'd have more informal conversations about what was going on in their lives." During these conversations, Andy would break from the traditional, accepted methodologies, of which he was originally very protective, in order to help people understand the teachings. He would tell his students how he thought about these lessons and how he tried to apply them to his own life. "There's so much emphasis on protecting the teachings and not projecting your own stuff onto them," Andy explained, "but I found more often than not that this resonated with people far more than the traditional methods."

It was this demonstrable gap in effectiveness between his casual layman's explanations and the authentic traditions Andy represented as a monk that inspired him to hand back his robes after a decade of dedicated training — to give up the monk's life and return home to the United Kingdom. "I was finding a way of talking about meditation that I had never experienced myself but that seemed to really resonate with people," Andy said, "and that's what got me thinking about this whole idea of demystifying meditation and trying to make it more accessible."

The first step on the journey once he was back in the United Kingdom was to figure out the *how* and the *why* of this whole experience and then to find a place where he could teach clients one-on-one, much the way he did with those first students at the meditation center in Moscow. "Every available moment, I was up writing content and trying to work out what is this thing that I want to do," he said.

It wasn't easy. Andy still had an affinity for, and a deep connection to, the tradition to which he'd given the first decade of his adult life. He wasn't just going to disregard everything because he had left the order. But even the things he knew would work, like the Tibetans' use of storytelling and metaphor, he would have to tweak. The question was, how? The answer, of course, was in the mission: whatever would demystify the teaching and make it more accessible.

The goal, he said, "was to give people just enough to be inspired or to get excited to try meditation, because a lot of people had heard about and read about it, but it's only really in the experience of it that you can get them to make that leap in terms of actually getting the benefit." So he started to use a lot more storytelling in his practice. He took a lot of metaphors and analogies from the Tibetan tradition, but he changed them just enough to make them "more approachable and accessible."

All of this he fine-tuned in his first teaching space, a clinic room in a London integrative health center run by a doctor who had heard a lot of good things about "mindfulness" — the catchall Western term for Eastern meditation techniques — and was "very interested in how it could complement some of the other things at the clinic," Andy said. Starting there, in a clinic in London's financial district, was a very intentional choice on Andy's part. If he was going to be successful in demystifying meditation, not only did the teachings have to feel accessible to students, but the place where they learned them had to feel accessible as well. "I deliberately chose that clinic because I didn't want [the place] to sit in the spaces where people traditionally see meditation," he said. "I didn't want it to be in an alternative health clinic or something like that. I wanted it to feel mainstream."

Before too long, Andy was seeing six to ten people every day, all with very mainstream problems. "They were struggling with depression, anxiety, insomnia, stress, migraines — many of the things that we all suffer with now in a life of just sheer overload," he said. He'd see each person for an hour a week for ten weeks, gradually developing in the process a ten-week-long modular course from which everyone can benefit. And by "everyone," I mean *everyone,* because "everything you hear in the Headspace app now is built on the content and the language that was developed during that time," Andy explained. "It was a really important training ground in terms of understanding what worked and what didn't, what language connected and what didn't."

But before he got to the Headspace app — which, by mid-2018, had more than 30 million users and a million paying subscribers — Andy first had to figure out how to move beyond the one-on-one clinic experience. Not to make more money, though he certainly could have used it, but to reach more people more quickly. "I wanted to get meditation out. I wanted to get more people meditating. I just didn't know how to do it outside of the clinic," he said.

Andy did a few workshops here and there on weekends, but that was as far as he'd gotten when, in early 2009, he was introduced by a mutual acquaintance to his eventual Headspace co-founder, a young former advertising executive named Rich Pierson, who had burned out from the booze-soaked, hard-living ad agency world and was learning acupuncture to combat his mounting anxiety in the very same clinic where Andy was working. Rich needed more help with his anxiety if he was going to make the transition out of advertising into sobriety and more purposeful living. Andy needed help branding and building beyond the clinic if it was ever going to fulfill his larger mission.

"I could see that it was working for people, even people who previously wouldn't have looked at meditation and gained benefit from it," Andy said. "But it was still one-to-one in the clinic. And I just didn't know: Do I start trying to train other people to teach meditation? Do I try and take this into workplaces? I had no idea, no business experience. And I just thought that Rich could help take this idea outside of the clinic and beyond."

Rich agreed to help. Andy agreed to put Rich through his meditation course. It was an ideal fit. And in 2010, after several months kicking around ideas, they formed Headspace. Not as an app mind you, but as a live events company that put on meditation workshops all over the United Kingdom.

It wasn't a great business to start, as you might imagine. Unless you're Oprah Winfrey or Dave Ramsey, live event workshops are a tough business and tough to scale. There is only one Andy Puddicombe, after all. And there were only so many workshops he could do in one day — not that they didn't try to push the limits on that number. But what was more important was that they were on track. They were executing Andy's mission. They were putting more and more people, in greater and greater concentrations, through the meditation lessons he'd developed over the previous years. And eventually, in 2012, it only made sense for them to turn his ten weeks of well-tested content into a 365-day meditation program that could live digitally online and be accessible to literally billions of people, all at once right there on their phones, at the press of a button.

Knowing where they'd been and in what direction they wanted to go with meditation, Andy Puddicombe and Rich Pierson knew that an app was the only logical way they were going to get there. The essence of the deeper purpose that was driving them had foreclosed other, possibly shinier, options.

That is how powerful having a larger mission can be for a founder and their business. A mission guided a former monk — a man who had given away all his worldly possessions and forsworn money for most of his adult life — all the way up to the summit of modern entrepreneurial achievement, along the only traversable path that would protect him from the pull of easy paydays, insulate him from the invidiousness of skeptical investors, and not just allow him to keep his principles but make them an essential part of his climb.

20

Build a Culture, Not a Cult

There has been a famous document floating around the internet since 2009 known in Silicon Valley as the "culture deck." It's made up of approximately 130 PowerPoint slides, compiled over a ten-year period by the serial entrepreneur Reed Hastings as he and his team went about building a little company called Netflix. The document began as an internal training tool. Hastings and his managers would take new hires through it as they were being onboarded, during the period just after Netflix went public and started to turn a profit, and its leaders were starting to focus more intently on "what we wanted to be, how we wanted to operate," Hastings has said.

Reaction to the deck in those first years was mixed. Some new employees loved it; others were scared to death of it for reasons that were wholly their own. What was clear to Hastings, though, was that the deck could be more than a training document; it could be a recruiting and vetting tool as well. "We realized we should give it to every candidate," Hastings told the other famous Reid in Silicon Valley (Hoffman) on his podcast, *Masters of Scale,* in 2017. Two years earlier, in 2015, Hastings said, "We wanted to make sure everyone who applied really got it." They did this by posting the presentation on SlideShare back in 2009, which is how it began to ricochet around the internet like a Super Ball shot out of a T-shirt cannon, and the results were profound.

By defining exactly who they were, what they believed, and how they would operate, and then putting it down on paper and out into the world, Netflix not only screened out suboptimal job candidates before they even applied, but they also got "many people becoming candidates that might not have otherwise thought about Netflix." In a predatory hiring environment like Silicon Valley in the late 2000s and early 2010s, selecting for culture became a competitive advantage. It helped Netflix grow into a $150 billion media company that has some of the highest employee compensation numbers and lowest turnover rates in the valley and, in less than twenty years, has disrupted the film and television industries in ways not seen since the introduction of sound and color.

This "culture first" approach didn't come naturally to Reed Hastings. At his first company, Pure Software, he did things another way — which is to say, "me first." Not that he was selfish; just the opposite was true. He did everything, or at least he *tried* to do everything, himself. "I thought if I could just do more sales calls, more travel, write more code, do more interviews, that somehow it would work out better," he said. In his mind, if there was a problem to be solved or a bug in the code to be fixed, as the founder and CEO of the company, which was his brainchild, he was the obvious and best choice for doing what needed to get done. Eventually, wearing all those hats got to be too much. "I was coding all night, trying to be CEO in the day, and once in a while, I'd squeeze in a shower," he said. It wasn't working. Hastings had to figure out a better way.

This is when he made the mistake from which the culture deck would eventually be born. Now whenever they had a problem at Pure Software, instead of trying to fix it himself, he tried to implement a process that would prevent the problem from ever happening again. In an interview with Chris Anderson at the TED Conference in 2018,* he called it a "very semiconductor yield orientation," which is

---

* I was fortunate enough to be in the audience for this interview. It was a fascinating conversation.

about as far as he could get from "culture first" without actually trying. The real problem, Hastings said to Anderson, "was that we were trying to dummy-proof the system, and then eventually only dummies wanted to work there. Then, of course, the market shifted, and the company was unable to adapt."

Pure Software was eventually acquired by its largest competitor, and Reed Hastings used the financial windfall from that sale to co-found Netflix, where he made sure not to repeat his process-obsessed, founder-centric mistakes. He was fortunate. Many founders have not been so lucky. Any successful founder will tell you that the impulse to do everything yourself, to believe that only you know best and then to build processes that reflect that belief, is endemic to entrepreneurship and has the potential to be incredibly destructive. When the processes don't work and your conclusions continually prove wrong, your assumption is that if you just take on a little more and work a little harder, everything will be fine. But that approach can wear you down physically and mentally. Plus, as Reid Hoffman put it in his episode with Hastings, "more work is never the real answer. To succeed as you scale, you have to leverage every person in the organization. And to do that, you have to be very intentional about how you craft the culture." This may sound like common sense — because it is! — but I've been surprised at how often entrepreneurs I've encountered make the mistake of trying to do everything themselves as the company begins to grow. What happens in the end is that everything about the business starts to be about the founder rather than the business.

This is one of the hardest traps for even the most well-intentioned entrepreneur to avoid, let alone spot. For the longest time in the beginning, it can feel like it's just you and your idea. The seed gets planted in your mind; you water it with inspiration until it germinates into an idea; you feed it with research until it pokes up through the soil and sees the light of day as a product, which is when it first finds the warmth of attention from an audience; and then, if you're lucky, it starts to blossom into a full-fledged business.

Getting to that point is an all-consuming process. It takes all your time, energy, and focus. It's all you think about, and after a while the line between you and your idea can start to blur. It becomes difficult to know where you end and the company begins. It becomes *impossible,* especially in the leaner, trying times, to fathom that anyone could understand the business or its problems in the way that you can. So when someone on your team levels the charge that you're making everything about yourself, it almost doesn't compute. Everything you do, you do for the business. You've given everything you have to it. If you could give more, you would. But when you and the business are indistinguishable, when you've allowed your identity to merge with the company's, how does it *not* appear to be the case, from the outside at least, that your singular focus on the business is also a singular focus on yourself?

It turns out there is a name for founders who fall into this trap. They're called "monarch CEOs," according to Professor Jeffrey Sonnenfeld, who studies CEOs at the Yale School of Management. "Their business is defined around them and their life is defined around the business," he told the *Washington Post.* The most notorious of these figures in recent years was Dov Charney, the controversial founder of the now-defunct clothing retailer American Apparel.

American Apparel was a juggernaut in the clothing business and in the culture during the first decade of the twenty-first century. Their advertisements were edgy and sexually provocative. Their retail stores were on the best streets in all the right cities. They manufactured their clothes out of a large, old factory building in downtown Los Angeles. Their clothes were everywhere and on everyone the entire decade. I still own a couple American Apparel T-shirts and hoodies that I wear in regular rotation.

American Apparel's rise from a domestic clothing manufacturer and wholesaler into an international retail brand was as fast as its fall. They moved into their famous downtown LA factory in 2000. By 2005, they were one of the fastest-growing companies in America. By 2011, the company had more than 250 stores with revenue well north of $500 million. And then, by 2014, amidst a tangle of sexual harassment lawsuits and bad financial deals, Dov was kicked off the board of the company he founded. By 2015, American Apparel was in Chapter 11 bankruptcy. By 2017, the company as Dov Charney knew it was gone: all ties to the founder severed; its intellectual property sold at auction to a competitor, Gildan Activewear, for less than $100 million; its retail stores shuttered.

It's a sad, cautionary tale. Dov Charney was American Apparel. American Apparel was Dov Charney. And that was the whole problem. Everyone saw it. The *New York Times* said, "Charney himself had no other interests outside his company. He viewed himself as indispensable." The *Financial Times* said, "It is almost as if Mr Charney believes that the scandalous behaviour he has so often been accused of is inextricably tied up with the image of his often lauded but deeply unconventional fashion label." It's a sentiment Charney would not reject. He told the *Financial Times* reporter, "I am a deep part of the brand."

The depth of their synchronicity is where the trouble for American Apparel started. At various points well into the history of the company, Charney was the CEO, the designer, the main photographer, the male fit model, a centerpiece of their advertising, and their biggest liability. Not just legally either. As often happens when a founder loses themselves inside their business, he became a control freak. He had store managers calling him directly. He famously moved into a warehouse that was having some problems and had a shower installed so he could live there twenty-four hours a day monitoring the work. Once, when there was a traffic jam in the parking lot of American Apparel's LA headquarters, Charney went downstairs and personally directed traffic until it cleared.

These might be humble, romantic gestures of a leader willing to do whatever it takes if they weren't actually a reflection of a founder who had turned into a relentless micromanager as the company grew. "A lot of founders have difficulty making this transition," said Professor Sydney Finkelstein of the Tuck School of Business at Dartmouth in the wake of Charney's ouster from the board. "When you're a smaller company, micromanagement is not necessarily a terrible thing. It's when you cross the line and you have to grow, you've got to have management talent around you."

American Apparel didn't have management talent. Or when they did, it didn't last long. Finkelstein called the place a "revolving door."

Executives at the company described Charney to the *New York Times* as "relentlessly controlling." In the same article, industry analysts commented that American Apparel had "developed a reputation as a place where talented people did not want to work," to the point where the ensuing brain drain created a power vacuum inside upper management.

Upper management—or in the early growth days, the founding team—is critical to the long-term success of a business because that is how the roots of a company's culture grow and spread. This is something that Reed Hastings began to understand deeply with Netflix around the same time that Dov Charney was turning inward and going the other way. While the culture is certainly a reflection of the founder in the beginning, Hastings would admit to venture capitalist John Doerr in an interview at a Kleiner Perkins Caufield & Byers CEO Workshop in 2015, "If the cultural roots are strong, then new leadership is developed in that model, and will often continue the culture." If the roots are unstable, however, and the leadership is constantly changing, the culture will be, too. By consistently firing or driving away talented leaders, Charney managed to yank out by the roots whatever culture there was to speak of at American Apparel, and in filling the vacuum with himself, the culture of American Apparel became the Cult of Dov. As Dov imploded, so did American Apparel.

Which brings me back to Reid Hoffman's point about succeeding at scale. As a founder, you have to be very intentional and deliberate about how you create the culture of the company. It starts and ends, I have come to understand, with shared values.

Brian Scudamore, the founder of 1-800-GOT-JUNK?, figured this out about five years into his junk removal business when it was doing about $500,000 in annual revenue (and growing), with five trucks and eleven employees. His epiphany seems pretty benign. "I realized I wasn't having fun any longer," he said, to the point that "I was avoiding spending time with my employees." There are worse things in the world than a CEO who doesn't want to hang out with the crew after work, but this was more than that. "I just had the wrong people," he said. "I realized that one bad apple spoils the whole bunch, and nine of my eleven staff were bad apples." He didn't mean they were bad *people,* just bad for the company and the culture he was trying to build. "They didn't see what I saw," Brian said. "They were hauling away the junk, taking it to the dump, but they didn't have that sense of allowing the customer to feel a sense of relief that their junk is gone and they've got their space back."

This was Brian's vision for the company and the values he was trying to build into its culture. The business was supposed to be a caring, affirming pursuit. They were unburdening their customers, liberating them from old baggage that had been weighing them down and closing in around them, sometimes for years. They were adding to their customers' lives by subtracting from their accumulated possessions. There was an emotional, psychological component to what they were doing at 1-800-GOT-JUNK?.

But Brian's first employees didn't see that. They were just tossing out garbage, so they felt and acted like garbagemen. They weren't aligned with Brian's vision, so he fired them. *All of them.* In one sitting. And he took full responsibility for it. "As their leader I said, 'Hey I've let you guys down and I'm sorry, but this isn't going to work out.'"

The irony, of course, was that at least for the time being, Brian now had to do all the work himself. "I went from five trucks down to the ability to only run one at a time," he said. "I was the call center. I did the booking, the dispatch, the junk hauling. I did everything." He had to go backward, to that familiar Swiss Army knife phase of entrepreneurship, in order to move forward in the right direction and to lay down the roots of a culture that, twenty-five years later, is responsible for $250 million in annual revenue across hundreds of franchises in every major metropolitan area in Canada, Australia, and the United States. "When you build a company, it's all about people," Brian said. "Find the right people and treat them right."

How do you do that? You start by looking for people who share your values. That's how Alice Waters built Chez Panisse, perhaps the most important restaurant in modern American gastronomy. Opened in Berkeley, California, in 1971, in an old arts and crafts house that used to be a plumber's shop just south of the UC Berkeley campus, Chez Panisse became the birthplace of California cuisine. It was the beginning of what today we call farm-to-table cuisine. Alice's singular focus on ingredients rather than technique changed the way cooks approached food and restaurant patrons approached dining. Not surprisingly, this wasn't Alice's goal for Chez Panisse. She only wanted to replicate what she'd been doing in her home and the homes of her friends — creating a space where people could gather and talk, and where they could eat very simple, very delicious food.

In the late 1960s and early 1970s, when the idea for Chez Panisse was taking shape, these notions could not have been any more countercultural. This was the golden age of canned foods and ready-to-eat meals. Fast-food franchises were popping up everywhere. Two years after Chez Panisse opened, Swanson would launch its Hungry-Man dinners. By 1975, there would be 1 million microwaves in American homes. When Alice spoke to people about her idea, the possibility that they would come out, in 1971, and actually *pay* for simply prepared French-inspired dishes such as pâté en croûte, duck with olives, and apple tart (the first night's menu) was insane. Even more nuts was that Alice and her partners, they didn't want your money!

"I would have been ashamed if I had been looking to make money," Alice told me. "Nobody who was involved with this project expected to make money. We hoped to. But we didn't expect it. And we almost didn't want it. This was a labor of love."

That's what you need from the people around you when you're growing a business of any kind. "Everybody who worked at Chez Panisse was passionate about the same idea," Alice said. It's how she hired, and why she employed so many of her friends in the beginning. "Because when you're working in a business fifteen hours a day, you want to be with people you like and with whom you share values."

That shared sense of purpose and values, more so than money or profitability, is also what explains the longevity of Chez Panisse — it's still open today — in an industry where the average life span of an independent restaurant is five years, and 90 percent of them close in the first year. Alice isn't trying to become a billionaire. She isn't trying to create Alice, Inc., and franchise her name and face all over the globe. She doesn't own any other restaurants. "I couldn't ever imagine flying around the world to visit my restaurants," she told me. Her goals, like her food, are much simpler.

"I've always wanted a place that I wanted to be in and that was constantly growing and changing," Alice said of her decision not to franchise, but rather to keep Chez Panisse as a single restaurant, to expand its influence in other ways. "And that happened when different people brought ideas into the restaurant. That's why I really feel like it's important that you find people who share your values. When they do, they're the ones who breathe life into the business."

That's the whole purpose of the Netflix culture deck, when you think about it. Netflix wants to find people who believe in the ideas expressed on those 130 plainly designed presentation slides, who share the same values as people, as an organization, as a culture. They want the next generation of leaders who can extend what Reed Hastings and his co-founder Marc Randolph launched in the spring of 1998 far into the future.

It's a simple notion — to create a lasting culture by building a business with a shared set of values — but it is one plenty of founders struggle with, because they allow themselves to get buried in the minutiae of the day-to-day. Or they lose themselves inside the business entirely. Or, worse, they come to believe that only they know what the company needs (which is usually just more of them). Whereas Reed Hastings published a training tool to share with the world and now aspires to go entire quarters without making a single decision, far too many founders are tempted to go the Dov Charney route: have a shower built in the warehouse and sleep with a walkie-talkie on your chest — if you sleep at all. The scary part is that when you're in the thick of things, it is much easier to become a Dov Charney than a Reed Hastings.

At the very end of my interview with Tristan Walker in Washington, DC, in 2019, I asked him what the one thing was he wished he knew fifteen years earlier that he knows now. His answer was simple and clear: "Know your values." But don't just know them, *write them down.* That's what he did, three weeks before raising the first round of funding that turned his idea for a shaving solution for men of color into a multimillion-dollar business with his name on the door — Walker & Company.

There were six of them: courage, inspiration, respect, judgment, wellness, and loyalty. What makes this list remarkable isn't that he could rattle off the values like the names of his children; it is that they existed so clearly in the mind of a thirty-six-year-old who, for most of his life, had the singular goal of becoming wealthy. Growing up in Queens, then earning a scholarship to the Hotchkiss School, one of the most prestigious boarding schools in America, Tristan saw every day the difference between being rich and being wealthy. He witnessed the doors that true wealth could open, and he wanted that for himself and for his family. From the moment he graduated high school, that goal drove every decision he made: what he majored in at college (economics), where he went to graduate school (Stanford business), where he interned (Twitter), and what companies he worked for after he graduated into the real world (Foursquare and Andreessen Horowitz).

If he hadn't been careful, Tristan could have very easily found himself on a self-absorbed Dov Charney–style trajectory. Instead, he found a problem to solve "for people who looked like me," as he put it. He developed a set of solutions that could become a business that employed a lot of people, if he just cultivated the seed of the idea and tended to the soil with enough care to make sure the idea blossomed and flourished. Almost immediately, Tristan's goals changed. Instead of being singular and self-focused, they were multiple and communal. He recognized that for a business to last 100 years, which was one of his new goals, it can't be about you, because "*you* don't scale." Only your idea, and your story, and your values do. As long as you know them and share them.

"Knowing your values gets you on the same page with your employees. They get you on the same page in this noisy world with your consumers, but more importantly they give you your purpose," Tristan said. "Without knowing your values, you're going to make decisions that are inconsistent, and you have to have consistency to inspire your sanity."

I would argue that you also need consistency to inspire your people. And there is nothing more consistent than a set of clear values written down on the page for everyone to see. Just ask Reed Hastings — or, better yet, ask his 7,000 employees.

21

Think Small to Get Big

When we moved our family from Washington, DC, to the Bay Area, one of the first things we did was to take the ferry from Jack London Square in Oakland across the bay to San Francisco and spend the day walking around. My boys wanted to do the typical San Francisco stuff — watch the sea lions at Fisherman's Wharf, ride a cable car down Powell Street, visit Alcatraz — but as we disembarked at the iconic Ferry Building, walked out onto the Embarcadero, and looked up Market Street toward downtown, I was taken by a view of the city I'd never seen before as a visitor when I'd come in from the airport or across the Bay Bridge.

To one side was the San Francisco we know from movies: the two identical beige buildings of One Market Plaza; the Transamerica Pyramid; the four towers of the Embarcadero Center, which look like Earth reached up to give the sign of the horns using buildings instead of fingers.

To the other side was a patchwork of construction cranes and glass towers, alternately suspended in the sky and rising up from the ground like so many stalactites and stalagmites. A number of the buildings were residential condo complexes, but they were anchored by a sixty-one-story bullet-shaped building reminiscent in both shape and visually transformative effect of London's Gherkin. It's called the Salesforce Tower, so named for the massive cloud-based software company that occupies it and a number of other smaller buildings on Mission Street.

I was looking at a view of a city in flux. A city undergoing a historic seismic shift, the fault lines of which ran in parallel right down Mission and Market Streets. To the south were the headquarters of many of the tech companies that hit the mother lode during the internet gold rush of the early 2000s and became the dominant forces in their respective spaces: Salesforce, Twitter, Instacart, Airbnb, Pinterest, Zynga, Trulia, DocuSign, Lyft, Uber. To the north were landmarks to the legacy companies that actually built the city — Ghirardelli Chocolate, Wells Fargo, Levi Strauss — and got their start during the *actual* gold rush in the late 1840s and 1850s, striking it rich not by mining for gold, but by operating on the periphery servicing the interests of those who did.

Domingo Ghirardelli immigrated to California from Italy in 1849 after hearing about the discovery of gold at Sutter's Mill. He tried his hand at mining, like just about everyone who came to California those first years, and he failed rather miserably, also like most of them. With mercantile roots, he gave up his fantasy of finding gold and decided instead to open a store selling mining supplies and sweets in Stockton, a town at the midpoint on the road from San Francisco to the nearest mining claims in the Sierra foothills. Over the next few years, as that store flourished, he opened a second one in San Francisco, then a hotel, and when that burned down in 1851, he built a stand-alone confectionery that would become the Ghirardelli Chocolate Company.

In 1852, as San Francisco began to explode with growth, Henry Wells and William Fargo came out from New York to form Wells, Fargo & Co. to service the banking needs of miners and merchants alike. They opened locations all over gold country within a couple years. Their focus on keeping money in the region and serving local clients, rather than sending deposits back east to New York as was the habit of many banking interests, not only earned them loyalty and a reputation for dependability, but it also helped them survive the panic of 1855, which wiped out virtually all of their competition.

By hyper-focusing on San Francisco, on the miners and merchants who were building it up, Wells, Fargo became the only game in town for a while, which allowed them to consolidate even more control of the local banking business and then expand rapidly outward into other areas from there.

Levi Strauss took a page out of both the Ghirardelli and Wells, Fargo playbooks and moved to San Francisco from New York in 1853 to open a store selling dry goods to prospectors and the burgeoning local population. Quickly he began wholesaling to other stores in the area — dry goods, fabric, mining supplies — before finally getting into what we now call blue jeans in the early 1870s. That occurred when a tailor in Reno, Nevada, bought some of his denim, figured out a way to fashion it into more durable pants by using metal rivets on the pockets and the zipper, and then asked Strauss to front the money to file patents on the new design, making them partners and eventually multimillionaires.

It has struck me on more than a few occasions when talking to founders that taking Levi's route through a gold rush is far cheaper, much less risky, and potentially just as profitable as going all in to mine for the mother lode itself — or to chase a unicorn, in the language of modern-day entrepreneurship. Just think about the hundreds of millions of venture dollars required to launch the handful of tech companies lining Mission Street, filling the office space south of Market. Uber alone has raised $20 billion in the ten years since its founding, and yet for every Uber, there are a hundred Uber competitors or "Uber for _____" companies that never made it. The possibility of succeeding in that kind of capital-intensive, winner-take-all environment has always been much lower than in finding a small niche related but adjacent to a massive boom and building a business there.

That was certainly the conclusion Chet Pipkin, the founder of the consumer electronics maker Belkin International, arrived at in the early 1980s when he was a young student at UCLA. It was the beginning of the very first tech gold rush — the personal computing revolution — and Chet was learning everything he could about computers in search of a good business idea. He thought about becoming a

PC maker for a minute, though that was "pretty quickly dismissed," he said, because "the amount of capital it would have taken would have been more than I could have imagined, and there seemed to be a lot of people going after that space."

By 1982, there were already a half dozen PC manufacturers with a machine on the market, including IBM and Commodore. By 1984, there would be four more, including Apple. That's a lot of big-time competition for a twenty-two-year-old living at home with his parents in South Los Angeles. And IBM wasn't just a computer maker; they had built and programmed the computing engine behind much of the Apollo moon landing mission thirteen years earlier. The Commodore 64 had the best graphics and sound that anyone had ever seen or heard to that point. And, well, we all know what would become of Apple. This was not a business you could just dip your toe into and not expect to lose your shirt.

That was not of much concern to Chet, however, because one of his earliest realizations, as he worked to understand the nascent personal computing industry, was that there would be gaps in the marketplace that someone like him could fill. "It's inevitable," he thought, "that there were going to be things to do that people were not thinking about. I didn't know exactly what those were, but I knew that was the kind of thing I was looking for."

He found his niche by immersing himself in the scene and hanging out at local computer stores. "I just watched," he remembered, "and one of the things that was impossible to miss, almost from day one, was folks who would buy a PC and a printer and then they would say, 'Well, how do I make this work?'"

Today, that question feels like an anachronism. If you have a computer and a printer that are reasonably new, you plug them in and turn them on, and they find each other over Wi-Fi and connect. Things could not have been more different in 1982. "Computers were being made by all these different manufacturers," Chet explained. "They had different connectors on them; the printers had different connectors on them. It was an absolute nightmare for folks who were just trying to get this stuff to work for them."

It was like the early days of the railroad in Great Britain and the

United States, when train tracks were of different widths in different parts of the country and railcars had different linkage mechanisms depending on who manufactured and who owned the cars. For the entire giant network to function and reach its vast economic potential, all those systems had to be either standardized or made compatible, which is eventually what the railroad companies did. They agreed on a standard set of railway gauges and widths, then started deploying a set of coupling mechanisms to more easily join their railcars, based on the 1873 design of an enterprising American inventor named Eli Janney.

The opportunity Chet Pipkin saw when he watched customers struggle to make their machines connect was the chance to be the Eli Janney of personal computing. "There was no missing that the big void here was providing an elegant tool to make this stuff work together the way that it should," he said. It was an opportunity that, in his words, "looked even more compelling and more exciting than making the hardware."

So that is the path Chet took. With the help of his brother and his father, who was a great toolmaker, he pulled together a makeshift workbench in his parents' garage using a four-by-eight-foot piece of plywood and a laminate overlay, then set to frankensteining a bunch of wires and prefabricated connectors into cables that allowed the first generation of PCs to work with the first generation of printers.

They weren't pretty, by Chet's own admission, but they functioned, and they very quickly found customers, even if he had to go out and hustle to find buyers in the beginning. Eventually, though, customers started finding him. When he ran Belkin's first ad in *Computer Dealer* magazine, they got an order from the student store at Carnegie Mellon University for 100 cables that went from the parallel port on an IBM PC to an Epson printer.

"It was one of our biggest orders ever," Chet said of their early progress in 1982, at which point the only constraint on their success, as far as he was concerned, was their ability to make cables quickly enough. Chet solved that problem by hiring a couple *dozen* people, who helped him grow sales to $180,000 by the end of 1983, Belkin's first full year in business.

That kind of early, explosive success from a small group working out of a garage in a young industry that shows tremendous growth potential is not to be dismissed. Which begs the question: Why wouldn't (or didn't) the big players in the space identify this opportunity the way Chet did and then move to capture all that value at a scale Belkin wouldn't be able to for a number of years? The answer, according to Chet, is one of the reasons that finding and owning a small niche is such a valuable strategy for an entrepreneur during a boom time.

"IBM had their hands full just making enough PCs," Chet explained. "For years there were just not enough of them getting built, and they had no idea what printer any given small business or consumer was going to choose anyway, so they wouldn't even know which one thing to make."

His point was that, on the one hand, IBM and other PC makers like them had too much work to do in their principal business to care about or even understand something they felt was too small of an opportunity. On the other hand, this niche was the "perfect size and just the right amount of work" for a company like Belkin International.

It helped, of course, that Chet was not a threat to PC makers. He was not trying to take market share from them. If anything, the products he chose to manufacture as time went along and he became more established were bellwethers for the PC makers he was really trying to help. After all, the entire goal of his business was to make more PCs work with more peripheral devices for more consumers. So if Belkin decided to make fewer cables for your machines than it did for your competitors', it was an indication that it might be time to look in the mirror and examine your business.

It was in this capacity, as a manufacturer of cables and other connectivity devices, that Chet found his Janney coupler; his blue jeans and pickaxes and shovels; his banking services. In carving out a space for himself on the fringe of the PC revolution, and in providing some of the fuel for it to go mainstream in the process, he was able to follow in the footsteps of men like Eli Janney, Levi Strauss, Domingo Ghirardelli, and Henry Wells and William Fargo. In 2018, Chet hit his own version of the mother lode when he sold Belkin to a subsidiary of the Chinese conglomerate Foxconn for $800 million.

Interestingly, as I listened to Chet tell the story of Belkin's improbable rise from his parents' garage in 1982 to the shelves of every Apple Store today, my mind was drawn back to one of the first interviews I ever conducted for *How I Built This,* with Herb Kelleher. Specifically, it was Herb's constant focus on not trying to do too much, and its direct relationship to Southwest Airlines' unlikely growth into an international air carrier, that made Chet's story resonate so strongly with me.

"I wrote a letter to our employees about my ten foremost concerns for the next decade of Southwest Airlines," Herb told me of an early critical phase in the company's history, "and number one was that we ignore competition and get complacent."

Except he meant it in a way that most people wouldn't expect. Herb had endured years of larger regional air carriers in Texas trying to smother Southwest in the cradle, to sue the airline out of existence before it had ever taken flight. Once he survived that and got Southwest off the ground, he watched over the next thirty years as major airline after major airline either spent themselves into bankruptcy or mismanaged themselves into unfavorable mergers.

TWA, Eastern, Swissair, Aloha, Pan Am, Continental, Northwest, America West. Herb most definitely did not want Southwest Airlines to meet the same fate. "So I used the line 'Think small and act small and we'll get bigger. Think big and act big and we'll get smaller,'" he told me of that letter to his employees. He cautioned them not to think or act like the bigger airlines; not to be enamored of what it *appeared* they had; not to *compete* with them on their terms. Instead, if Southwest just stuck to what they did best, he believed, if they operated within their means and according to their founding principles, if they stayed in their lane, everything would work out, and major opportunities would present themselves. In short, if they thought small and acted small, the sky would be the limit.

This is really where the most valuable lessons and inspiring stories are to be found from the technological and industrial gold rushes that have pockmarked modern business history. They're not with Cornelius Vanderbilt or Jay Gould or any of the other railroad tycoons from the late nineteenth and early twentieth centuries. They're not with IBM or Apple or any of the giant software companies that rose to prominence in the 1980s and 1990s. And they're not with Uber or Salesforce or Twitter or any of the other tech companies born out of the internet boom in the early 2000s, whose headquarters line San Francisco's Mission Street and define one side of the boundary between where we are going and where we have been.

If you want to find an example of an entrepreneur or an innovator who built a sturdy, profitable business connected to a booming industry, you could do far worse than the stories of Levi Strauss, Eli Janney, Chet Pipkin, and even Herb Kelleher. Not only are they a testament to the profitability of a small niche that can, like a vein of gold, appear only an inch wide but run a mile deep. They are also evidence of the possibility for that niche to be a foothold from which an ambitious founder might stake their claim on what could very well be the next gold rush.

22

Manage Partnership Tensions

C ompanies are like families. From the outside they all look similar and sometimes sort of boring, but on the inside they're all uniquely complicated. They have very specific ways of doing things that seem peculiar to anyone else. They have rules and traditions and terminology that mean a lot to them and define significant aspects of how they function. They also have weird internal rivalries and quarreling cliques. They have baggage and secrets and skeletons in their closets. And with all of that shared history, they end up constructing a shared identity; a common banner they can wrap themselves in during good times or rally around through tough stretches, whether they have to come together to accomplish a mission or respond to a threat.

The people holding that banner, directing operations, charting a course for the future — those are the leaders. In a family, it's the parents. In a startup, it's the founders. And just as with parents in any normally complicated family, relationships between founders can get complicated. They can get strained, even break down. Founders can love each other, care deeply for each other, want nothing more than for their business to succeed, and still they will fight. Maybe they don't see eye to eye on how to run things; maybe their leadership styles are at odds; maybe their personal goals change. Or maybe they're just exhausted from working an entrepreneur's schedule year after year.

Whatever the case, as a founder you have to be ready for the honeymoon phase of your partnership to end, for the romance of entrepreneurship to fade away and leave the mundane obligations of running a business in its place. That will be less sexy and less exciting, as tends to happen with anything that becomes part of a daily routine, but you will still have to do the work to make it work, while also being prepared to make difficult decisions if the work isn't enough. Decisions that are perhaps the most difficult you've ever made in your life, but also the most important for the long-term viability of this thing you've worked so hard to build.

Katrina Lake had to make a decision earlier than most. In the summer of 2012, less than eighteen months into the life of the personal styling service Stitch Fix, she and her co-founder, Erin Morrison Flynn, split. Flynn was a buyer for J.Crew and the wife of one of Katrina's college friends. They founded Stitch Fix in February 2011 on the strength of that connection and a shared interest in disrupting the fashion industry, but it quickly became apparent that they didn't share much else with regard to the trajectory of the company.

"You can be in a place where you really, deeply care for somebody and at the same time you see things so differently that you just can't see it from the other person's seat," Katrina said.

Their differences in vision and opinion, unfortunately, resulted in difficult litigation that took longer to resolve than Katrina and Erin were officially co-founding partners. That's a place no founders ever expect to find themselves in when they embark on building their business, which is why every founder story is different. When I touched on the unwinding of their relationship in my interview with Katrina, she was naturally circumspect, but she described the experience in what will become familiar language.

"It's like in a divorce when they talk about irreconcilable differences," she said, "feeling like you've been in it with somebody and you just can't see the future in the same way."

What else can you do in a situation like Katrina and Erin's? If the business is working even though you're not? You have to at least consider the possibility of a split. Because without a resolution, the relationship may become increasingly toxic. That's why it's so important to manage any significant tension with your co-founder properly. It can be a momentum killer. It can eat at the foundation of your company culture, and if it gets bad enough, it can cause your employees to question everything they are working toward. To make sure that doesn't happen, you either have to squash petty power plays and surrender your ego, or accept that your partnership has reached the end of its utility and find a way to consciously uncouple.

In an ideal world, of course, founders don't just have two choices. They often find a third way and work through their problems, for the sake of both the business and their relationship. That is what Eric Ryan and Adam Lowry did when they ran into a rough patch trying to expand Method into the trailblazer in eco-chic household cleaning products that would eventually generate more than $80 million in sales and be sold to the Belgian consumer products manufacturer Ecover.

The tension started around 2008, when they developed a new line of personal care products called Bloq that failed miserably. "It was like a plane crash. It's not one thing that goes wrong. It's like ten things that go wrong. And that's exactly what we did there," Eric said of the shower-related products that retailers liked but consumers seemed to have no time for. "It was nailed to the shelf, it didn't move."

Method took a pretty big hit as a result of the failure, and not just financially. "It was in the low millions that we lit on fire," Adam said. "The bigger thing, though, with a product failure is the reputational risk. The customers — meaning, for us, a retailer — were not excited about that. It's something that you have to dig yourself out of."

In the military there is a saying: "Proper preparation prevents poor performance" — the five Ps. In business you might say, "Product plane crashes produce partnership problems," because that's what happened with Adam and Eric.

"There was a time for a couple of years where we were at each other's throats," Adam said in the aftermath of the Bloq fiasco.

"It was like a marriage," Eric said.

That description was not inaccurate. These two people — who were great, almost lifelong friends, who knew each other incredibly well — were confronted by a difficult problem they'd never faced before, with both a lot invested and people counting on them. You'd think that with their shared history and the complementary skill sets that made them such great co-founders, Eric and Adam would have been able to get through this treacherous moment with minimal aggravation.

But the irony is, everything that made them perfect partners in developing the Method brand also made solving problems and resolving disagreements within the operation of the business incredibly complicated.

"We knew how to be friends," Eric said, "but we didn't know how to be colleagues and partners together."

This was partly a personality issue — Adam is an introvert, Eric is an extrovert — and partly a matter of differing professional styles that result from their personalities.

"Eric and I approach problems from very different angles, and that is a huge asset, but it also can be a huge rub," Adam said.

"We would be in these deep moments of stress," Eric explained, "and my instinct is to just engage and run at it. Adam needs a little bit more space to kind of think it through."

That's a recipe for conflict, and it was a lot to manage for a couple twentysomethings from Grosse Pointe, Michigan, who basically stumbled into a rekindled friendship aboard a plane one year and ended up in business together the next. To get through it — to make their differences in approach an asset and not a liability — would require acceptance and understanding, and then dedicated effort to accommodate for their unique working styles.

"It required a lot of open-mindedness. It required a lot of self-awareness. It required a lot of listening," Adam said. "It was a very conscious effort to say, 'We've got to work on this, or this is going to end badly.'"

For Steve Huffman and Alexis Ohanian, the founders of the news aggregation website Reddit, what threatened to end badly for them was not their business partnership but their friendship — in the years *after* they sold to Condé Nast in 2006 and then exited the company in 2009. By that point, Steve and Alexis had lived together for eight years, first as roommates at the University of Virginia, where they conceived of Reddit, and then in New York when Condé Nast acquired Reddit. They'd graduated college and Paul Graham's Y Combinator together; they'd negotiated the sale of their business together (less than eighteen months after they founded it); and they'd endured three years under the yoke of a corporate overlord for the first time. Alexis and Steve had basically become adults together, and millionaires on top of it.

"We'd been through a lot together, and we had never really discussed it," Steve said. "So by the time we left Reddit, we were not on the best of terms." On one level, Steve was talking about what had gone on inside the company during the previous five years. "We had never discussed our roles at Reddit, the boundaries. Who was responsible for what. We didn't really have a way of resolving disputes." But listening to him and Alexis recount those early days, and knowing that they were excited about selling to Condé Nast at the time ("This was 16 months of work that was going to mean more money for me than my mother and father had made their entire lives," Alexis said), I could clearly see that at the bottom of their professional problems were actually personal ones.

"We never really exercised the muscles that founders have to exercise [but] that best friends don't," Alexis explained. "It's great to be able to start a company with one of your best friends, but the conversations you have to have as co-founders are very different from the conversations you have to have as friends, and we didn't have enough of the hard ones often enough."

It turns out this was precisely the issue Andy Dunn and Brian Spaly were encountering inside the online menswear business Bonobos at pretty much the same time as Alexis and Steve were silently growing apart. "Once you get into a business partnership with a friend, the friendship gets totally sublimated into the business partnership," Andy said. "So a lot of the stuff that you used to talk about, you don't have time for, because you've got to work on this little, growing baby company." Then what happens, when things get difficult at the office, is that founder-friends don't get the support or the patience they need from each other because the friendship muscle has atrophied.

It's the worst kind of negative feedback loop. Andy and Brian's friendship made conversations about conflicting business roles and differences of professional opinion very uncomfortable, and so the issues festered. Those unresolved issues increased the amount of attention each founder had to pay to the business — the energy for which they inevitably took from their friendship, sending their relationship into a downward spiral. When Brian left Bonobos in 2008, there was no personal or professional relationship left to speak of. (Later, the two co-founders would reconcile, and today they are close friends again.) When Alexis and Steve left Reddit in 2009 and their professional relationship ended, all that remained was a friendship in pretty bad shape.

"When our contracts expired, we just kind of said, 'Hey, you know, great, see you later,' and left it that way," Steve said.

"I didn't feel animosity," Alexis clarified. "It was just neglect."

Neglect is among the worst things that can happen to a partnership or a friendship. Everything around it tends to rot and die, including the essential things that partners and friends build together. That's certainly what almost happened to Reddit in 2015 when the site went through a series of crises. The CEO quit with a midlife crisis. His replacement, Ellen Pao, took over and then very publicly resigned after enduring a torrent of abuse from scores of toxic users (trolls) who had gotten out of hand.

Fortunately, just as the site was going through the worst of it, Steve and Alexis started to repair their relationship. "I don't remember exactly how it started, but I know from my point of view I just had this thought, like, 'Hey, where is my best friend?'" Steve said. "And we just started kind of talking through things." Talking through them in ways they never had in the first few years of Reddit's existence. Eventually, Steve and Alexis even went to see Steve's therapist together, in an effort to resolve what five years of neglect and then five years of distance had done to their friendship. This brought them into closer and closer contact right as the Reddit they had built started to go haywire and, as Steve put it, became unrecognizable to them.

It was perfect timing. Repairing their friendship reanimated their partnership. It reminded them how much they cared about Reddit, and it helped them convince each other to come back full-time and save it from the trolls. In 2014, the year before their return — with Steve installed as CEO — Reddit was valued at $500 million, and things were trending downward. In 2019, under their leadership, Reddit was able to raise $300 million at a $3 *billion* valuation. Alexis and Steve would never take the credit for that turnaround, but it would also be a mistake to ignore the fact that by finally managing the tensions that had developed in their personal and professional relationships, they put themselves in a position to rescue what they'd built and save the self-proclaimed "front page of the internet."

When Adam Lowry said it would end badly if he and Eric Ryan didn't work on their relationship — *on their work marriage* — it wasn't immediately obvious whether he was talking about the partnership or the business itself. I've spoken to enough co-founders who've gone through periods of difficulty, however, to know that both are at risk for collapse, sometimes in quick succession, if the work doesn't get done and hard decisions don't get made.

Nowhere is this clearer than with co-founders who are *actually* married. The work they have to do is harder and more urgent because there is no avoiding whatever issues they might have. Think about it: Adam and Eric had separate homes to go to at the end of the day. So did Andy Dunn and Brian Spaly, Katrina Lake and Erin Flynn, and eventually Alexis Ohanian and Steve Huffman. But married couples? They bring work issues home and marital issues to work. There's no escape!

That's what makes the married founders of the San Francisco–based personal care company EO Products, Susan Griffin-Black and Brad Black, so exceptional. Their marriage ended in the midst of their professional success, and yet they somehow found a way to navigate the traditional pitfalls of divorce — not just to protect their business but also to protect their partnership and the human relationship that sat at the foundation of both of them.

Now, it bears stating that neither Susan nor Brad had to endure the trauma of a personal transgression in the dissolution of their marriage. This certainly made it easier to find a way forward than if they'd also had to wrestle with overcoming a violation of deep trust. Betrayal is not one of those things that sits quietly and waits for you to get home from the office. It follows you everywhere, which is why the *typical* story of a co-founder breakup — whether the founders are friends or spouses — is much messier and usually ends more sadly than the story of Susan and Brad, whose personal relationship simply unraveled over time. The financial pressure of starting and running a business together, on top of the demands that come with raising kids and just being married, took a lot out of them. "We lost our way in our personal relationship through it all," Susan said, "but we really cared about each other."

And that was key to what happened next. Like Alexis Ohanian and Steve Huffman, the underlying respect and compassion Susan and Brad felt for each other got them into therapy. Counseling wasn't going to save their marriage, and they both knew that. But it was very helpful in the long term because it taught them how to work through their differences — a skill they would need as co-founders *and* co-parents if they wanted to keep their business and their kids on track, both of whom were thriving at the time despite Susan and Brad's personal struggles.

"It was difficult. It was painful. We could have sold. We could have bought each other out. We had options," Susan said. But as a product of divorce herself, she was very aware of the importance of protecting children from the actions of parents when things aren't going well, so she and Brad weren't going to move a thousand miles away from each other (they still travel together as a family on Christmas) and they weren't going to sell the business, if that wasn't what was best for everyone. "We both had the capacity to take the highest road for the kids and then also the employees," Susan said of their ultimate decision to keep the business going. "With all the people that we were responsible for, it was a very conscious choice."

That doesn't mean it was easy, of course, for anyone. "The first two years were tough, and certainly the first six months were the hardest. Absolutely our employees said that. Yet it's always felt like the right thing to do," Brad said of their decision to divorce but continue running the company together. It wasn't like their divorce came as much of a shock to their employees anyway. "We had side conversations first with folks, then we had a meeting about it, but it wasn't *not* obvious either. We don't really hide our honesty from each other."

Employees, like children, know when something is wrong, even if everything else around them is going well. And they can manage for a while. Eventually, though, the unresolved issues, unmanaged tension, and unspoken conflicts begin to reveal themselves in the form of internal dysfunction and suboptimal business performance. I think if you asked Steve Huffman and Alexis Ohanian whether their deteriorating relationship leading up to their exit from Reddit in 2009 sowed the seeds for the chaos that burst to the surface among the site's users in 2014 and 2015, they would reluctantly agree that you couldn't separate the two things. Similarly, you can draw a straight line between the personality conflicts between Andy Dunn and Brian Spaly and the fight within Bonobos for the soul of the company. You can keep the lid on a pressure cooker for only so long. Eventually, all that pressure has to go somewhere. And if you don't turn down the heat or press the release valve, all you're really doing is setting the timer on a scalding explosion.

Susan and Brad's decision to divorce was a release of years of built-up pressure that actually enabled EO Products to grow and to thrive in a better, faster way. It also gave them the personal space they needed to figure out who they were individually and to build a healthier, more robust relationship as friends, parents, and business partners.

"We did the best we could when we were married," Brad said, "and the depth of our relationship is much more meaningful now than we were able to get to when we were married."

"It also made our roles very clear in terms of what we were accountable for at work," Susan added, "and then our care for each other and similar values supported that."

"It doesn't mean we get along all the time now. It's not that we don't get into fights," Brad said of their current partnership, "but we do tend to get out of fights pretty quickly.

You know, of all the lessons I have learned in talking to co-founders, the extent to which nearly all of them have gone through extended periods of profound difficulty with each other, and the way so many of them used the language of marriage and family to describe how they navigated those periods, was among the most enlightening and empowering for me. And it's probably because I identify with the parallels as a husband, father, and entrepreneur.

Thinking like a parent and a partner is a skill every aspiring founder should cultivate in preparation for the challenges they will face with potential co-founders, because they will invariably pour as much of their heart and soul and energy and money into building their business as they will into starting a family. If you would gladly sacrifice and do whatever it takes to protect your family, why would you not do the same for your business?

23

Know Thyself

When I left *Weekend All Things Considered* to become the host of *TED Radio Hour* in 2012, more than a few of my friends in the news business thought I'd lost my mind. I was the host of a very popular show that aired on 800 radio stations across the country every week. And I was giving that up to do *what?* A *podcast?* Who listens to podcasts? It was as if I had decided to leave all my worldly possessions behind and walk alone into the wilderness.

They were right to be skeptical. We were still a few years away from the podcast boom that began to swallow traditional radio in the second half of the 2010s. People listened to podcasts, but not nearly as much as they do today. There were no major podcast apps. There were no podcast millionaires. There was iTunes and ads for Stamps .com, and that was about it.

What my colleagues didn't understand was that while I was technically changing jobs and leaving the news, I wasn't really changing what I did or who I was. In fact, I was doing and becoming *more* of those things that were authentically me. I may have worked in journalism for more than a decade, but I never felt like a "newsman." I was a storyteller, and *TED Radio Hour* — then *How I Built This* and

Wow in the World and the other shows I would create with Spotify and Luminary — would allow me to more fully express that core part of my identity in a way that news, by its nature, never could.

Podcasting let me be the most genuine version of my personal and professional self, and it unexpectedly put my career into ascendancy as a result. Embracing my storytelling sensibilities helped put my production company on the same track. It guided me to, and through, every decision in every phase of our growth — whom to hire, whom to profile on the show, what to say no to — and it also kept us from falling off the right track.

When growth begins to accelerate, it's even more critical to know who you are as a founder and who you are as a company. That understanding helps point you in the right direction when you have opportunities to pursue lots of different things. It's a constant reminder of what business you're actually in, which is something that is surprisingly easy to forget or lose sight of once your business starts to expand, evolve, and change shape. Believe me, I've been there, and so have most of the founders I've interviewed.

This is the issue Andy Dunn faced during the first five tumultuous yet thriving years of Bonobos. In that time, he'd founded the company with his Stanford business school roommate, Brian Spaly, and moved the entire operation to New York City to be closer to fabric suppliers and the fashion PR industry. They'd built sales from $10,000 in October 2007, their first month in operation, to $7 million in annual sales in 2009. In between, however, Andy had split from Brian (Brian went on to found Trunk Club), then raised two rounds of angel money, only to lose his first and most trusted investor, thanks to an overly aggressive valuation and a condescending "you either get it or you don't" kind of pitch email he sent to prospective investors. In 2010, Andy bounced back from what he called the worst year of his life to wrap up an $18 million Series A fundraise, which he used to expand offerings and operations over the next few years.

In the midst of all this Shakespearean startup drama, there was also, in Andy's words, "a battle over the soul of the company." Were they a technology company, or were they a retail menswear com-

pany? The answer, of course, is that they were both, but it was figuring that out for themselves "which was the challenge," Andy conceded.

The early failure of Bonobos to overcome this challenge, to reconcile and converge these two sides of the company into a single
unified brand, was, by Andy's own admission, his fault as the company's CEO. "If I had been a better leader, maybe I could have figured
it out," he said. But his wasn't strictly a strategic leadership issue,
which Andy also acknowledged, because the cracks had first begun
to show in him *personally* as he worked to know and to better understand himself.

"I was a confused person," Andy told me in the fall of 2018. "I got
depressed, and I kind of had to fake it at work that I was doing okay.
It was super tough to navigate."

He also struggled with direct conflict and confrontation. "I valued harmony over the difficult conversations until the situation became really difficult," he said, "and then I'd take it on." Combined
with the normal stress and insecurity that come with running a successful startup — one that wasn't even his idea to begin with* — these
personal issues started to steer Andy toward poor decisions, including fighting with his co-founder in front of the team, which exacer-
bated the company's identity crisis.

"I thought we were doing a pretty good job of talking in private
and then presenting a unified front," Andy said. But then he got a call
from one of their investors, who told him he'd been hearing things
about their fighting. "I thought, 'Wow, how did that happen? What
do I do?'" The investor told him that he and Brian had to get to the
bottom of their issues. They had to resolve whatever was dividing
them and to figure out a way to work together more effectively. They
had to stop fighting in front of the kids, as it were.

Andy saw things a little more starkly. For him (to borrow from

---

* Two of Andy's earliest ideas were to bring to the United States a Guatemalan
rum and an uncured South African beef jerky called biltong, the latter of which
violated a bunch of federal regulations on importing uncooked meat. The original
concept for Bonobos — better-fitting men's pants — was Brian Spaly's.

the language of marriage in the previous chapter), they were beyond couples therapy and trial separations. "We needed a clear CEO," he said, "so it was more, 'Should I leave or should Brian leave?'"

You could say the battle for the soul of Bonobos actually began there, within Andy, then radiated outward to include Brian—his friend, roommate, classmate, and co-founder. Eventually, Brian would leave. "He was unbelievably dignified about the whole thing," Andy said. But that didn't end the battle, because Andy continued to make missteps.

First, he gave a company-wide presentation titled "23," based on the Hall of Fame speeches of two very different athletes, Ryne Sandberg (formerly of the Cubs) and Michael Jordan (formerly of the Bulls), who wore the number 23 for their respective teams in Chicago, where Andy grew up. Sandberg's speech focused on respect. Jordan's was notoriously hostile and retributive, all about settling scores and "being better than everyone and dominating everyone." Andy compared and connected the speeches thematically in an attempt to inspire his troops toward a more unified purpose. On the one hand, "we need to all have respect for all the people here and the sacrifices they are making," he said. On the other hand, like Jordan, people needed to do more to achieve, to grow, to kill the competition. "It was kind of convoluted," Andy admitted, "and it totally didn't work."

The troops didn't feel an increased sense of esprit de corps. Instead, they felt demoralized. "It was the opposite of what you want to see from a leader," he said. "You want to be recognized for how hard you're working, not scolded that you're not working hard enough."

What made the presentation a real flash point, though, wasn't just that everyone inside Bonobos felt like they were busting their butts to make the company a success (rightly, in Andy's estimation); some also thought they were busting their butts *more* than others. "The folks who did all the customer service and fulfillment were working around the clock. The apparel folks were working the second most. And there was a perception that the engineering team, who were getting paid the most, were not working as hard," Andy explained. This complaint, which went both spoken and unspoken by the retail-side employees, was actually what motivated Andy to create the "23" presentation. And it is why the product folks took it so personally. It felt to them like a slap in the face, since *they were the ones* killing themselves to bring truly innovative menswear options to market, while the engineers were strolling in late, leaving early, and earning sometimes three times as much for their trouble. In short, grumblings indicating poor morale were bubbling up from the ranks.

Andy's big miscalculation was magnified by the divide between the tech side and the fashion-product-retail side of the business, but it was grounded fundamentally in *another* identity issue altogether. This was brought squarely to his attention after the presentation by a brilliant, ex-Zappos engineer whom Andy and Brian had hired early on to lead the tech team. "He called me and said, 'I wish you could have seen the spirit of joy that Tony Hsieh created at Zappos. I wish you could see the way a spirit of positivity actually creates a much better work environment at a startup.'"

What this engineer had landed upon without realizing it was the disconnect between the type of business Bonobos was in and the type of businesses Andy had come from. In the five years before going to business school, Andy had worked in consulting with Bain and in private equity with a firm out of Chicago called Wind Point. He was assigned to projects for a cardboard packaging company and a South American airline. He assisted with the Lands' End acquisition by Sears. These were industries with notoriously thin margins where companies hired consultants or sold to private equity firms because they were ruthless about efficiencies and laser focused on profits. In effect, Andy had come from the opposite of the startup world and was unconsciously bringing that cutthroat sensibility to his leadership of Bonobos.

The engineer's message was "a wake-up call," Andy said. "This isn't consulting or private equity, where people are motivated by fear. This is a startup, where people are motivated by joy. It's about creating something versus making sure that you're working hard enough to get to the next rung."

This realization would turn out to be more than a wake-up call. First, the ex-Zappos engineer's point wasn't just a friendly piece of advice. It was his parting thought. He quit, leaving the tech team unguided and the whole business potentially underpowered. At the time, the website was the only entry point for Bonobos customers. If that broke down, it could be incredibly costly. So Andy started to recruit a similar level of programming talent to New York. Or I should say, he *tried*. This was 2010. The economy was coming out of the recession, and a new wave of technological innovation, in the form of mobile devices and mobile apps, was about to arrive and upend large swaths of the industry. For an experienced programmer or engineer, the big action and the opportunities were unequivocally in Silicon Valley. It would take a lot to lure an engineer with a Zappos-level pedigree to Manhattan for the opportunity to sell pants on the computer. Whatever Andy was offering in those first months after their lead engineer left clearly wasn't enough.

For a while, the business subsisted on the work of outside technology consultants, but eventually the challenges this arrangement presented outweighed the benefits. Near the end of 2011, Andy finally decided to go where the talent was instead of trying to coax it 3,000 miles across the continent. He hired a Netflix engineering director named Michael Hart to be chief technology officer, then installed him in a brand-new Palo Alto office that Bonobos opened at the beginning of 2012.

As well-intentioned as this decision was, "it turned out to be a catastrophic error," Andy said. It had the effect of taking the tribal instincts already present between the two sides of the business and institutionalizing them — not just widening the internal divide between tech and retail, but deepening each side's sense that they represented the core of the business. "The New York office saw this as a menswear retailer," he explained. "The Palo Alto office saw this as the beginning of a multibrand technology platform that they were going to power with technology." And both sides believed they had the strongest claim to the company's finite resources, which were being made *more finite* by the day, not surprisingly, as a result of the cost of maintaining and managing two locations instead of one.

With dedicated offices on opposite sides of the country beginning in 2012, each group now had their own house to protect — as though

Bonobos was Hogwarts and they were Slytherin and Gryffindor! — and seemingly very little incentive to cooperate. "People were not seeing eye to eye at all," Andy said. "They just weren't interacting enough to resolve their differences about what the strategy was and what the company was about."

But that raises the question: What exactly *was* Bonobos about? Because this kind of thing that Andy Dunn and his team were experiencing doesn't often happen in a company that knows who it is and what it does. Only a company that has lost its way a little bit, that doesn't know precisely what business it's actually in, tends to fight itself like this. Andy only needed to look twenty blocks uptown from his New York office and a few years into the past, at AOL Time Warner and the titanic merger that created the company in 2000, to see what the worst possible version of this might look like.

When AOL and Time Warner merged, a lot was made of the new media entity's size and market cap. The potential created by both teams leveraging the assets they brought to the table was difficult to contemplate let alone calculate. The merger was valued at $165 billion, but that was probably just a guess. The business press struggled to come up with adjectives grandiose enough to describe it. In the frenzy around the merger, however, something went unnoticed, or at least underappreciated: AOL Time Warner was opening its sails into some very stiff headwinds. The dot-com bubble was about to burst. Ad sales would then slump, which would inevitably cast doubt on the future viability of the internet (whose arrival this huge merger officially signaled) right as the one element that would ultimately release its true potential — high-speed broadband — was about to come online, catching the company off guard and fully broadsiding its leadership.

These obstacles could have been surmounted by a company that knew what it was about, to paraphrase Andy Dunn. With a strong culture unified by a larger mission and propelled by people who were all rowing in the same direction, they could have even leveraged the obstacles they faced into opportunities. Except inside AOL Time Warner, there was no unity to be found, and within a decade the merger would be dead. Both companies would lose more than

85 percent of their premerger value. Time Warner would eventually spin off its cable business (Time Warner Cable), it's publishing business (Time Inc.), and, of course, AOL, which would reenter a radically transformed digital media landscape as a wandering shell of its former self. The smaller Time Warner rebranded itself as WarnerMedia, which was ultimately sold to AT&T for around $85 billion in 2018.

In the aftermath of the merger's unwinding (which occurred at roughly the same time Andy and Brian unwound their partnership at Bonobos, coincidentally), analysts and participants alike pointed to the schism between the AOL folks down in Virginia and the Time Warner folks up in New York as one of the principal reasons for the company's failure to find its way through the turbulent waters of the dot-com recession. There was always great talk about "building synergy" between AOL and Time Warner, but in the end that turned out to be an illusory goal.

"Some of it was the fights within the company," Steve Case, AOL's chairman, told me. "It was a mix of different factors but at the end of the day it's about people and it's about teams."

On the ten-year anniversary of the announcement of the merger, the *New York Times* ran a retrospective oral history, titled "How the AOL–Time Warner Merger Went So Wrong," that featured insights from many of the executives involved in the deal and in the operation of the resulting enterprise. It concluded with Richard Parsons, the president of Time Warner at the time of the merger.

"The business model sort of collapsed under us, and then finally this cultural matter," Parsons said. ". . . It was beyond certainly my abilities to figure out how to blend the old media and the new media culture. They were like different species, and in fact, they were species that were inherently at war."

Once AOL Time Warner started to sink, there was no saving it, because each side was more interested in blaming the other for why the ship wasn't seaworthy rather than working together to patch the holes in the hull, bail out the water, and maybe get the thing upright and sailing again.

Bonobos was nowhere close to a sinking ship in 2013, but it was definitely listing. It was struggling to figure out who it was and what it did. Andy's vision at the time was to create a whole portfolio of brands beyond Bonobos, using the "digitally native vertical brand model" they'd effectively invented and leaning heavily on personalization, since the more brands they added, the richer their data sets would be and the better their product offerings and services would become. "The mandate to New York was to build the best men's clothing brand we can," he said, "and the mandate to California was to build the best technology platform we can." A platform that, he hoped, would power Bonobos first but then, over time, would become the backbone of the many other brands they developed.

It sounds amazing, right? But you can imagine, at this point, the wide differences in responses and reactions Andy received when talking about it to the Palo Alto office versus the New York office. The West Coast folks were ready. They felt strongly that the company should invest deeply in building this robust personalization functionality. The retail side, though, was skeptical, and that is being charitable. "The viewpoint in New York was, 'Can I just get the product page updated to include reviews?'" Andy recounted.

It was clear to Andy then that this hybrid thing was no longer working and something had to change. "The organizational harmony at the company was being destroyed by this cross-coastal conflict," he said. "The culture was deteriorating, and it was becoming harder by the day."

I have great empathy and admiration for Andy Dunn. "I'm just the sum of cumulative terrible mistakes," he once told me, describing how he views himself as a leader. But what is remarkable about him as well is that he had the emotional maturity to reflect on his struggles. So much so that he sought help — in the form of therapy — to help him figure out who he was and what he really wanted to do.

In January of that year, he gathered the Bonobos board of directors and informed them that he'd decided to shutter the Palo Alto office barely a year after opening it. The closure was the first step toward resolving what Andy called a "broader error" he was making in trying to turn the company into a multibrand technology platform: getting away from who Bonobos was and what it did. There is a major difference, he believed, between experimenting around the core of a business and jumping into new core businesses.

The fit-to-ship Guideshops they began opening in 2012, the retail partnership they entered into with Nordstrom, and the other categories of menswear like dress shirts and suits they developed—all of those built around the Bonobos brand and, unsurprisingly, did quite well from the start.

The high-cost Palo Alto office filled with West Coast tech people who had different ideas for what Bonobos should be, and the derivative golf (Maide) and women's clothing (AYR) brands they launched—those were experiments that were "outside the scope of the Bonobos brand." Maide hung on to become Bonobos Golf in 2017, but AYR was successfully spun out, as were the technology functions of the Palo Alto office, into a personalization SaaS (software as a service) company with their former chief technology officer, Michael Hart, as CEO.

By 2014, Bonobos was already "massively turning the corner," to use Andy's phrase. The key mover that did it for them was twofold: they finally owned what the brand was, and then they took it multichannel beyond e-commerce into physical brick-and-mortar with their Guideshops and Nordstrom partnership. "That was another really fun board meeting," Andy said of yet another debate over the identity of the business. In this one, the question was: "Is this an e-commerce company, or is this a menswear experience company?" Andy made the case that they weren't an e-commerce business at all. Just as you might say Google isn't a search company, it's an ad sales company that uses search, Andy said Bonobos was a retail customer service business that utilized an e-commerce platform. And if they could "invent a way to deliver the same level of fit and service" as a traditional brick-and-mortar retailer, then that would only get them closer to their soul as a business.

Without abandoning technology, which was never his intention, Andy had leaned into their retail menswear roots and managed to solve the challenge that had vexed him as a leader since he first took the reins in 2009. He had, at last, put Bonobos in a position to deliver on his and Brian Spaly's original pitch to investors—it's Ralph Lauren meets Zappos — and to let everyone know — inside and outside the company, investor or customer, analyst or employer — who they are and what they do.

Once everyone was on the same page, the work really began to pay off, and in early 2017 Bonobos caught the eye of Walmart, which purchased the business that summer for more than $300 million. Smartly, Walmart's leadership has allowed Bonobos to continue to do what it does, because they know who they are and what business Walmart is in, and they fully understand the same thing about Bonobos. Thankfully, Andy Dunn understands that, too, and he has finally been able to experience the power of becoming more of the things that are authentically him.

24

When to Sell and When to Stay

In February 2008, the popular Harvard Business School professor Noam Wasserman published an article in the *Harvard Business Review* that would become the basis for a best-selling book of the same name a few years later. It was called "The Founder's Dilemma." The thesis, based on reams of research Wasserman had conducted on thousands of entrepreneurs, was that at some critical point in the growth of their companies, all founders will find themselves with a choice between two competing interests — money and control — and they will often choose poorly. They will act either against their own self-interest or, in some instances, against the best interests of their companies, and sometimes both.

The backdrop for Wasserman's argument was the landscape of fundraising and the management trade-offs many entrepreneurs are unprepared to make in exchange for the capital they need in order to grow. Specifically, they resist the level of control that investors demand. "Founders don't let go easily," Wasserman wrote. In fact, 80 percent of the entrepreneurs he analyzed were forced out of their founding leadership positions before they were ready to leave, and "most [were] shocked" when it happened.

This is a product of the entrepreneurial personality, Wasserman argued. Entrepreneurs tend to be single-minded in their focus. They are extra passionate. They are sometimes confident beyond their abilities, to the point of naïveté. These are the attributes of a great startup founder, though less so of a CEO charged with scaling a business. And still, when confronted with this analysis by professional investors or even their own board of directors, "founders are usually convinced that only they can lead their start-ups to success," Wasserman wrote. "'Since I've gotten us to the stage where the product is ready, that should tell them that I can lead this company' is a common refrain."

Now, entrepreneurs don't *have* to raise professional money if they don't want to. They don't *have* to accept it in the amounts or at the valuation that may be available to them. They don't *have* to realize the potential idling within their ideas as quickly as others may want either. They can take it slow. They can defer compensation. They can wait to make a lot of money and let the company grow at a more natural pace. It wouldn't be an unfamiliar place from which to operate for most entrepreneurs, since founders typically pay themselves about as much as they would make if they were employees, and much less on average than a CEO would make coming into the company. Fundamentally, it comes down to what a founder thinks is best for the company and best for themselves.

"Entrepreneurs face a choice, at every step, between making money and managing their ventures," Wasserman wrote. "This fundamental tension yields 'rich' versus 'king' trade-offs. The 'rich' options enable the company to become more valuable but [may] sideline the founder by taking away the CEO position and control over major decisions. The 'king' choices allow the founder to retain control of decision making by staying CEO and maintaining control over the board — but often only by building a less valuable company."

Neither choice is, by definition, better than the other. It all depends on what a founder's goals were when they started their company, and where those goals have evolved in light of their success.

Except I don't think money and control are your only choices when you are wrangling with a growing and successful business. I don't believe they are the only two major forces that motivate an entrepreneur's decision making either. I think there is a third. A consideration that tends to play a lesser role during the fundraising part of growth, but is especially active once a founder has grown their business beyond what they ever imagined possible and the opportunity to sell presents itself.

I'm talking about happiness. Contentment. Making a decision that feels *right*.

In 2000, Gary Erickson and his partner at the time, Lisa Thomas, had to make a decision about whether or not they were going to sell Clif Bar to a big food company. A number of them were sniffing around trying to get into the energy bar game after Nestlé bought PowerBar for $375 million and Kraft snapped up Balance Bar for $268 million earlier that year. Gary wasn't necessarily looking to sell, but watching their two biggest competitors be acquired within months of each other, for more than a quarter of a billion dollars each, had a big impact on Lisa.

"I can remember the exact moment that I got a call from her and she said, 'I want to sell the company,'" Gary recounted. "And I said all right, I guess this is what you do."

It was inarguable that there was a ton of money to be made here. Clif Bar had been in business for eight years by then; they had a growing staff and annual sales north of $40 million. They were the biggest privately held energy bar company left on the market. One of these multinational conglomerates was going to pay nine figures for them without a doubt. So they hired an investment banker, who went out onto the market and put the company up for sale, and then they hit the road.

"We started traveling all over the country, visiting these large companies that wanted us to be part of their portfolio," Gary said, "and we got an amazing deal from one of them." The Quaker Oats Company, which already had Chewy granola bars in its portfolio and was itself barely more than a year away from selling to PepsiCo, offered Gary and Lisa $120 million. That would mean $60 million for each of them. They could walk away, set for life.

They said yes.

The signing of the papers was set for April 17, 2000. Gary and Lisa informed all their employees. Their investment banker, the people from Quaker Oats, and the lawyers were all gathered on the thirtieth floor of the Bank of America building in San Francisco. Lisa was on the phone with some of them nailing down the last few details in the contract. "The deal was essentially done," Gary said. And then, less than an hour before he and Lisa were scheduled to jump in the car and drive from their headquarters in Emeryville, across the Bay Bridge, and into the city, Gary decided to take a walk around the block.

"I went out to the parking lot, and I just started weeping. I put everything into this. This is my life. These are my employees, and this is my family. It was named after my dad!" Gary said, describing the emotions flowing out of him. "Halfway around the block, I decided not to sell."

To Lisa this would seem like a total about-face. The deal was done as far as she was concerned. What she didn't know was that for the previous three months, as the deal was being negotiated, Gary had been living in total darkness. "I was not sleeping well. I was not riding my bike. I was probably not very fun to be around," he said. He spent every waking moment of those three months fighting himself over the deal. And on top of all that, when telling the employees about their plans to sell, Gary felt like he'd sold them a lie. "I said things would not change. And it was not true. Of course it was going to change. It could be better, it could be worse — but you can't say it is not going to change," Gary said.

That's the control part of the founder's dilemma that Noam Wasserman described. The price Gary Erickson would have to pay for his $60 million cut of the sale was the inability to reassure his employees — *his family* — that everything was going to be how it always was. That everything was going to be okay. It was a price he wasn't willing to pay. Not because he thought whoever Quaker Oats installed to run Clif Bar would do a bad job, but because it was a job that he loved and still wanted, even if it cost him $60 million.

Which it would, because Lisa still wanted out. Gary spent the next seven months "dialing for dollars," looking for $60 million to buy out his partner. It's what she was expecting, it's what she was losing, and it was only fair. At the same time, Gary was back running the company day to day, and it was growing like crazy. "This isn't something you want to deal with as you are growing your business," Gary said. He already had his normal Clif Bar duties to fulfill. But now he had $60 million in debt to cover and a workforce that, at least for a time, was "convinced this would be a short-term deal and I would go back and sell the company." He was taking calls from private equity groups who'd heard what had happened and were putting out feelers by way of telling Gary that he was out of his mind for turning down Quaker Oats and that Clif Bar was never going to make it, *even without the debt.*

And yet, nine years later, Gary paid off the entire debt. Nine years after that, Clif Bar did more than *$6 billion* in sales. And today, it's the leading energy bar in the United States.

For Gary, none of this was about the money, or even the control. "There was something deeper about wanting to grow this business. The power of a business done the right way is way more powerful than two rich people," Gary said. It's a power that comes from freedom and contentment. The freedom to do whatever you want because you are content with the fact that you've already done what you know is right. In that moment back in April 2000, halfway through his walk around the block, when Gary decided not to sell Clif Bar, he "felt completely free." Free, ironically enough, to stay right where he was, to take on even more responsibility than he had before, and to do right by his employees. That decision would eventually make him rich, and it would immediately make him happy.

Angie and Dan Bastian wanted to do right by their employees as well. That was a big part of the reason they chose to sell their popcorn company, Angie's BOOMCHICKAPOP. First, a majority stake was sold to the private equity firm TPG Capital in 2014, then the whole thing was sold to Conagra in 2017. Unlike the three months of torment that Gary Erickson endured prior to pulling the pin on the sale of Clif Bar to Quaker Oats, it wasn't so hard for Angie and Dan to let go. It was easier than the road they had taken to get to a place where a major multinational corporation would even consider buying them, that was for sure.

Angie and Dan had been at it since 2003. Eleven years! Initially, just as an outdoor events company, popping kettle corn in their garage and selling it outside supermarkets, Little League baseball games, and Minnesota Vikings football games in the freezing Minnesota winter. That they would end up building a business defined by beautifully branded and packaged *popcorn* that flies off grocery store shelves across North America was as much a shock to them as to anyone, because in the beginning this whole thing was just a side hustle.

A psychiatric nurse practitioner and middle school teacher, respectively, Angie and Dan were looking for a way to make a little extra money that they could put away for their children's college educations. The kids were just three and five years old when their parents started to kick around ideas.

"We are successfully employed, but we don't have any savings — we haven't started yet — and everybody's already got a college fund and a 401-whatever-that-is," Angie said of their financial situation at the time, to a roar of laughter from the audience during our live interview in Minneapolis in 2019. "We don't have anything. We have to figure out how to create something here."

The fact that it was kettle corn they landed on was pure chance — a product of Dan's intrepid late-night googling. "Somehow I stumbled across a site that said, 'Make thousands of dollars every weekend popping kettle corn,'" Dan said. "I didn't even know what it was."

His ignorance of the sweet-and-salty treat did little to suppress his appetite for the offer this website presented. For the low, low price of $10,000, a couple in Gig Harbor, Washington, who'd made this *their* side hustle, would send them a big kettle with all the equipment, a tent, and a table. No recipe.

"I remember distinctly the phone call," Angie said. "I'm in the middle of a patient takedown, and my husband's on the line. So I run back to the nurses' station, and he's on the other end and he says, 'Ange what do you think about kettle corn?' I'm like, 'I like kettle corn.'"

So they bought it. Over the phone. On a credit card.

For the next two years, during the week Dan taught Spanish and social studies to thirteen-year-olds while Angie worked at the local clinic,* then at night and on weekends they would fire up the kettle, hand-pack the kettle corn into cheap Ziploc bags, and set out around the greater Minneapolis area with their folding table and their tent, selling bags of their delicious $3 snack.

There is a well-known African proverb that says it takes a village to raise a child. The next ten years for Angie and Dan Bastian would prove that it also takes a village to build a popcorn business.

In 2003, they were introduced by a friend to the buyer for a local grocery chain. The buyer took a liking to them (and their kettle corn) and gave them the kick in the pants they needed to make their side hustle legitimate. "They said, 'Get your act together. Get a nutritional panel. Get packaging—twist ties don't work in grocery stores,'" Dan said. "'Then come back and talk to us.'" So over the next six months, they bought some equipment, they rented out a small commercial kitchen—they "moved the operation indoors," as Angie likes to put it—and they came back to the grocery chain to officially launch "Angie's Kettle Corn."

They were licensed, and they were roofed, but they were still just kind of making it work with whomever and what they had around them. Their logo was drawn by a local woman named Chris Higginbotham, who lived in a small town just north of theirs. "We sat in her basement and drew out the logo," Angie said of their very formal business arrangement. They were able to get the labels for the packaging printed locally as well. When it came time to manufacture the kettle corn, it was mostly Dan in the kitchen, but he and Angie and their kids "and whoever else we could find" would hand-pack and label the bags every night. Dan would wake up early every morning and pack up the day's product into old banana boxes that he'd liberated from the very grocery stores to which he was about to make deliveries. Then, every Thursday through Sunday, he and Angie would do product demos in a half dozen of their first grocery clients with the help of a couple named Don and Jeannie Boyer, who would eventually become their employees, but at the time were just

* Angie kept her job at the clinic for *seven years* before finally leaving to concentrate full-time on their business.

a couple retired third-grade teachers who wanted to do something together. Unable to afford actual employees just yet, Dan and Angie offered the Boyers $8 an hour ... combined. "They said, 'We don't care what you pay us,'" Angie recalled, "because they were kind people and they wanted to help."

Within a couple years, Angie and Dan would need financial and organizational help as well. They'd been putting most of their business expenses on credit cards, and by 2006 they had so much credit card debt that they were technically in worse financial shape than when they started. That's when a family friend who was also an accountant came to their aid. "He looked at our books and said, 'Why don't I just give you a loan here, and we can relieve your credit card debt and you can pay me back?'" Angie recalled. A year later, Dan's brother, Greg, would join the business and continue the work their accountant-friend had begun by helping to clean things up from a financial perspective. Greg would become "the rock of the company," Dan said.

The support and guidance these people offered could not have come at a better time, because while Angie and Dan weren't making any money yet, it was clear by the time Greg joined the company in 2007 that they were onto something. They couldn't keep up with demand. There weren't enough hours in the day for Dan to do the cooking and to complete everything else on his daily to-do lists. As a stopgap, they hired three students from Minnesota State University — two of whom were relatives — and paid them minimum wage. They put a cooler of beer at the end of the production line as an incentive. It was the kind of fringe benefit that only a college student could love. Soon, in order to ramp up production, they had to move into a bigger building, which the North Mankato Port Authority agreed to help them finance if they guaranteed they would create at least eight new jobs. (They blew that number out of the water.)

In the spring of 2008, they got their first taste of the grocery store big leagues. The buyer for Trader Joe's, whom Dan had been harassing for months with phone calls and shipments of sample product, ordered twenty-five *trucks* worth of kettle corn to be distributed through all of the Trader Joe's stores nationwide. It was an order worth $400,000 or $500,000. And they had neither the money nor the staff to fulfill it. Thankfully, Greg was able to convince a credit card company that had recently sent Dan an offer for an instant $100,000 line of credit (it was one of those fake-looking checks you get in the mail — apparently they're real!) to wire the money right into Dan and Angie's business account. Then their friend Colette, who owned a human resources company, helped them hire a bunch of people.* With the money and the muscle secured, they were able to meet the manufacturing demands of their first Trader Joe's order and set themselves up for a second one, and then a third, and a fourth, each coming more quickly than the one before it.

By 2009, the revenue of Angie's Kettle Corn reached $3 million to $4 million, the lion's share coming from Trader Joe's. Things took off from there. They got into Target, into regional grocery chains, and then into Costco. In 2011, when they went through a rebrand to become Angie's BOOMCHICKAPOP, with a renewed focus on healthy popcorn snacks, their growth rate was approximately 4,000 percent.

In 2014, they caught the eye of TPG, a very large private equity firm with a reputation for smart acquisitions of responsible companies. TPG bought out the interest of a smaller firm that had taken a minority stake back in 2010 and took a majority stake themselves. It allowed Dan and Angie, for the first time, to take money off the table for themselves and to distribute some of the wealth among their employees. The people who had helped them take their little kettle corn operation from stripped-down demos in local grocery stores to an entire product line with eye-level shelf placement at Target and end-cap displays at Trader Joe's. The people who had taken a risk to help them get out of debt and teach them how to run a real business. The people who had made it possible for them to reach their goal of securing their children's college educations and to achieve so, so much more.

When they finalized the deal with TPG in 2014, "those granted equity shares became liquid for our staff," Angie said. "It was the best

---

* Colette would eventually join the company as the vice president of human resources.

three days of my career." They were able to distribute millions of dollars to "everyone who had given everything to us," Dan said, choking up as we neared the end of our interview. "It was kind of a thank-you to everybody."

And then they got to do it again in 2017 when Conagra bought the whole business for a quarter of a billion dollars.

"That was really fun," Angie said, because it gave them a chance to reward those employees who hadn't been granted equity yet. "We did a calculation, and they got a check, too."

What made their exit so smooth, I think, was that they were able to do it slowly, over time. The three years between the TPG deal and the Conagra acquisition allowed Dan and Angie to "take a big step back and let new leadership come in," Dan said. "We were able to participate as much as we wanted and as much as the staff needed us, so that when 2017 came, it wasn't as emotional as the 2014 sale." Exiting slowly and selling with an eye toward others cut through the tensions of the typical founder's dilemma. Angie and Dan didn't have to choose between money and control, "rich" and "king"; they just had to think about happy or not happy.

"We started this to put our kids through college," Dan said, "and now we're doing it for all these other people." That was much more rewarding. It offered a sense of contentment and true happiness, and even *that* they were able to share with their old company's new leadership. When Angie and Dan calculated the distributions from the Conagra sale for their non-equity employees, they gave the checks to the leadership to pass out. "They got to experience what it felt like to give," Angie said.

It's the kind of gesture that stays with your people long after you, the company founder and their leader, have gone.

25

Be Kind

Starting a business is hard. Growing a business is harder. Sustaining that business for a long time, at or above the standards you set for it at the beginning, for many founders seems hardest of all. Mostly because it requires so much buy-in — on mission, on values, on identity, on dozens of constantly changing things — from every employee who walks through your doors every day as they come to work.

Inspiring your employees to exhibit that kind of unity can be incredibly difficult — not because of their lack of interest, but because of your lack of time and know-how. As founder and CEO, you're going to be busy. So very busy. There are going to be products to launch, strategies to build, meetings to lead, people to hire, fires to put out, investors to woo and to answer to. Your natural instinct will be to focus the majority of your time on the things you're good at — the business stuff, the product stuff. You'll prioritize cultivating the things that add to the bottom line while mitigating those that subtract from it.

As you should. That's your job. But it is not your *only* job.

You are also the mission maker, the values setter, the morale booster. You are responsible for creating an environment in which your employees can thrive, work can get done, customers' needs can be met, and you can be proud of what your company has accomplished at the end of each day.

There are a thousand management and leadership books out there that will give you advice on how to do all of this. They have systems and multistep plans and case studies with data to back it all up. There is something valuable to be gleaned from each of them. But I honestly don't think it needs to be that complicated. I don't believe you need to take a personality inventory of your entire team in order to know what motivates people or to get their buy-in on the business. I think it's all much, much simpler than that.

I didn't always believe that. Before I went into podcasting, I spent my entire career in large media organizations with strong cultures defined by difficult work environments. Whether it was the actual physical place, like the war zones I reported from for a number of years, or the general atmosphere, with its competing personal ambitions, tight deadlines, and even tighter budgets, the only thing you could get a group of journalists to agree on was that they didn't agree on anything.

My opinion began to change on this subject as I interviewed more and more entrepreneurs. Many of them struggled with hiring early in the growth process, but comparatively few struggled with retention once they got their businesses figured out. Initially, the reason for this was hard to pin down. These founders came from across the entrepreneurial spectrum, and they had very little in common besides the fact that they all started businesses. They were doing *something* differently, though — that I knew. I just didn't have the entrepreneurial language to describe it. Eventually, my thinking crystallized when I realized that I didn't need business jargon to understand them, since what they were doing differently wasn't entrepreneurial at all; it was just quintessentially human.

One of the first opportunities I had to express this idea publicly was, of all places, as a guest on *The Tonight Show Starring Jimmy Fallon* in the summer of 2019. As he wrapped up our interview, Jimmy asked me if I could offer one piece of advice to aspiring entrepreneurs in the audience — one thing I'd learned from all these amazing people I'd interviewed that I could share with them. What I told Jimmy, the people assembled in Studio 6B, and the viewers at home across the country was to be kind; that kind leaders have kind companies; that kindness is a powerful tool; that kindness is *free* — it costs nothing! — and that the return on investment for kindness is bigger than that for any financial investment an entrepreneur can make.

I believe in the truth of that message a little more each day. It doesn't mean every single person is kind every second of the day. Believe me, I have my moments. So much so, that as I write this, I am looking at a small pennant I bought on Etsy that simply says BE KIND. I have it up on the wall in my studio to remind me of this message as an aspiration and a daily goal. Sometimes I fall short, but I use it as my North Star nonetheless, and every day that I keep myself pointed in that general direction is a good day.

Fundamentally, I don't believe a company can stand the test of time if people will not stand for the company. And I find one of the most reliable ways the vast majority of entrepreneurs inspire people to do that is with kindness. I don't know any other way to put it. So many of them are just kind! They treat their people well. They do the little things *and* the big things. They pay their success forward.

And with rare exceptions, they are also highly ethical. They act with an integrity that seems to come from a place of deep morality. When I ask founders about how they built their teams or how they managed through tough times, for example, more often than not their answers begin with the words "I believe" or "we believe." What they believe isn't always the same, but it always feels profoundly personal. It's not clinical or calculated. It's compassionate. There is an empathy present in their decisions that often extends all the way out to the customer.

In the late 1980s and early 1990s, when Marcia Kilgore was building the skin care and facial business that would become Bliss out of a tiny studio apartment in Manhattan's East Village, she developed a reputation as more than just an expert on clearing up bad skin. She was also someone you could count on to do whatever it took to get you to that fresh-faced place.

"A facial is generally an hour, but I might be in there for two hours with somebody if they really needed it," Marcia said. "I think it's really important to be thorough and do the best job you can. And I think you get results when you put time in."

For Marcia, those results took the shape of a sixteen-month waiting list and a client roster that included Madonna, Nicole Kidman, Uma Thurman, Demi Moore, Annie Leibovitz, and half the models in Manhattan.

When the online eyewear retailer Warby Parker launched in 2010, they were not so excited about *their* wait list, because it was the result of being utterly unprepared for the onslaught of orders they received, thanks to the attention they got from two magazine features — one in *GQ*, one in *Vogue* — that ran just prior to their site going live. They ended up having to put 20,000 potential customers onto a wait list that took them upwards of nine months to clear. It could have been a disaster for the young company. You don't get too many second chances in entrepreneurship, especially if you're an online business. But even more than that, co-founder Neil Blumenthal said, they wanted to "create a business that had a positive impact on the world, and part of that is treating customers fairly." So the founders reached out to every single person on the wait list who was disappointed or was having a bad experience. "These were early adopters that were excited to place an order from us, and we didn't have anything to sell them," Neil's partner, Dave Gilboa, explained. "We gave people discounts, we would give them free glasses, and we learned a lot of important lessons in terms of being empathetic to customers."

Kind founders don't just make every *customer* feel valued; they make every *employee* feel valued as well. They do things that make their employees feel like part of a family. They make it a point to give their employees something to call their own, in recognition of this larger journey they are on together as a business, *as a unit.* That could mean giving them a piece of the company itself, offering opportunities that help them grow as people, or just doing something as simple as recognizing their basic human dignity by trusting them with the freedom to use their time the way they see fit.

These are not my ideas. They are the kinds of decisions you hear about again and again from people describing why they love their jobs. They are choices made by entrepreneurs whose businesses, unsurprisingly, continue to thrive, in some cases several decades after their founding. People like Eileen Fisher, of the eponymously named fashion brand, and Kim Jordan, of New Belgium Brewing Company, who both decided in the midst of their early success in the 1990s to give an ownership stake to their employees.

For Eileen, her decision was born as much from the belief that Eileen Fisher — *the business* — should be a shared, communal experience as it was an expression of gratitude to all those people who helped lead the company through its early explosive growth while Eileen was going through a difficult divorce.

"I struggled a lot with being in two different places at once," she said. "Wanting to be at work or worrying about work when I was at home, and at the same time worrying about my kids when I was at work." It's a seemingly timeless struggle that is familiar to millions of working parents. "I think about all the women out there trying to start businesses and work in the business world, and just how hard it is to manage families," Eileen said. "I did the best I could. I had to let go a lot. I really had to rely on the people in the company and our teams and try to sort of lead loosely."

A lighter leadership touch when it came to managing people wasn't unnatural for Eileen. "I saw myself more as a designer and an artist rather than a businessperson," she said. To this day, she is uncomfortable with the idea of being a CEO. "Chief creative officer" was the closest she could ever bring herself to come to any executive leadership title. And it was a fitting description because she never "liked telling people what to do. I liked being given a problem and let me do it my way."

By the late 1990s, both Eileen Fishers had survived the divorce and her private turmoil to become huge successes. They had a showroom on Madison Avenue. Eileen's clothes were in Bloomingdale's, Saks Fifth Avenue, and Nordstrom. At a certain point, the company was doing $100 million in top-line revenue. At that stage, with everything Eileen had endured stress-wise over the previous few years, she could very easily have sold the company or found a strategic partner and taken some money off the table for herself. I think that's what a lot of people would have done in her shoes. More to the point, selling Eileen Fisher was not a creative enough way — in the opinion of its chief creative officer (aka Eileen) — to bring the company into the next decade in a way that reflected where they'd come from and what she wanted the company to be.

"It was never about the money," she said of the evolution of the business. "It was personal. I wanted it to be how *I* wanted it to be." And for Eileen that meant sharing the wealth. "I wanted the people who are a part of the business to participate and feel like owners and *be owners.*" So she sold part of the company to her employees. Today, with roughly 60 stores around the world and 1,200 direct employees (including employee number one, who is still with the company more than thirty-five years later), Eileen Fisher is 40 percent employee owned.

At New Belgium Brewing Company, Kim Jordan and her cofounder, then-husband Jeff Lebesch, were dedicated to the concept of giving equity to their employees even earlier in the growth of the business. For Kim, it was a way of acknowledging that building this beer company into what they believed it could become was going to take a lot of work.

Beer is a live food product, Kim explained to me during our conversation in front of a live audience in her hometown of Denver, Colorado. "You can't bottle half a batch and say, 'Well, we'll pick that up tomorrow.' You have to finish," she said. "If the machine breaks down six times, or twenty times, in between the beginning and the end, you stay and you finish it."

Like any business, they were going to have some of those days. Long, hard, sixteen-hour days. If New Belgium was going to be successful, Kim thought, they would have to get through those days together. That's why it was important to her to recognize the dedication and the sacrifice it would demand from all the people whose job it was to fix those machines and finish those batches and do whatever it took to get product into bottles, out the door, and onto shelves.

"I really felt this deep sense of wanting to acknowledge that we were building this community," Kim said. "And I wanted to see how we could test this model where people in America get to own something, where they build value and they build equity and they're all in it together."

Kim and Jeff started by setting up a phantom stock plan and distributing shares to employees pro rata every six months. But this wasn't just some perfunctory stock issuance that got stapled to the back of a paycheck twice a year. This was an *event*. They made new employees stand up in front of their co-workers — and now *fellow owners* — to talk about why they wanted to be an owner. "We'd ask them questions," Kim said. And not just her or Jeff, but the entire staff would get in on the act. "How long are you going to be here? What kind of skills are you going to work on in the next six months?" Questions that would test whether these men and women about to join the ranks of ownership were in it for the long haul.

The system Kim and Jeff set up worked so well that eventually, after Jeff left the company and Kim assumed complete control, she sold her entire stake in the company to her employees. All of it went right into the employee stock ownership plan (ESOP). Any ownership Kim retained was in her capacity as an ESOP account holder, just like all her co-workers, and her stake sat right alongside theirs within the ESOP trust.

New Belgium Brewing Company, today worth north of $250 million, had become a fully employee-owned company. One where, beyond equity (and one would assume free beer), employees also got a free cruiser bike after a year of employment and an all-expenses trip to Belgium after five years, where they'd get to visit the bar in Bruges where the idea for New Belgium was originally sparked. Like I said, it's the little things *and* the big things that keep people around.

From a strategic perspective, what is so underappreciated about treating your employees well and creating a kind work environment is that people pay attention. Employees feel it, obviously, as do their families, which makes talent retention appreciably easier. People looking for better job opportunities or something they can make a career out of see it, too, which is great for recruiting. And customers notice, which is excellent for brand loyalty and word of mouth. "I've had thousands of people say to me, 'I came to New Belgium for a tour, and you can just tell that these people are into it. They like this thing,'" Kim said.

They like this thing. Her co-workers love building a beer brand together. They like coming in to work. "One of the things that I knew early on is that people want to be connected to something bigger," Kim said. "We spend a lot of time at this thing called work, so it should feel good."

Time is one of those resources that kind companies recognize has value far beyond money. For Yvon Chouinard, founder of the outdoor clothing company Patagonia, time is something he values above most everything else. He protects it religiously for himself, spending five months out of the office every year at his home in Jackson Hole, Wyoming, fly-fishing and not answering his phone. "People know if the warehouse burns down, don't call me," he said. "What can I do? [They] know what to do."

They know what to do because he has empowered them to do their jobs however works best for them. "I don't care when you work as long as the job gets done," he explained. What his employees do with the rest of their time is up to them. There are no hard-and-fast rules other than that. The extent to which anything is codified at all is the explicit understanding, made famous in Yvon's 2005 bestselling memoir, *Let My People Go Surfing,* that "when the surf comes up, you drop working and you go surfing."

I would argue that this generosity of spirit, this confidence in his people to manage their own time, is Yvon's primary means of expressing the sort of kindness and respect that create a positive work environment and a loyal, productive workforce. Like Kim Jordan, Yvon knows the average person spends a third of their life at work. Kim's way of honoring that commitment is to share ownership in the business. Yvon's approach is to give as much of that time back to his employees as he can, so they can live their lives, be their whole selves, and bring those whole selves into the workplace with them every day.

That impulse to build a business with a fully actualized workforce has been the driver, almost since day one, for a number of company-wide policies — mostly related to families — that have made Patagonia consistently one of the great places to work since its founding in Southern California in 1973. The company has had flexible work schedules and extensive maternity and paternity leave *since the seventies.** In the early days, when a woman's maternity leave was up, Yvon would let her bring her infant to work with her. "We wanted to have our kids with us at work," Yvon said plainly, "so we put them in a cardboard box on your desk, and that worked for a while. But then we got some screamers, so my wife started a childcare center." Not some impersonal babysitting service staffed by a faceless third-party vendor either, but an honest-to-goodness childcare center. "We recognized that two to five years old is the most important learning time of a person's life," Yvon said. "The kids that come out of our company are the best product that we make." Some have been so good, Patagonia has even hired them. That's how long their childcare center has been around. They have employees today who grew up in it!

While Yvon, an avid outdoorsman and bona fide free spirit, has always considered himself a reluctant businessman (it's in the subtitle of his book), decisions like these were not acts of pure charity. Patagonia's policy of hiring nannies to go on business trips with employees who are new parents and don't want to be away from their young children is as much about the importance of family as it is about the value of employee productivity. Policies like this one have a deep business logic, grounded in Yvon's desire to build a company that will last. "I have probably 70 percent women working for me. I have more women than men in all upper management, and I don't want to lose them," he said. "If we are going to be here 100 years, it's good business."

What makes these policies good business is not simply that they

---

* There are numerous Fortune 500 companies today that don't give new parents the time Patagonia did forty-plus years ago.

are kind and human gestures, though both things are true. It's that they remove the traditional trade-offs between time and money that most working parents have to make as they attempt to strike a balance between work and family. When you eliminate that trade-off altogether, you reduce the pull many working parents feel to choose one or the other. You give them back time, and you increase their ability to be present in all aspects of their lives as their whole selves.

That was Eileen Fisher's big regret when she reflected on how she navigated trying to be the best mom she could be and running her company, all while she went through a divorce. Knowing what she does now, she confessed, she would have done things differently. "I would have just worked harder at being where I was, doing what I was doing in the moment, stop trying to be two places at once, and just do the best I can." She would have worked harder at being her whole self. Instead, Eileen felt the constant pull of obligation in both directions, and any time she gave in to one side, she felt like she was letting down the other. She was losing or forgetting part of herself no matter which way she went. And she was the boss! Imagine what that is like for normal employees.

That push and pull is not something Yvon is interested in for his employees. "We want them to be who they are," Patagonia's chief human resources officer said at a management conference in the spring of 2019, in the simplest articulation of a forty-year policy that has produced not only some of the highest-quality outerwear on the market but an industry-defying 4 percent employee turnover rate and a 100 percent retention rate for new mothers returning to work. If you can get your employees to stick around the way Yvon Chouinard has, it might just be possible to build a company that will last 100 years as he hopes Patagonia will.

To be clear, there is no one right way to treat your people well. Starbucks offers benefits and college tuition opportunities to its part-time employees. Burton Snowboards lets you bring your dog to work. (They had 132 dogs registered to employees when we talked in 2017.) And if it snows more than two feet in Vermont, the office shuts down, and everyone at Burton hits the slopes. At Clif Bar head-quarters in Emeryville, California, Gary Erickson and his wife and co-CEO, Kit Crawford, have on-site daycare, a gym, personal train-ers, and boxes of Clif Bars all around campus, with the full under-standing that employees can take as many as they want any time they want.

Whatever your choices as founder, a robust set of ethics should sit at their foundation. Beyond that, only two things are truly nec-essary when it comes to building a kind, long-lasting company. One, that the things you do advance your mission and match your values. And two, that you do them from the beginning, precisely because mission, values, and culture generally are so hard to change. This was largely the undoing of AOL Time Warner, remember, and the reason nothing could pull American Apparel out of its tailspin after Dov Charney lost the trust of his board and his employees.

This was also something that Yvon Chouinard was made to un-derstand after numerous CEOs came to him over the years to learn how he built Patagonia and how they might copy his model at their own companies. In each case, he'd run them through Patagonia's unique policies and his philosophy on management and service. They'd love one or another idea and get excited about bringing it back to their own teams. Then Yvon would tell them to forget it. "It will fail," he'd say, "because you have to start with it, with the very first person you hire."

He had come to this conclusion after a number of years trying to help companies struggling to motivate and reenergize their work-force, having seen the same movie play out a dozen times, each time ending poorly. But there was another reason he felt that way—this one having less to do with other people's companies and more to do with his own. "I have had psychologists study our employees," Yvon told me, "and they said, 'Your employees are the most independent we have ever seen in any company. In fact, they're so independent, they're unemployable anywhere else.'"

The unkind reading of the psychologists' message is that Yvon Chouinard has managed to build a business where the inmates run the asylum. But I think the more accurate interpretation, and the reason he believes that Patagonia's principles won't translate to other companies unless the owners are starting from scratch, is that Yvon has cultivated a workforce that can't imagine working anywhere else. It is the ultimate testament to the power of kindness, generosity, dignity, and respect in the building of a long-lasting business.

26

What You Do with Your Luck

I still remember my very first interview for *How I Built This,* which we released in September 2016. Sara Blakely. The inimitable, indefatigable billionaire founder of Spanx. She was a huge get for us. And she was placing a tremendous amount of trust in me. I believed in the concept of the show and in my abilities as an interviewer and a host, but this was still my first foray into a show exclusively about entrepreneurship, and it was still very much an experiment. Sara had graciously agreed to be the guinea pig, and I didn't want to blow it.

As a war reporter and host of *Weekend All Things Considered* and *TED Radio Hour,* I'd interviewed more than 6,000 people — Nobel laureates, world leaders, pop stars, Olympic champions, business and industry titans, novelists, and many more — but in preparing to discuss the business story of one of the most successful female entrepreneurs ever, I couldn't help but feel nervous. I was still a little fuzzy, for instance, on some of the acronyms I would come to know over the next four years — CPG, P&L, and LTV, for instance — and what actually goes into calculating COGS.

Beyond surviving the interview with my professional dignity intact, I was equally concerned about the show's survival after its first few weeks out in the world. I didn't *really* know if people would care about the stories I was trying to help entrepreneurs tell. I knew listeners would benefit from them, but only if we could get this right. Only if I could make my guests comfortable enough to be honest and vulnerable. I had no way of knowing whether my normal approach as an interviewer would work to make that happen. And having spent my entire professional career as a journalist, with a healthy dose of skepticism toward business vibrating underneath it, I was worried about giving listeners the wrong message about entrepreneurship.

Looking back almost four years later, I can happily say that I no longer worry about these things. As it turns out, people *do* care about entrepreneurial stories and the hero's journeys at their core, and entrepreneurs appreciate the chance to be transparent and forthright about the events in their lives that shaped who they have become and the businesses they have built.

The fact that we have been able to turn all that into a successful podcast has left me with lots of different feelings. I'm extremely grateful for the listeners and fans. I'm inspired by the brave, resilient entrepreneurs I've had the chance to meet, to interview, and in some cases even to befriend. And I'm incredibly proud of what my team and I have done with the show in just a few years. But most of all, I feel lucky.

See, I started at NPR many years ago as an intern, with a bunch of other interns who were much more accomplished and much more sophisticated than me. Every day for the first year or so, I was convinced I could never compete with these brilliant people who would probably one day ascend to the anchor chairs of all the great NPR programs. And yet, somehow I built a successful career in broadcasting. It's a set of circumstances I can only make sense of when I recognize that although I worked hard, I also got very lucky. Lucky that people discovered my shows. Lucky that NPR gave me the opportunity to try something new. Lucky that I had two loving parents and a good education. Lucky that I grew up in the United States, where the mere thought of building something from nothing, of taking a chance at doing something you love, isn't some absurd fantasy, but is baked into the nation's founding promise.

I am a big believer in luck. When I look back at the trajectory of my life, I feel like luck has played an outsized role in much of the professional success I have enjoyed. I'm even lucky I was rejected for jobs at NPR I desperately wanted — rejections that were painful and difficult at the time. Because had I gotten those jobs, I wouldn't be making the shows I make today. That's one of the reasons I end every interview on *How I Built This* by asking my guests to what extent they feel luck played a part in their success, compared with things like hard work and skill and intelligence. Not because I think there is a right answer, or even that there is an answer at all, but because in attempting to answer this question, they must take a moment to reflect. After spending many hours walking me through every little detail of their entrepreneurial journey — from the call of their idea for a business, to the all-is-lost moments they were able to overcome, all the way to their present-day involvement in the company they have worked tirelessly to shape — founders have a chance to think one more time about everything we've just talked about, everything they thought about before coming in to the studio, and to reevaluate how all the pieces of their story fit together. Almost without fail, this question has produced some of the most revealing parts of my interviews.

In a way, the question functions like the big, blank, cavernous lobby atriums you find in most of the world's great museums. It's a transitional space between everything you've just absorbed from history and everything in present-day life you're about to step back into. It's a place to pause, to gather yourself and to synthesize all of it into a better understanding of your world. I watched this happen in real time with Rod Canion, the founder of Compaq Computer, for example, when I asked him about the nature of his success and he took a long beat before responding.

"If you'd asked me that in the late eighties, I would probably have said it was 90 percent intelligence and insight and work, and 10 percent luck. But I would say today it was the other way around," Rod said. "That tells you how perspective changes with time."

What changes, I think, is the appreciation for just how many people out there are smarter or work harder or have more money or possess a more resilient personality, and are still less successful despite their best efforts. Every successful entrepreneur I've met has a story about working eighteen-hour days for months on end or eating ramen and cereal and rice to get by, but none of them has ever worked harder in their capacity as a founder than a dishwasher or a gardener or a construction worker or a waitress works every single day.

Now, I'm not trying to take away from the difficulty of starting a business. The conversations I've had since I started *How I Built This* have opened my eyes to what a remarkable challenge it is just to stand up an idea, let alone to grow it into a company that can function successfully without its founder at the helm. It's hard work. The point is, you can do everything right, you can make all the plays, and still you can lose the game. Convincingly so. In fact, most people do lose. Most businesses fail within a year or two. The cards are generally stacked against anyone thinking about starting a business. And yet, at the same time, if one or two bounces go your way, all of a sudden you can come out of the game as the big winner.

That is luck.

Just look at someone like the late Herb Kelleher. Herb was an incredibly hard worker. But Herb also got lucky in ways that were entirely out of his control. During their first seven years in service, Southwest Airlines flew only within the state of Texas, but the deregulation of the airline industry in 1978 enabled them to break the monopolistic stranglehold that the big airlines had on domestic routes by offering staggeringly cheap cross-country flights. Southwest also launched during a transitional period in the culture when more and more people became interested in air travel. Previously, air travel was something that was accessible only to a small number of people. The Don Drapers of the world. By undercutting the bigger airlines and offering affordable airfare — courtesy of deregulation — Herb and his team were able to tap into that pent-up demand and turn massive profits from a customer base that didn't exist only a few years earlier. It was a brilliant move by Herb, no question; one that required relentless hard work to execute. But Southwest was also in the right place at the right time. They were lucky. Herb was lucky.

So was Tobi Lütke, the founder of Shopify, though his luck came disguised inside misfortune. What propelled Tobi's e-commerce platform to its initial massive success were the millions of people who were suddenly out of work because of the 2008 financial crisis and were turning to online businesses as a way to pay the bills. While other internet properties and media companies suffered losses, Shopify exploded. Could it have succeeded without the rush of customers from the financial crisis? Yes, absolutely. But as much? Or as quickly? It's hard to say. What isn't is that Tobi's timing was very lucky.

A number of founders I interviewed found luck within the financial crisis as well. Ron Shaich saw it as a chance to invest even more heavily in the Panera brand and grow it much more quickly than originally planned, ultimately tripling the stock price. Carley Roney and David Liu saw their site, The Knot, grow 5 percent while other media companies shrank by as much as 20 percent. They were lucky to be in the right business. "Weddings were truly recession-proof," David said. Kendra Scott considers the recession the greatest gift her eponymous jewelry company ever received, because it gave her the permission she would never grant herself to pivot the company away from wholesale to consumer retail, where she ultimately found massive success. "For all these years, I'd been worrying about what the buyers wanted. I wasn't thinking as much about the customer," Kendra said. "Then the whole world changed, and I realized I had to refocus all of my attention on the customer."

Each of these stories has a strong strain of luck running through it. But I'm not talking about luck in this context as any sort of admonition against these founders being proud of all the hard work they put in. I mention it in order to, I hope, help aspiring entrepreneurs understand that the luck these founders experienced was not some disembodied magical force. It didn't happen in a vacuum. It didn't happen to them. Luck, when it comes right down to it, is really just an opportunity waiting to be taken advantage of, and they took advantage of it. Herb's strategy for Southwest wasn't a directionless guess. The airline didn't run headlong into the good fortune of deregulation and changing travel habits by chance. Herb was open to the luck that was unfolding in front of him. He recognized it for the opportunity that it was, and he developed a strategy to maximize it. The same is true of Ron Shaich, Kendra Scott, Tobi Lütke, and The Knot founders.

Kevin Systrom, one of the Instagram founders, has a simple theory about luck. He shared it as part of his answer to my final question at the end of my interview with him and co-founder Mike Krieger. "The whole world runs on luck. The question is, what you do with it."

I think he's right. I think everyone is lucky in some number of ways for some amount of time in their life, and it's what you do with your luck while you have it that determines whether you succeed or you fail or you even try.

Maybe you have a good network, like John Foley, the co-founder of Peloton, who raised $400,000 as a seed round from eight people who "knew me and trusted me and loved me," as he described them, including his brother-in-law, who was the CEO of Ticketmaster.

Maybe you were born into a stable home like Chet Pipkin, who lived with his parents, in the same house he'd grown up in, while he started Belkin International on the dining room table before moving into the garage. "Chet, I love you very, very much," his mother said, "but you're going to get this stuff off of this table." That is what counted for tough love in the Pipkin household!

Maybe you had the privilege of a good education like a significant number of the entrepreneurs I've interviewed. Jenn Hyman is double Harvard. Jim Koch is triple Harvard. Ron Shaich, Susan Tynan of Framebridge, Katrina Lake, and Alexa von Tobel of LearnVest all went to Harvard Business School. Andy Dunn and Randy Hetrick went to the Stanford Graduate School of Business. The Warby Parker guys went to Penn. There is no arguing how lucky you should consider yourself if you find your way into one of those institutions. All of those entrepreneurs certainly did.

Or maybe you were lucky enough to be born with the kind of personality that makes you more resilient, more willing to accept rejection, more willing to do whatever it takes, without the massive ego that prevents so many from sticking with it during hard times. A personality like Daymond John's, with the drive to work hard and the resilience to push forward through all the nos until he got to a yes.

Whatever the case, the question you will need to answer for yourself as an aspiring entrepreneur isn't whether you will ever have any luck — you will, you probably already do. It's what you are going to do with the luck that you have. Are you going to take advantage of it? Are you going to do the work? Are you going to take the leap? Are you going to write that twenty-fifth investor email? What about the twenty-sixth? Are you going to pay all the friends in your network to buy your product so the stores think its super popular right away, like Sara Blakely did with the first five stores she got Spanx into? Are you going to physically move your product in those stores to a more optimal location like she did, too? Those are choices you will have when you realize how lucky you are and you spot the opportunities that come with that luck.

The most important opportunity I ever spotted was the chance to meet this beautiful and brilliant woman at a friend's barbecue I was lucky enough to attend in Washington, DC, in the summer of 2000. Her name was Hannah. And while I didn't actually talk to her that day, I engineered it so that my friend who was hosting the barbecue, who was also Hannah's roommate, would bring her along to another party I was invited to the following day.

This is the other thing about luck that you can't forget: you have some agency over it. As Brian Scudamore said to me when he was talking about pestering the Idaho Transportation Board into giving him the phone number "1-800-GOT-JUNK," sometimes "you make your own luck." Recruiting our mutual friend to my cause was one of those times for me.

The following night, Hannah showed up at the party, though not without some initial misgivings that were completely unrelated to me and that I only learned about after the fact. She just didn't feel like going. Then, right as her roommate was getting ready to leave their house, Hannah reversed herself. She shouted down to the front door, "Hang on, I'm coming!" — and arrived just in time for me to fall in love with her. Two months later, I left for Berlin to become NPR's bureau chief. We were separated by an ocean for two more years. Yet we stayed together.

Twenty years later, we are married, we have two children, and she has become the single most important influence in my life. So much of what I've done and the opportunities I have had have been directly connected to her support, guidance, and wisdom. The opportunity to meet her was the luckiest thing that has ever happened to me.

You and I, we are both lucky. I had the opportunity to write this book; you had the money to buy it (or the patience to wait for it at the library) and the time and inclination to read it. I've had the privilege of meeting and interviewing some of the world's most successful innovators, entrepreneurs, and idealists in order to help them tell their stories; you somehow found your way here, where you can learn from the lessons their stories hold. In 2015, I had an idea for a podcast that a few key folks at NPR and my partner in life, Hannah, encouraged me to pursue; today, or someday soon, I hope you are lucky enough to have your own idea that this book helps you to pursue.

If it does, please let me know, because I really want to hear about how you built it.

AFTERWORD

Here's something you may not know: what you hear on *How I Built This* and my other interview shows is an edited version of a much longer conversation. I spend two, three, sometimes four or more hours guiding my interview partners through the small details and big moments of their life journeys. It's an intense and often emotional experience — for them and for me.

My rule is simple: nothing is off-limits, and everything is on the table. Because all of us are complicated. Everyone has embarrassing episodes in their life they'd rather not talk about. But those moments are part of the journey, and, when contextualized, they help to give us a more detailed picture of who a person is.

As you might imagine, when you spend a concentrated period of time with another person's voice in your head — asking about your most challenging moments, your vulnerabilities, failures, mistakes, and lapses of judgment (along with your triumphs and successes, of course!) — it's hard to walk away without feeling an unusually strong and deep connection.

In most cases, I receive an email from my interviewees a few days later, and they describe the experience as a form of therapy. As catharsis and reflection. It makes total sense to me, because our instinct as humans is to push forward and to never look back. We rarely get a chance to reflect on the journey that is life, or, in the case of my guests on *How I Built This,* the journey that is entrepreneurship.

But those moments of reflection are crucial. Because if there's one critical thing I've learned from the entrepreneurs I've interviewed — and from my own journey as an entrepreneur — it's that you will have moments when you truly feel alone.

Starting a business — starting anything creative, for that matter — is difficult. It is a twisting road with hours, days, weeks, and months filled with struggle and failure and self-doubt and even tears. When you add a sense of isolation to the mix, it's "Hello, anxiety!"

It happened to me a while back after weeks of sleepless nights. We were getting ready to move across the country, I was producing three shows with two more in the works, and I was starting to worry about everything. My family, my kids, my staff, the shows, partnerships, deadlines, my health. The fate of all these things felt as though it sat squarely and solely on my shoulders.

Finally one night, my wife, Hannah, pulled out a notebook and asked me to tell her what was on my mind. I poured out everything in my head, and she wrote every word of it down. The act of emptying my anxieties onto the page was itself a therapeutic act that helped me get back to sleep, but the real salvation came three months later when Hannah pulled out the notebook and read my list of worries back to me.

Not a single item on that list was relevant any longer! Not one of my worries had materialized in any meaningful way. Most things had worked out with the passage of time. But at the time, it felt like the world was collapsing around me. I would love to tell you this was just a "me" problem, but it's part of the human condition. Our brains have a natural safety mechanism designed to help us react in times of stress and moments of threat. It was useful in prehistoric times when we had to escape from wild animals. The struggle today, as humans in a modern world, is to figure out how to flip that safety switch to neutral, how to step back from our lives and take the long view on our journeys.

That, really, is what I try to do every time I sit down with an entrepreneur for *How I Built This.*

As you read this book, you may have already heard and answered the call to entrepreneurship. You may be smack in the middle of navigating the crucible of its tests, trying to figure out exactly what kind of company you want to build and what kind of founder you want to become. Wherever you are on your journey, you will almost certainly face a moment like the one I experienced. A period of crippling anxiety and despair that no one could possibly understand what you're dealing with, that everything is riding on the decisions you make, that it's all up to you.

When that happens, I want you to pull out a notebook and write those worries down. I want you to trap them on the page, so that you can look at them the next day, the next week, the next month, the next year, and realize that while every challenge and crisis you face in the pursuit of your idea feels like it could be the end of it all, it's not. I promise.

How do I know? *You are still here, aren't you?* And not only are you still here, but you have everyone who is helping you bring your idea to life. You have everyone who wants to see you succeed. You have every single entrepreneur who has come before you and has made the mistakes you can now learn from without having to make those mistakes yourself. And you have this book, which I hope has given you a little bit of extra support and confidence to know that as you build your business, you are not alone.

ACKNOWLEDGMENTS

This book is based primarily on my four years of interviews on the *How I Built This* podcast. Most of the people profiled here sat down with me for many hours. One of the hardest parts of producing the show is deciding what to keep and what to edit out. Same story with this book. There are a hundred other stories I could share — and hopefully will in a future book! In the end, I hope what remains here will help to inspire you along your journey.

This book would still be a pile of notes, unruly paragraphs, disorganized ideas, and transcripts on my desk without the support of my brilliant writing partner, Nils Parker. Over the course of a year, I probably spent more time with Nils (on the phone or in person) than with nearly anyone other than my wife and kids. I will cherish these conversations, intellectual exchanges, and brainstorming sessions forever. This book is as much Nils's as it is mine. We benefited greatly from the wisdom of Ryan Holiday, who provided critical feedback. Joseph Karnes and Billy Oppenheimer offered excellent research support, and Tessa Abrahams gave the manuscript a close read to make it better at every turn. Barbara Jatkola combed through the draft with a penetrating eye, and her feedback was incredibly helpful. My agents at UTA, Oren Rosenbaum and Byrd Leavell, have been huge champions and supporters of my work from the day I met them. My editor at Houghton Mifflin Harcourt, Rick Wolff, was an early and enthusiastic backer of this idea and helped guide the writing process over the past two years.

As I mentioned in the introduction, *How I Built This* began as an idea I had back in 2008 when I took a class at Harvard Business School during a sabbatical year as a Nieman journalism fellow after nearly eight years as a foreign correspondent. I spent the next seven years hosting *Weekend All Things Considered* and then *TED Radio Hour.* Finally, in late 2015, I pitched the idea for *How I Built This* to NPR's head of programming, Anya Grundmann — a true visionary in the world of podcasting and the architect of NPR's podcast revolution. I worked on the show at night and on weekends with the help of a DJ-producer named Ramtin Arablouei. (Ramtin now co-hosts another NPR program, *Throughline.*) My editor, Neva Grant, helped us craft my raw interviews into episodes. Jeff Rogers, our senior producer, gave us crucial feedback and support, along with my longtime collaborator Sanaz Meshkinpour, and producers Casey Herman and Rund Abdelfatah (the other co-host of NPR's *Throughline*). There was healthy (and justified) skepticism within NPR over whether the show would work and whether to give it a shot. But after almost a year of pursuing the idea in earnest, we were able to get the show off the ground. Today, four years since its debut in 2016, *How I Built This* has an incredibly talented team and millions of weekly listeners. Though you hear my voice and my interviews, the amazing team (past and present) behind the podcast and our live events includes Jed Anderson, Sequoia Carrillo, Elaine Coates, James Delahoussaye, Rachel Faulkner, Jessica Goldstein, J. C. Howard, John Isabella, Candice Lim, Diba Mohtasham, Allie Prescott, Daniel Shukhin, and Jinae West.

Books don't happen without lots of help. I'm so thankful for my dear friend and mentor Sara Sarasohn; her wife, Ellen Evangeliste; and their daugther, Ruth; along with Yangchen Dolma, who have been there for us on so many occasions over the past two years.

Thanks also to my mom and dad. They came to this country in the early 1970s with a dream to build a better life. They raised four kids and gave us all the tools of independence and the support of a nurturing childhood. Finally, my deepest thanks to my wife, Hannah, and my boys, Henry and Bram, for their love and understanding throughout this process. As I've written in this book, I'm a big believer in luck. And the luckiest day of my life was the day I met Hannah.

NOTES

1. Be Open to Ideas

page

4   *north of mid–eight figures:* Jolie A. Doggett, "L'Oreal Signs Agreement to Buy Carol's Daughter," *Essence,* October 20, 2014, https://www.essence.com/hair/loreal-signs-agreement-buy-carols-daughter/.

10 *the most common mistake:* Paul Graham, "How to Get Startup Ideas," Paulgraham.com (blog), November 2012, http://www.paulgraham.com/startupideas.html.

2. Is It Dangerous or Just Scary?

13 *the odds of which:* Aric Jenkins, "Which Is Safer: Airplanes or Cars?," *Fortune,* July 20, 2017, https://fortune.com/2017/07/20/are-airplanes-safer-than-cars/.
    bathtubs claim one American life: James Fallows, "Telling the Difference Between Danger and Fear," *The Atlantic,* May 23, 2014, https://www.theatlantic.com/technology/archive/2014/05/telling-the-difference-between-danger-and-fear/371211/.
    "Bathtubs should be 365": Ibid.

3. Leave Your Safety Zone . . . but Do It Safely

27 *"putting in six days":* Phil Knight, *Shoe Dog: A Memoir by the Creator of Nike* (New York: Scribner, 2016).

5. Find Your Co-founder

42   *"It seems unlikely":* Paul Graham, "The 18 Mistakes That Kill Startups," Paulgraham.com, October 2006, http://paulgraham.com/startupmistakes .html.

48   *"My best business decisions":* "Buffett & Gates on Success," University of Washington, 1997, YouTube, https://www.youtube.com/watch?v=ldPh0 _zEykU&feature=youtu.be&t=2583.
      "Neither of us had any idea": David Sheff, *"Playboy* Interview: Steve Jobs," *Playboy,* February 1985, available at Atavist, http://reprints.longform.org/ playboy-interview-steve-jobs.

50   *"Starting a startup":* Graham, "The 18 Mistakes That Kill Startups."

6. Fund the Business, Part 1: Bootstrapping

54   *"i thought of a way":* Rebecca Aydin, "How 3 Guys Turned Renting Air Mattresses in Their Apartment Into a $31 Billion Company, Airbnb," Business Insider, September 20, 2019, https://www.businessinsider.com/how -airbnb-was-founded-a-visual-history-2016-2.

61   *"bootstrapping as long as you can":* "Investing with the Godfather of Silicon Valley," ZURB, n.d., accessed April 12, 2019, https://zurb.com/ soapbox/ron-conway-zurbsoapbox-investing-with-the-godfather-of -silicon-valley.
      "In our experience": Sam Altman, Twitter post, October 13, 2015, 2:02 p.m., https://twitter.com/sama/status/654039449538457600?s=20.
      "We especially love companies": Sam Altman, Twitter post, October 13, 2015, 2:06 p.m., https://twitter.com/sama/status/654040512266039296?s=20.

7. Get Your Story Straight

65   *"the keeper of the vision":* Ben Horowitz, "How Andreessen Horowitz Evaluates CEOs" (blog post), *a16z,* May 31, 2010, https://a16z.com/2010/05/31/ how-andreessen-horowitz-evaluates-ceos/.
      "The story must explain": Carmine Gallo, "'Your Story Is Your Strategy' Says VC Who Backed Facebook and Twitter," *Forbes,* April 29, 2014, https://www .forbes.com/sites/carminegallo/2014/04/29/your-story-is-your-strategy -says-vc-who-backed-facebook-and-twitter/#59014a4f1dd8.

66   *which Whitney co-founded:* Alyson Shontell, "Ousted Tinder Cofounder Sues for Sexual Harassment, and She's Using These Nasty Texts as Evidence," Business Insider, July 1, 2014, https://www.businessinsider.com/ tinder-lawsuit-and-sexual-harassment-text-messages-2014-7.
      worst possible circumstances: Abby Phillip, "Read the Most Surprising Al-

legations from the Tinder Sexual Harassment Lawsuit," *Washington Post,* April 24, 2019, https://www.washingtonpost.com/news/the-switch/wp/2014/07/01/read-the-most-surprising-allegations-from-the-tinder-sexual-harassment-lawsuit/.

a professional and a romantic split: Ibid.

a very public sexual harassment lawsuit: Jacob Kastrenakes, "Former Tinder Exec Sues Company for Sexual Harassment and Discrimination," The Verge, July 1, 2014, https://www.theverge.com/2014/7/1/5860512/tinder-sued-sex-harassment-discrimination-of-former-exec.

despicably hurtful online vitriol: "Bumble CEO: Backlash from Tinder Lawsuit Was 'Extremely Invasive,'" interview by Kristen Bellstrom, *Fortune,* November 13, 2017, YouTube, https://www.youtube.com/watch?v=OwneQiw4HfU.

left Tinder in early 2014: Stuart Dredge, "Dating App Tinder Facing Sexual Harassment Lawsuit from Co-founder," *The Guardian,* July 1, 2014, https://www.theguardian.com/technology/2014/jul/01/tinder-sexual-harassment-lawsuit-whitney-wolfe.

8. Fund the Business, Part 2: Other People's Money

78   *A year later:* "Jeff Bezos Convinced 22 Investors to Back His New Company Amazon in 1994. Their Returns? Mind-Boggling," *South China Morning Post,* April 26, 2018, https://www.scmp.com/news/world/united-states-canada/article/2143375/1994-he-convinced-22-family-and-friends-each-pay.

     each has been made a billionaire: Bloomberg, "Runs in the Family: Jeff Bezos's Parents Might Also Be Ridiculously Rich," *Fortune,* July 31, 2018, https://fortune.com/2018/07/31/jeff-bezos-family-investment-amazon/.

10. Go In Through the Side Door

97   *invest in the company:* A month to the day before Jeff Raikes sent his email to Warren Buffett, Microsoft announced record annual revenue of $11.36 billion for fiscal year 1997. "Microsoft Announces Record Fiscal 1997 Revenues and Income," *Microsoft News,* July 17, 1997, https://news.microsoft.com/1997/07/17/microsoft-announces-record-fiscal-1997-revenues-and-income/.

99   *"Don't always go through":* Peter Thiel, "Competition Is for Losers" (How to Start a Startup, lecture 5, Stanford Center for Professional Development, Stanford University, October 7, 2014), YouTube, https://www.youtube.com/watch?v=3Fx5Q8xGU8k&t=1163s.

103   *Today, RXBar, which was acquired:* Samantha Bomkamp, "Chicago-Born Company RXBar Drives $110M in Sales for Kellogg," *Chicago Tribune,*

August 2, 2018, https://www.chicagotribune.com/business/ct-biz-kellogg
-rxbar-earnings-20180802-story.html.

104 *"I have a single idée fixe":* "Microsoft Announces Record Fiscal 1997 Revenues."

11. It's All About Location

109 *more than 820,000 merchants:* Emil Protalinski, "Shopify Announces New
Partner and Developer Tools, Plus an AI-Powered Fulfillment Network,"
VentureBeat, June 19, 2019, https://venturebeat.com/2019/06/19/shopify
-announces-new-partner-and-developer-tools-plus-an-ai-powered
-fulfillment-network/.

175 different countries: Shopify, "Shopify Announces Third-Quarter 2018
Financial Results," press release, October 25, 2018, https://news.shopify
.com/shopify-announces-third-quarter-2018-financial-results.

111 *"Where you live matters":* "Drew Houston's Commencement Address," MIT
News, June 7, 2013, http://news.mit.edu/2013/commencement-address
-houston-0607.

113 *"more than 140 franchise studios":* "Barre3 Founder: Sadie Lincoln," barre3,
https://barre3.com/sadie.

12. Get Attention, Part 1: Building Buzz

115 *roughly 850,000 new businesses:* US Department of Labor, Bureau of Labor
Statistics, "Entrepreneurship and the U.S. Economy," chart 1, April 28, 2016,
https://www.bls.gov/bdm/entrepreneurship/bdm_chart1.htm.

Across the five biggest app stores: "App Stores: Number of Apps in Leading
App Stores 2019," Statista, n.d., https://www.statista.com/statistics/
276623/number-of-apps-available-in-leading-app-stores/.

116 *In 2018, those apps produced:* Mansoor Iqbal, "App Download and Usage
Statistics (2019)," Business of Apps, November 19, 2019, https://www
.businessofapps.com/data/app-statistics/#1.

$365 billion in revenue: "Worldwide Mobile App Revenues in 2014 to 2023,"
Statista, n.d., https://www.statista.com/statistics/269025/worldwide-mob
ile-app-revenue-forecast/.

In 2019, while I was writing this book: Iqbal, "App Download and Usage Statistics (2019)."

Mobile apps have become: Matt Miller, "Top Predictions for the App Economy in 2018," *App Annie* (blog), December 5, 2017, https://www.appannie
.com/en/insights/market-data/predictions-app-economy-2018/.

Nearly 800,000 existing businesses: US Department of Labor, Bureau of Labor Statistics, "Entrepreneurship and the U.S. Economy," chart 5, April 28,
2016, https://www.bls.gov/bdm/entrepreneurship/bdm_chart5.htm.

80 percent of new businesses: US Department of Labor, Bureau of Labor Statistics, "Entrepreneurship and the U.S. Economy," chart 3, April 28, 2016, https://www.bls.gov/bdm/entrepreneurship/bdm_chart3.htm.

The top five apps: Peter LaBerge, "The 2018 Mobile App Store Download Statistics Report," *Branch* (blog), October 4, 2018, https://blog.branch.io/the-2018-mobile-app-store-download-statistics-report/.

13. Get Attention, Part 2: Engineering Word of Mouth

127   *"I would create the perception":* "A Lesson in Self Promotion with Tim Ferriss," Soapbox, ZURB, 2011, accessed December 6, 2019, https://zurb.com/soapbox/tim-ferriss-s-soapbox-a-lesson-in-self-promotion-with-tim-ferriss.

      "There's a hidden power": Reid Hoffman and Sam Altman, "Why Customer Love Is All You Need," *Masters of Scale* (podcast), January 30, 2018, https://mastersofscale.com/sam-altman-why-customer-love-is-all-you-need/.

128   *"nothing influences people more":* Louise Story, "Facebook Is Marketing Your Brand Preferences (with Your Permission)," *New York Times,* November 7, 2007, https://www.nytimes.com/2007/11/07/technology/07iht-07adco.8230630.html. Story called the ad program "a twist on word-of-mouth marketing."

131   *With a single forum post:* Kelsey Meany, "Blow-Dry Bars Are a Thriving Industry Disrupting the Salon Business," Daily Beast, July 13, 2013, https://www.thedailybeast.com/blow-dry-bars-are-a-thriving-industry-disrupting-the-salon-business.

134   *The year before:* "McDonald's Opened a Record 597 Restaurants in 1985, Giving...," UPI, April 9, 1986, https://www.upi.com/Archives/1986/04/09/McDonalds-opened-a-record-597-restaurants-in-1985-giving/3085513406800/.

      Wendy's had booked: Katy Waldman, "How Wendy's 1980s Turnaround Changed the Fast Food Industry," *Slate,* October 5, 2012, https://slate.com/business/2012/10/wheres-the-beef-how-wendys-1980s-turnaround-changed-the-fast-food-business.html.

14. Survive the Crucible

142   *"the customers aren't quite":* Marc Andreessen, "The Pmarca Guide to Startups," *Pmarca* (blog), June 25, 2007, https://pmarchive.com/guide_to_startups_part4.html.

145   *"the only way you can gain":* Ronald A. Heifitz and Martin Linsky, *Leadership on the Line: Staying Alive Through the Dangers of Leading* (Boston: Harvard Business School Press, 2017), 53.

15. Fund the Business, Part 3: Professional Money

147 *fewer than twenty employees:* U.S. Small Business Administration Office of Advocacy, "United States Small Business Profile, 2018," https://www.sba.gov/sites/default/files/advocacy/2018-Small-Business-Profiles-US.pdf.

between $300,000 and $2 million: Nina Godlewski, "Small Business Revenue Statistics (2019): Annual Sales and Earnings," Fundera, November 20, 2019, https://fundera.com/resources/small-business-revenue-statistics/.

16. Protect What You've Built

160 *He formed a company:* "My Biggest Mistake: James Dyson," *The Independent,* February 6, 1994, https://www.independent.co.uk/news/business/my-biggest-mistake-james-dyson-1392336.html.

161 *After he returned:* Jeff Stibel, "James Dyson: A Profile in Failure," LinkedIn, June 16, 2015, https://www.linkedin.com/pulse/james-dyson-profile-failure-jeff-stibel/.

after a three-year battle: Clare Dyer, "Hoover Taken to Cleaners in £4m Dyson Case," *The Guardian,* October 4, 2002, https://www.theguardian.com/uk/2002/oct/04/claredyer.

"terrible mistake": "My Biggest Mistake: James Dyson."

"It was like giving birth": Quoted in Stibel, "James Dyson: A Profile in Failure."

17. When Catastrophe Strikes

169 *In 1981, after several years:* Michael Decourcy Hinds, "Tylenol Spotlights a $6 Billion Industry," *New York Times,* October 10, 1982, https://www.nytimes.com/1982/10/10/weekinreview/tylenol-spotlights-a-6-billion-industry.html.

They expected Tylenol: Thomas Moore, "The Fight to Save Tylenol (*Fortune,* 1982)," *Fortune,* June 30, 2014, https://fortune.com/2012/10/07/the-fight-to-save-tylenol-fortune-1982/.

170 *The story led the news:* Knowledge@Wharton, "Tylenol and the Legacy of J&J's James Burke," *Time,* October 5, 2012, http://business.time.com/2012/10/05/tylenol-and-the-legacy-of-jjs-james-burke/.

"triple-seal": Eric Pace, "Tylenol Will Reappear in Triple-Seal Package," *New York Times,* November 12, 1982, https://www.nytimes.com/1982/11/12/business/tylenol-will-reappear-in-triple-seal-package.html.

"Before 1982, nobody ever": Judith Rehak, "Tylenol Made a Hero of Johnson & Johnson: The Recall That Started Them All," *New York Times,*

March 23, 2002, https://www.nytimes.com/2002/03/23/your-money/IHT
-tylenol-made-a-hero-of-johnson-johnson-the-recall-that-started.html.

171   *"The FBI didn't want":* Moore, "The Fight to Save Tylenol."
Their net income: Phillip H. Wiggins, "Tylenol Recall Expense Is Put at $100
Million," *New York Times,* October 29, 1982, https://www.nytimes.com/
1982/10/29/business/tylenol-recall-expense-is-put-at-100-million.html.
"There were many people": Knowledge@Wharton, "Tylenol and the Legacy
of J&J's James Burke."
Within two months: Rehak, "Tylenol Made a Hero of Johnson & Johnson."
Within eight months: Mukul Pandya and Robbie Shell, *Nightly Business Re-
port Presents Lasting Leadership: What You Can Learn from the Top 25 Business People of Our Times* (Upper Saddle River, NJ: Wharton School Publishing, 2004), 38–41.
by the end of 1983: Knowledge@Wharton, "Tylenol and the Legacy of J&J's
James Burke."
"We believe our first responsibility": "Our Credo," Johnson & Johnson, n.d.,
accessed November 14, 2019, https://www.jnj.com/credo/.
"The credo made it very clear": Pandya and Shell, *Nightly Business Report
Presents Lasting Leadership,* 38–41.

172   *"almost everything you can":* Ibid.
"Often our society": Moore, "The Fight to Save Tylenol."

175   *"almost 200 swabs every day":* Jeni Britton Bauer, "Change, Listeria, and the
Re-Opening of Our Kitchen," Jeni's, April 4, 2016, https://jenis.com/blog/
change-listeria-and-the-re-opening-of-our-kitchen/.

176   *"lives on in my memory":* Lisa Everson and Kim Bainbridge, "How Jeni's
Splendid Ice Creams Handled a Listeria Crisis," NBC News, August 15, 2018,
https://www.nbcnews.com/business/your-business/how-jeni-s-splendid
-ice-creams-handled-listeria-crisis-n851336.
Beginning in 1996: Keith Bradsher, "S.U.V. Tire Defects Were Known in '96
but Not Reported," *New York Times,* June 24, 2001, https://www.nytimes
.com/2001/06/24/business/suv-tire-defects-were-known-in-96-but-not
-reported.html.
But the recall: Matthew L. Wald, "Tread Failures Lead to Recall of 6.5 Million Firestone Tires," *New York Times,* August 10, 2000, https://www
.nytimes.com/2000/08/10/business/tread-failures-lead-to-recall-of-6.5
-million-firestone-tires.html.

177   *"series of lawsuits he filed":* Bradsher, "S.U.V. Tire Defects Were Known in
'96."
it took another six months: "Firestone Tire Recall," National Highway Traffic
Safety Administration, September 1, 2000, https://one.nhtsa.gov/Vehicle
-Safety/Tires/Firestone-Tire-Recall.

178   *"Business relationships, like personal ones":* "Text of Letter to Ford from

Bridgestone," *New York Times,* May 22, 2001, https://www.nytimes.com/ 2001/05/22/business/text-of-letter-to-ford-from-bridgestone.html.

18. The Art of the Pivot

185 *"lots of other people":* Adam Lashinsky, "Why Twitch Pivoted to Video Games, and Why It Worked," *Fortune,* March 28, 2019, https://fortune.com/ 2019/03/28/twitch-startup-pivot/.
"capped out growth": Ibid.
At the same time: Greg Kumparak, "Justin.tv Shuts Down to Let the Company Focus on Twitch," TechCrunch, August 5, 2014, https://techcrunch.com/ 2014/08/05/justin-tv-shuts-down-to-let-the-company-focus-on-twitch/.
"The only content on Justin.tv": Lashinsky, "Why Twitch Pivoted to Video Games."

19. It Can't Be All About the Money

200 *But before he got:* Ann-Marie Alcántara, "Meditation App Expands Its Subscription Membership to Google Assistant and Alexa," *Adweek,* June 29, 2018, https://www.adweek.com/digital/meditation-app-expands-its-subscription -membership-to-google-assistant-and-alexa/.

20. Build a Culture, Not a Cult

203 *"what we wanted to be":* Reed Hastings, "Culture Shock," interview by Reid Hoffman, *Masters of Scale* (podcast), June 27, 2017, https://mastersofscale .com/reed-hastings-culture-shock/.
"We realized we should": Ibid.
"We wanted to make sure": "Reed Hastings: Building an Iconic Company," interview with John Doerr, Kleiner Perkins Caufield & Byers CEO Workshop, September 15, 2015, YouTube, https://www.youtube.com/watch?v= BsXXIfqbnRk.
204 *"many people becoming candidates":* Hastings, "Culture Shock."
It helped Netflix grow into: Reed Hastings, "How Netflix Changed Entertainment—and Where It's Headed," interview by Chris Anderson, TED Conference, July 12, 2018, YouTube, https://www.youtube.com/watch?v= LsAN-TEJfN0.
"I thought if I could": Hastings, "Culture Shock."
"I was coding all night": Ibid.
"very semiconductor yield orientation": Hastings, "How Netflix Changed Entertainment."
205 *"more work is never":* Hastings, "Culture Shock."
206 *"monarch CEOs":* Jena McGregor, "When Company Founders Fight Back,"

Washington Post, April 23, 2019, https://www.washingtonpost.com/news/on-leadership/wp/2014/06/27/when-company-founders-fight-back/.

207 *"Charney himself had no other interests":* Joe Nocera, "American Apparel Is a Lesson in How Not to Run a Company," *New York Times,* July 12, 2014, https://www.nytimes.com/2014/07/12/opinion/joe-nocera-american-apparel-is-a-lesson-in-how-not-to-run-a-company.html.

"It is almost as if": Elizabeth Paton, "American Apparel Founder Wears His Defiance Proudly," *Financial Times,* June 24, 2014, https://www.ft.com/content/5c656fd6-fb76-11e3-9a03-00144feab7de#axzz35aM4l4YP.

He famously moved: Ryan Holiday, *Stillness Is the Key* (New York: Portfolio, 2019), 229.

"When you're a smaller company": American Apparel's Dov Charney One of the Worst CEOs: Finkelstein," *Bloomberg Surveillance,* December 17, 2014, YouTube, https://www.youtube.com/watch?v=QjhoZBvNqU0.

208 *"relentlessly controlling":* Elizabeth A. Harris and Steven Greenhouse, "The Road to Dov Charney's Ouster at American Apparel," *New York Times,* June 27, 2014, https://www.nytimes.com/2014/06/27/business/road-to-dov-charneys-ouster-at-american-apparel.html?_r=0.

"If the cultural roots": "Reed Hastings: Building an Iconic Company."

210 *That shared sense of purpose:* Hannah Wickford, "The Average Life Span of a Restaurant," Azcentral.com, April 13, 2018, https://yourbusiness.azcentral.com/average-life-span-restaurant-6024.html.

23. Know Thyself

233 *In 2010, Andy bounced back:* Sam Parr, "Here's How the Founder of a Men's Clothing Company Made $100m in Revenue," *The Hustle* (blog), January 25, 2016, https://thehustle.co/bonobos-andy-dunn.

239 *"The business model":* Tim Arango, "How the AOL–Time Warner Merger Went So Wrong," *New York Times,* January 20, 2010, https://www.nytimes.com/2010/01/11/business/media/11merger.html.

24. When to Sell and When to Stay

243 *"Founders don't let go":* Noam Wasserman, "The Founder's Dilemma," *Harvard Business Review,* February 2008, https://hbr.org/2008/02/the-founders-dilemma.

244 *It wouldn't be an unfamiliar place:* Ibid.

25. Be Kind

261 *Patagonia's policy of hiring:* Lila MacLellan, "At Patagonia, Exit Interviews Are Rare — but They Go Deep," Quartz at Work, March 19, 2019, https://qz

.com/work/1574375/patagonias-hr-leader-has-been-moved-to-tears-in
-exit-interviews/.

262 *"We want them to be"*: Scott Mautz, "Patagonia Has Only 4 Percent Employee Turnover Because They Value This 1 Thing So Much," *Inc.*, March
30, 2019, https://www.inc.com/scott-mautz/how-can-patagonia-have-only
-4-percent-worker-turnover-hint-they-pay-activist-employees-bail.html.

4 percent employee turnover rate: Ibid.

100 percent retention rate: Jenny Anderson, "This Is What Work-Life Balance Looks Like at a Company with 100% Retention of Moms," Quartz
at Work, October 16, 2016, https://qz.com/work/806516/the-secret-to
-patagonias-success-keeping-moms-and-onsite-child-care-and-paid
-parental-leave/.

INDEX

HOW I BUILT THIS

Guy Raz is the co-creator of NPR's *How I Built This*, *TED Radio Hour* and *Wow in the World*, and the creator of Luminary's *Wisdom From The Top* and *The Rewind* on Spotify. He received the Edward R. Murrow Award, the Daniel Schorr Journalism Prize, the National Headliner Award and the NABJ Award, among many others, and was a Nieman journalism fellow at Harvard. He lives in the Bay Area.